*The Limits of
Social Democracy*

A volume in the series

Cornell Studies in Political Economy

EDITED BY PETER J. KATZENSTEIN

A full list of titles in the series appears at the end of the book.

The Limits of Social Democracy

INVESTMENT POLITICS IN SWEDEN

JONAS PONTUSSON

CORNELL UNIVERSITY PRESS

Ithaca and London

THIS BOOK HAS BEEN PUBLISHED WITH THE AID OF A GRANT
FROM THE HULL MEMORIAL PUBLICATION FUND OF CORNELL UNIVERSITY.

First published 1992 by Cornell University Press.

International Standard Book Number 0-8014-2652-9

Library of Congress Catalog Card Number 92-2694

Printed in the United States of America

*Librarians: Library of Congress cataloging information
appears on the last page of the book.*

⊗ The paper in this book meets the minimum requirements
of the American National Standard for Information Sciences—
Permanence of Paper for Printed Library Materials, ANSI Z39.48-1984.

Contents

Acknowledgments   VII

Introduction   1

1. Theoretical Perspectives on Social Democracy   10

PART I. THE RISE AND FALL OF THE HISTORICAL COMPROMISE

2. The Politics of Planning   37
3. Labor Strategy and Investment Politics in the Postwar Era   57
4. The Changing Economic Context of Reformism   97

PART II. INVESTMENT POLITICS IN THE 1970S AND 1980S

5. Active Industrial Policy   127
6. Codetermination   161
7. Collective Shareownership   186
8. The Limits of Social Democracy   220

References   239
Index   251

Acknowledgments

This book has been in the making for nearly a decade, and I have accumulated many debts. I did the initial research in 1982–83 as a visitor at the Swedish Center for Working Life, supported by fellowships from the Regents of the University of California and the Social Science Research Council. A fellowship from the German Marshall Fund of the United States let me do additional research in 1987–88, and another from the Swedish Collegium for Avanced Study in the Social Sciences enabled me to complete the final draft in spring 1991. The Collegium not only gave me much-needed financial support for the final push, it also provided a very stimulating working environment.

I am most grateful to my dissertation committee at the University of California, Berkeley: Giuseppe Di Palma, Michael Burawoy, Paul Thomas, Harold Wilensky, and John Zysman. Zysman deserves special mention: his work on financial systems and industrial policy inspired me to undertake the research project that culminated in this book and still informs my thinking. In a similar vein, I owe a great intellectual debt to Andrew Martin, whose insightful studies of Swedish political economy provided the foundation for my own research.

The three people most continuously involved in this project, and most deeply implicated in the final product, are Sven Steinmo, Peter Swenson, and Bo Rothstein. They have read virtually everything I have written, and at least one has taken issue with every part of it. Working on related topics, they have generously shared their research and ideas with me.

For comments on various drafts of the entire manuscript or particular chapters, I am also indebted to Bengt Abrahamson, Klas Åmark,

ACKNOWLEDGMENTS

David Cameron, Peter Galasi, Geoffrey Garrett, Miriam Golden, Michael Goldfield, Bo Gustafsson, Peter Hall, Geoffrey Hodgson, Peter Lange, Tomas Lappalainen, Rianne Mahon, Rudolf Meidner, Allan Pred, Hilary Rose, David Soskice, John Stephens, Sidney Tarrow, Kathleen Thelen, Timothy Tilton, Sten Wikander, and especially Peter Katzenstein.

Though I cannot recall that he ever read any of this book in manuscript, Lennart Erixon has been a great help and has offered many valuable suggestions regarding my analysis of economic restructuring. I have also benefited greatly from the help and insights of Christian Berggren, Anders Broström, and Ann-Britt Hellmark and from the cheerful encouragement and editorial advice of Roger Haydon.

My debts to my wife, Toni Marks, are simply too extensive to describe, but I thank her for putting up with this project for so long.

JONAS PONTUSSON

Ithaca, New York

Introduction

Sweden is the advanced capitalist country with the longest experience of Left government. The Swedish Social Democrats lost the election of 1991; but by then they had governed the country for all but six of the previous sixty years. For several generations of Swedes, Social Democracy is the "natural party of government." Sweden is also the most thoroughly unionized of the advanced capitalist countries: union members account for roughly 85 percent of the labor force. In no other capitalist country, we can reasonably claim, has the labor movement been more influential.

Sweden is thus the locus classicus for discussing the achievements and limitations of Social Democratic reformism. How does the Swedish welfare state differ from other welfare states? Are income, wealth, and power distributed more equally in Sweden? How has the political and economic power by labor affected economic growth, employment, and inflation? What is the long-term path of Social Democracy? Does Social Democratic reformism heighten wage earners' expectations or promote an acceptance of capitalism?

This book focuses on a series of reform initiatives launched by the Swedish labor movement between 1968 and 1976.[1] First, the labor

---

1. The year 1976 represents the peak rather than the end of what I refer to as the "reform offensive of 1968–76." Also, the term "labor movement" ("labor" for short) is used here in the sense that Swedes use the term "worker movement" (*arbetarrörelsen*); that is, to designate the Social Democratic party (Socialdemokratiska arbetarpartiet; SAP), the confederation of blue-collar unions (Landsorganisationen; LO), various "auxiliary" Social Democratic organizations, and as an opposition force, the Communist party (known since 1990 as *Vänsterpartiet*, the party of the Left). The term does not encompass white-collar unions, which are organized into two confederated peak organizations: the Central Or-

movement introduced the idea of an *active industrial policy*, proposing institutional reforms to extend the state's capacity to intervene selectively in industrial restructuring. Second, to foster codetermination or *industrial democracy*, it proposed legislation designed to restrict managers and to help employee representatives influence corporate decisions. Finally, the labor movement introduced the idea of *collective shareownership* by endorsing the buildup of "wage-earner funds" through collective profit-sharing.

These initiatives challenged the power and prerogatives of corporate managers and owners of capital. Hence they departed from the essentially welfarist orientation of Swedish Social Democracy between 1948 and 1968. To use John Stephens's (1979) terminology, in the 1970s production politics became ascendant over consumption politics. I do not mean that traditional Social Democratic reformism can be adequately characterized as "redistributive." As Gösta Esping-Andersen (1985, 1989) has pointed out, the postwar expansion of the welfare state involved not only income redistribution but also the creation and extension of a sector in which public, nonprofit agencies provide services and goods in response to demand based on citizens' rights rather than on ability to pay. I mean simply that the postwar project of Swedish Social Democracy did not involve any sustained effort to reform the organization of the corporate, commodity-producing sector of the economy (what Swedes refer to as *näringslivet*).

The corporate sector includes cooperative and state-owned enterprises as well as privately owned business, the production of services as well as of industrial goods; but private ownership and industry are dominant. In the mid-1970s state-owned enterprises accounted for less than 6 percent of Sweden's gross domestic product (GDP), a share significantly smaller than in several other West European countries (Parris, Pestieau, and Saynor 1987:27). As the source of export earnings, the corporate sector is the engine of the Swedish economy and the point where the tension between politics and markets emerges most clearly.[2]

In Swedish Social Democracy we can discern two distinctive ideological traditions (Higgins 1988; Tilton 1990). One accepts the basic prem-

---

ganization of Salaried Employees (TCO) and the Swedish Confederation of Professional Associations (SACO-SR).

2. Following Swedish national accounting practices, I treat the housing sector as separate from the corporate sector. A significant segment of the housing sector is also characterized by commodity production, but like the public sector, the housing sector as a whole is sheltered from international competition. Compared with the corporate sector, the housing sector is more regulated, subsidies play a more important role, and public and cooperative forms of ownership are much more common.

ise of mainstream economics, that the pursuit of profit by private business yields the most efficient allocation of resources; it is hostile to selective state intervention in the corporate sector. This tradition seeks to satisfy working-class interests by combining Keynesian macroeconomic management to promote capitalist growth with welfare measures to offset the negative consequences of that growth. The other Social Democratic tradition is more critical of mainstream economics. It too favors Keynesian macroeconomic management and welfare, but it also seeks institutional reforms to alter the balance of power between business and the state and to give unions a direct role in decisions about production.[3]

The reform offensive of 1968–76 demonstrated the continued vitality of this latter tradition within Swedish Social Democracy. This tradition might be called socialist, but it need not entail system-transforming ambitions, let alone a coherent vision of the transition to socialism. It can be, and often is, just as preoccupied as its "Right" counterpart with solving immediate problems.

Moreover, the two traditions share a positive disposition toward restructuring and rationalizing the corporate sector. From a comparative perspective, the willingness of the Swedish labor movement to accommodate economic change is outstanding. Sweden's small population is important in this context. Ever since the late nineteenth century, the labor movement has looked to imports to reduce consumer prices and hence raise workers' purchasing power. Imports must be paid for with export earnings, of course, and so labor has always had to concern itself with the world competitiveness of Swedish industry. The labor movement did not see its reform offensive as a retreat from its commitment to free trade. On the contrary, it argued that active industrial policy, codetermination, and collective shareownership were needed to reconcile wage earners' interests with competitiveness.

The reform offensive challenged the power and prerogatives of managers and capitalists at different levels. Some initiatives addressed specific aspects of the relationship between wage earners and employers. For instance, the labor movement pushed through legislative measures that restricted employers' right to fire people (the Employment Security Act of 1974) and that allowed shop-floor safety stewards to shut down production if they determined conditions were hazardous or unhealthful (the Work Environment Act of 1977). Other reforms addressed systemic features of the labor-capital relationship. The wage-earner funds proposal endorsed in 1976 by LO, the confederation of

3. In the context of practical politics, the differences between these traditions often become a matter of emphasis, but the contrast emerges clearly if one compares Feldt (1984) with Hedborg and Meidner (1984).

3

blue-collar unions, usually called the Meidner Plan after its principal author, went furthest, by calling into question the very principle of private ownership. Had the proposal been enacted, collective funds would gradually have acquired ownership in all profitable corporations employing more that fifty or one hundred persons.[4]

I look on the reform initiatives of 1968–76 as attempts to democratize control of investment. More precisely, they tried to create institutional arrangements whereby unions, as representatives of wage earners, could influence allocative investment decisions within the corporate sector of the economy. Legislation on employment security, the work environment, and the like thus lies outside my analysis. The question of investment control—how investment decisions are made and who makes them—is the critical link between labor's pursuit of full employment, real-wage growth, and income redistribution within the framework of capitalism and any system-transforming political project. Investment decisions are strategic in that they entail a long-term commitment of resources, and business resistance to reformist initiatives is likely to be strongest when such initiatives impinge on the investment decisions of corporate managers or owners of capital. In short, if we are searching for the limits of Social Democracy, this is the place to look.

Predictably, the reform attempts made by the Swedish labor movement in 1968–76, especially the proposal about wage-earner funds, provoked a great deal of political controversy. Organized business and the bourgeois parties mobilized against the collectivization of ownership.[5]

In the 1970s it became common to speak of three stages in the evolution of the Swedish labor movement: having first achieved political democracy early in the century, labor had achieved social democracy by the late 1960s and then embarked on the struggle for economic democracy. Walter Korpi was perhaps the principal academic proponent of this interpretation. In 1978 Korpi referred to the realignment of Swedish politics in the 1930s as Sweden's "historical compromise," suggesting that Swedish Social Democrats had then achieved what the Italian Communists were seeking in the 1970s. He argued that this compromise was a necessary stage on the road to economic democracy (or

4. According to Meidner (1975:79), it would have taken wage-earner funds thirty-five years to acquire 49 percent of the equity of a corporation operating at an average annual rate of profit of 10 percent. The higher the profits, the faster the collectivization of ownership would have been.

5. In accordance with conventional Swedish usage, I use "bourgeois parties" as a collective label for the three parliamentary parties to the right of the Social Democrats: the Center party (formerly the Agrarian party), the Liberals (the "People's party"), and the Conservatives (the "Moderate Unity party").

democratic socialism) and that the labor movements of Southern Europe, despite their radical rhetoric, were really far behind the Swedish labor movement.

Some fifteen years have elapsed since LO endorsed the Meidner proposal for wage-earner funds and Parliament passed the Codetermination Act. Is Sweden today farther along the road to economic democracy than it was fifteen years ago? One would be hard put to make such a claim. Indeed, nobody does. Market forces and corporate choices still determine the allocation of investment within the corporate sector. While the unions' ability to influence corporate investment through codetermination has proved limited, market forces have become more important, and less subject to political regulation, as financial markets have been deregulated, the stock market has boomed, state subsidies to industry have been cut, and state enterprise has been reorganized and partially privatized. Joining the European Community will probably consolidate this "counterrevolution," at least in the short run.

What came of the reform initiatives of 1968–76? The literature in English includes several accounts of codetermination practices, and the Swedish literature on codetermination is huge, but I know of no account of the development of Swedish industrial policy beyond the late 1970s, nor of any systematic attempt to assess the significance of the wage-earner funds legislation the Social Democrats introduced in 1983. Given the excitement the idea of wage-earner funds generated, the latter absence is all the more remarkable. Perhaps scholarly inattention to implementation and consequences stems from the fact that these initiatives did not, in the end, amount to anything exciting. But if very little came of the new reformism, we need to ask why.

The experience of investment politics underlines two variables that are glossed over in conventional accounts of Sweden as a country where labor rules: business power and political divisions within the labor movement. What makes Sweden special from a comparative perspective, as Peter Katzenstein (1985) argues, is not only the strength of its unions and the electoral dominance of Social Democracy, but also the cohesive, highly organized character of its business community (see also Israel 1978). Most interpretations of Swedish politics downplay business power, treating it as a "structural constraint" on labor rather than as an active force in politics.

At the same time, most interpreters give us a Swedish labor movement that is virtually a monolithic actor in politics.[6] Distributive conflicts among unions figure prominently in recent literature, but politi-

6. This is more generally true of the literature on corporatism and labor politics in the advanced capitalist countries. See Golden and Pontusson (1992) for an alternative approach to comparative labor politics.

cal divisions among the unions and between the unions and the Social Democratic party (SAP) have typically been noted but not analyzed. As we shall see, the reform offensive of 1968–76 emanated from the union wing of the labor movement; party leaders never fully subscribed to its ambitions. This split within labor, most apparent in the case of wage-earner funds, provides an obvious explanation for the limits of reformism in investment politics, but we must also ask why this split occurred.

The reform offensive was not a complete failure. In each of the three areas I identified above—industrial policy, codetermination, and collective shareownership—labor's initiatives did lead to new institutional arrangements. Assessment depends, of course, on what standards we apply, and I return to this problem in the concluding chapter. But the outcomes in each case fell far short of the ambitions of the labor movement. The gap between expectations and outcomes was especially marked in the case of wage-earner funds. By comparison, labor's push for codetermination must be considered a qualified success. And as we shall see, the experience of industrial policy can be characterized as an intermediate case. This variation across cases makes possible a more nuanced and precise discussion of the limits of Social Democratic reformism.

This book takes on four tasks. The first is to describe the reform initiatives of 1968–76 and situate them in relation to postwar investment politics. The result is a description of the evolution of Social Democratic goals and strategy with respect to the issue of investment control. The second task is to explain the evolution of Social Democratic strategy and, specifically, why the labor movement began to challenge private control of investment in 1968–76. The third is to describe the institutions that resulted from labor's reform offensive and to assess their significance for the allocation of investment capital. The fourth is to explain why the institutional arrangements came to look and function as they did. I thus have two objects of analysis: on the one hand, Social Democratic goals and strategy; on the other, institutions created by the Social Democrats to enhance wage-earner influence over investment.

I proceed from the premise that control cannot be reduced to the issue of ownership (Zysman 1983). Corporate management always enjoys some autonomy from owners, and political actors may be able to influence corporate investment without holding ownership stakes. At the same time, public ownership or lending does not necessarily let political actors shape corporate decisions.[7] To assess the ability of political actors—in this case unions—to influence corporate decisions and the allocation of investment capital across firms, we must explore institutional arrangements that are variable rather than constant features of capitalism—that vary across advanced capitalist countries.

We can distinguish two levels of decision making about investment in a capitalist economy. First, individuals or institutions (possibly governments or state-owned institutions) invest by purchasing corporate equity or by lending capital to corporations and thus determine the interfirm allocation of investment. Second, corporations invest in products, plants, machinery, and employee skills and thus determine the intrafirm allocation of investment. Both types of investment decisions entail a long-term commitment of resources, shaping the future structure of the economy.

In a similar vein, we can distinguish between wage-earner or union influence exercised "from above" and "from below." Influence from above is exercised through the government or through capital-market institutions such as public pension funds and wage-earner funds. Influence from below, is exercised through representation on corporate boards of directors or through codetermination bargaining. The scope of influence from below is more limited, for it does not enable unions to influence the interfirm allocation of investment (except possibly for conglomerates). Exercising influence from above is necessarily more complicated, however. To Zysman's (1983) question, Can the state influence strategic corporate decisions? we must add a second question: Can labor influence the state? The problem before us makes it imperative to treat state institutions as mechanisms of representation as well as intervention.

Influence from above might be exercised through electoral-parliamentary or corporatist mechanisms of representation. The electoral-parliamentary route involves unions' participation in electoral politics and the representation of "wage-earner interests" by government officials (either elected officials or civil servants accountable to them). I use the term "corporatism" to designate direct representation of unions (and other interest groups) in the formulation of public policy in a broad sense; it encompasses policy-making by local governments, administrative state agencies, public pension funds, and wage-earner funds as well as the central government. Elected or not, the union offi-

7. At times Zysman goes so far as to suggest that ownership is irrelevant to control (e.g., Zysman 1983:185–87). I do not understand why one would adopt such a radical position: it seems more plausible to hold that collective ownership enhances the potential for public influence but is neither a necessary nor a sufficient condition.

cials involved in corporatist representation are invariably career officials. By contrast, union influence from below is exercised through participation in corporate decision making and involves shop-floor representatives as well as local officials (part time or full time, depending on the size of the firm).

The question of union influence over investment decisions is closely related to "public" or "democratic" influence over investment decisions, for the state provides one of the principal ways unions may influence investment. The term "democratic control of investment" should perhaps be reserved for control by elected government officials (Hadenius 1983:14–17), but it is not misleading to speak of "democratization" to the extent that broad societal interests are brought to bear on the decisions of capitalists and corporate managers irrespective of the representative mechanism involved. And in a society where wage earners constitute more than 90 percent of the economically active population and unions organize more than 85 percent of wage earners, unions must surely be considered the representatives of broad societal interest par excellence.

Chapter 1 provides an overview of the Swedish experience of investment politics, identifying more precisely what I want to explain. It sets out my basic arguments and situates them in relation to the existing literature on Social Democracy in general and Swedish Social Democracy in particular.

The chapters in part one follow a chronological order and together cover the entire period of Social Democratic rule (1932–91). Chapter 2 describes the labor movement's ambitions to institutionalize planning and the political struggles surrounding the question of planning in the 1930s and 1940s. Labor's retreat from planning in the late 1940s constitutes an important yet frequently neglected feature of the postwar settlement between labor and business. It also provides interesting parallels to the new reformism of the 1970s. The reform offensive of 1968–76 was, in effect, labor's second attempt to institutionalize democratic control of investment.

Chapter 3 describes how the labor movement sought to influence the pattern of investment without challenging private ownership, market forces, or the autonomy of corporate management in the 1950s and 1960s. The chapter presents the logic of the Rehn-Meidner model, briefly discusses the implementation of solidaristic wage policy and active labor market policy, then explores two institutional reforms bearing on investment control: the system of (tax-exempt) investment funds and the buildup of public pension funds. As we shall see, these reforms were not intended to provide for union influence over allocative investment decisions.

Chapter 4 situates the new labor reformism of the 1970s in the context of long-term changes in the structure of Swedish industry and the dynamics of the world economy. I argue that such changes undermined the viability of labor's postwar strategy and reintroduced the issue of investment control. Against this backdrop I briefly address the economic recovery of the 1980s.

The chapters in part 2 deal with the reform initiatives of 1968–76: industrial policy (chap. 5), codetermination (chap. 6), and collective shareownership (chap. 7). In each case I reconstruct labor's motives and ambitions, discuss the political struggles these initiatives gave rise to in the legislative phase, and explore the actual functioning of the institutions that were created. Although my treatment of the experiences of industrial policy and collective shareholding funds is comprehensive, my analysis of the practice of codetermination is restricted to single case study of Volvo (a limiting case of what the labor movement has been able to achieve through codetermination in the corporate sector).

Finally, the concluding chapter generalizes about the limits of Social Democracy based on the experiences described in part 2, addressing the variations across my three case studies.

CHAPTER ONE

Theoretical Perspectives on Social Democracy

Why did the Swedish labor movement begin to challenge private control of investment in 1968–76? And why did labor fail to democratize allocative investment decisions? These questions raise distinctive analytical problems. While the question about the impetus behind reformism calls for an analysis of labor's interests and of the circumstances in which private control of investment is compatible (or incompatible) with labor's interests, understanding the limits of reformism calls for analyzing the balance of power between labor and business and the strategic choices labor makes in pursuit of its interests. I believe it is important to address these questions in tandem.

Though our explanations of why labor turned left and why its left turn failed must be different, they should be compatible. Walter Korpi (1978) provides a plausible explanation of why labor turned left, but its theoretical framework renders labor's failure unintelligible. Adam Przeworski (1985) provides a parsimonious and compelling rationale for why reformist challenges to capitalism must fail, yet the logic of his explanation implies that mature, reformist labor movements would never undertake initiatives like those the Swedish labor movement launched in 1968–76.

This chapter sets out my approach to each of the questions posed above and situates my arguments in relation to Korpi's and Przeworski's interpretations of the historical relation between capitalism and Social Democracy. But let me first summarize the history of Swedish investment politics.

THE STORY OF SWEDISH INVESTMENT POLITICS

Between the wars, the idea of planning replaced the goal of nation-alizing industry as the linchpin of Social Democratic investment politics. By the time the Swedish Social Democrats consolidated control of the government in the 1930s, they had already adopted an essentially prag-matic approach to public ownership, treating it as one of several means for achieving public control of economic development. Their reliance on nonsocialist parliamentary support precluded even selective sociali-zation measures, however.

After World War II, planning became the subject of a heated ideo-logical debate. Faced with vociferous business opposition, the Social Democrats abandoned their efforts to institute planning as an indus-trial policy that would be both comprehensive and selective. Although the role of the state in regulating the economy and redistributing in-come expanded, in Sweden formalized planning never amounted to more than macroeconomic forecasting. In contrast to their French counterparts, the five-year plans that were elaborated from 1948 on-ward did not involve negotiations with business and did not specify how resources should be allocated within the corporate sector.[1]

The retreat from planning did not mean that labor abandoned its ambition to influence investment. Rather, labor's postwar strategy, commonly known as the Rehn-Meidner model, was to influence invest-ment decisions in ways that respected the autonomy of corporate man-agers and owners of capital. The strategic reorientation of the labor movement in the second half of the 1940s can be seen as a shift from an "anticapitalist" to a "pro-capitalist" approach to investment politics, yet the planning it advocated in the interwar period was not strictly anticapitalist, and elements of the pro-capitalist approach that later came to prevail were articulated before World War II. It is more accu-rate to say that the Social Democrats purged their approach of anti-capitalist elements in the second half of the 1940s.

Labor's postwar strategy was to promote industrial restructuring through soldaristic wage bargaining. Its logic is well known: on the one hand, above-average wage increases for the lowest paid would squeeze the profit margins of less efficient firms and sectors, forcing them to rationalize production or go out of business; on the other hand, wage restraint by the best paid would encourage capacity expansion in more efficient firms and sectors. The unions could not possibly assume this

1. On the contrast between postwar patterns of state intervention in Sweden and France, see Pontusson (1983a, 1991).

role unless the government pursued an active labor market policy, but there was no need for an active industrial policy within the framework of the Rehn-Meidner model. Indeed, selective state intervention to alter market incentives for allocating investment capital was anathema to the model's logic, at least as conceived in the 1950s. Solidaristic wage bargaining promoted the restructuring of capital by reinforcing market-determined profit differentials.

Active labor market policy emerged as the most important form of selective state intervention during the postwar boom and came to exemplify the "corporatism" of the new era, with unions and employers participating in policy implementation as well as policy formation. Although there is little doubt that active labor market policy eased the consequences of restructuring for workers and communities and contributed to Sweden's successful maintenance of full employment, its limits in steering industrial development are apparent. By definition, active labor market policy deals with the consequences of corporate investment decisions and seeks to adjust the supply of labor to the resulting changes in demand. (That policymakers try to anticipate future changes in demand does not alter this assessment.)

Two institutional reforms suggest that labor's postwar strategy did not concede private control of investment. First, the system of investment funds (IF) introduced in 1938 was reformed in 1955, greatly enhancing its significance. The "IF system" let corporations avoid taxes by setting profits aside for future investment, subject to government approval. That the Labor Market Board (Arbetsmarknadsstyrelsen; AMS) was responsible for releasing investment funds has led a number of observers to cite the IF system as an instance of the selective state intervention and corporatist policy bargaining that ensue when labor market policy "spills over" into the sphere of investment policy.

Second, the ATP (pension) reform of 1959 led to the buildup of huge public pension funds in the 1960s. At their peak in the early 1970s these funds, known as the AP funds, accounted for 35 percent of the total supply of credit (and 57 percent of credit with a maturity of more than seven years). Because the funds have tripartite boards of directors, it has also been common to see their growth as an extension of public influence and corporatist bargaining.[2]

A more careful analysis reveals that releasing investment funds and

2. Lewin (1967), Jones (1976), Scase (1977), Stephens (1979), and Esping-Andersen (1985) suggest such interpretations of the AP funds, and Shonfield (1965), Jones (1976), and Wickman (1980) interpret the IF system in a similar manner. Higgins (1980, 1983, 1985) argues most consistently that the Swedish labor movement sought to extend democratic control of investment throughout the postwar era (see also Higgins and Apple 1983). See Pontusson (1983b) for a critique of Higgins's argument.

lending ATP savings have rarely been used to influence investment patterns in a purposive and selective manner. The IF system was conceived as a tool of countercyclical management, and this remained its primary function until the economic crisis of the 1970s. As successive governments liberalized the release of investment funds from the early 1970s onward, the IF system acted as a general investment subsidy rather than an instrument of state intervention.

The lending practices of the AP funds altered the allocation of investment capital among aggregate economic sectors (central government, local government, housing, and business) in the 1960s and 1970s. However, investment steering at this level was achieved through the regulation of credit markets by the Central Bank, which required private insurance companies to allocate their lending in essentially the same fashion. The tripartite boards of the AP funds have met rarely and have never made significant allocative decisions. Most important, the AP funds have been confined to indirect lending to the corporate sector and have never influenced the investment decisions of corporate borrowers.

Although the formalities of tripartite interest representation are very similar, the absence of meaningful bargaining among interest representatives on the boards of the AP funds contrasts with the pattern of labor market policy, bringing out the asymmetry of the political economy of class compromise in postwar Sweden: whereas the restructuring of the labor force was subject to detailed state intervention and union influence through corporatist channels, the restructuring of capital remained for the most part beyond the reach of public policy and corporatist bargaining.

Against this background, the new reforms pushed by labor from 1968 to 1976—active industrial policy, codetermination, and wage-earner funds—can be seen as a return to anticapitalist investment politics. Again, this characterization must immediately be qualified, for the labor movement certainly did not abandon concern for providing a favorable climate for private investors. Like the immediate postwar period, when labor sought to institutionalize planning, the 1970s were distinguished by the presence of anticapitalist components rather than by the absence of pro-capitalist elements in labor's appproach to investment and production.

To the labor movement, activating industrial policy meant extending the principles of active labor market policy. Through ownership engagements as well as subsidies to both private and state-owned corporations, the state did indeed become much more directly involved in industrial restructuring during the 1970s, and its involvement continued under the bourgeois coalition governments of 1976–82. In fact, the bourgeois parties nationalized more industry during their first three years in power than the Social Democrats had done in forty-four years. The experience of industrial policy turned out very differently from that of labor market policy, however, for industrial policy became an essentially defensive adjustment policy, involving ad hoc measures to cope with the crises of declining sectors, and had little bearing on investment decisions in the growth sectors of the economy. Moreover, a different pattern of policy-making evolved as industrial policy came to depend on direct negotiations between government officials and corporate management. Corporatist arrangements were less prominent than in labor market policy, and organized labor played a much more marginal role.

When the Social Democrats returned to power in 1982, they eschewed selective state intervention in industrial restructuring and opted for a market-oriented, profit-led recovery strategy. Known as "the third way," this strategy was conceived as an alternative to the reflationary policy orientation of the French Socialists as well as the deflationary orientation of Margaret Thatcher. Its centerpiece was a "competitive" devaluation of 16 percent, coming on top of a 10 percent devaluation in 1981. To counteract the inflationary effects of the devaluation, the new Social Democratic government pressured the unions into wage restraint and strove to balance its budget primarily by cutting expenditures. By 1988 the Social Democrats had effectively balanced the central government budget, though they had inherited a budget deficit corresponding to more than 13 percent of GDP in 1982. Remarkably, they achieved a balanced budget without any major cuts in welfare entitlements or any increase in unemployment.

One of the principal ways the Social Democrats saved money was by slashing state subsidies to industry. At the same time, the government reorganized the lame-duck corporations it had acquired in the 1970s and embarked on a partial privatization of state enterprise. Whereas labor's industrial policy of the late 1960s was informed by a vaguely articulated but strong belief that state-owned corporations should behave differently from private ones, the new policy stressed that profitability, in a narrow, conventional sense, should be their overriding goal.

The reorganization of state enterprise demonstrated the new government's commitment to market-driven restructuring of the economy. The pro-capitalist approach the Social Democrats adopted in the 1980s also manifested itself in a far-reaching deregulation of financial markets, including the removal of various restrictions on the movement of capital abroad. Moreover, the tax reform of 1989 eliminated some of the structural biases of the system of corporate taxation as well as the potential for state intervention by abolishing the IF system while reducing taxes on profits.

The Social Democrats did introduce wage-earner funds shortly after they returned to power, but the funds enacted in 1983 bore little resemblance to those proposed in 1976. Wage-earner funds became a subject of intense political controversy in the late 1970s. In the face of a massive mobilization against them by organized business and the bourgeois parties, the labor movement retreated from the more radical features of the Meidner Plan. The Social Democrats nonetheless lost the struggle for public opinion. Clearly, they won the 1982 election despite rather than because of their advocacy of wage-earner funds. Unwilling to abandon the idea completely, the new government created five collective shareholding funds modeled on a pension fund that had been established in 1973 to invest ATP savings in the stock market, known as the Fourth AP Fund. The 1983 legislation limited the buildup of wage-earner funds to seven years. At the end of 1989, the five funds together held slightly more than 3 percent of corporate shares registered on the stock exchange, and the Fourth AP Fund held another 3 percent.

The experience of the Fourth AP Fund can be summarized as follows. The fund has behaved like private insurance companies in that it has built up a diversified portfolio and has assumed an essentially passive ownership role, but it has put more emphasis on long-term ownership engagements and manufacturing. Specific investment decisions have been made according to conventional calculations of return on investment, and the fund's management has shunned any entanglement with the government's industrial policies. At least a couple of the wage-earner funds created in 1983 have taken a more active ownership role than the Fourth AP Fund, but their ability to influence corporate decision making is even more limited. Considered as portfolio investors, the wage-earner funds have been more market-conformative than the Fourth AP fund: they have not invested disproportionately in manufacturing industry, nor have they distinguished themselves as long-term investors.

In its nature and outcome, the debate over wage-earner funds recalls the debate over planning following World War II. In both cases radical reform initiatives by labor precipitated a countermobilization by business: the Social Democrats prevailed electorally but retreated ideologically. Much like the election of 1948, the 1982 election represents the beginning of a new, pro-capitalist phase of Social Democratic investment and production politics. The policy orientation pursued by the Social Democratic governments of the 1980s must not be seen simply as a return to that of the 1950s and 1960s, however. In terms of macroeconomics, the logic of the third way diverged from labor's postwar strategy in emphasizing the need for higher corporate profits to regain competitiveness and in treating public spending as an obstacle to private-sector growth.

On the other hand, the Social Democrats did not abandon their commitment to codetermination in the 1980s. Their return to power in 1982 coincided with the signing of a private-sector agreement on codetermination procedures (Utvecklingsavtalet), to follow up the Codetermination Act of 1976, and in the 1980s firm-level codetermination bargaining was institutionalized within the corporate sector. With some justification, the Social Democrats commonly characterize their new approach to production politics as the pursuit of firm-level codetermination within the context of market-driven restructuring (see, e.g., SAP 1989). Whereas the labor movement originally broached codetermination as a challenge to the power structure of capitalist corporations, it now tends to treat it as a means of reconciling the need for productivity and quality improvement with reskilling and work humanization. Codetermination is no longer conceived as a struggle for power. Nonetheless, the codetermination offensive of the early 1970s has had important and enduring consequences.

A careful assessment of Swedish codetermination practices in the 1980s would require a separate book, for its reality varies across sectors, firms, and workplaces. But the secondary literature suggests that the conclusions of my case study of Volvo can be generalized. Although codetermination has indeed given the Volvo unions significant influence over corporate decisions about new technology and new forms of work organization, bargaining over such issues occurs within limits set by corporate decisions in which the unions hardly participate. In particular, the significance of codetermination is constrained by the multinational character of Volvo's operations.

To sum up, the period since the Social Democrats came to power in 1932 might be divided into four subperiods. From 1932 to 1948, and again from 1968 to 1982, investment control was high on labor's political agenda, and programmatic texts of the labor movement articulated certain anticapitalist ambitions. We might think of this historical pattern in terms of shifts in the balance between the two ideological traditions within Swedish Social Democracy. Again, what distinguishes 1932–48 and 1968–82 is the presence of anticapitalist ambitions rather than the absence of pro-capitalist concerns. Pro-capitalist investment politics constitutes a more or less permanent feature of Swedish Social Democracy in government.

The LO unions initiated the reform offensive of 1968–76, and the SAP leaders never fully subscribed to LO's ambitions. This divergence between the two wings of the labor movement distinguishes the experience of the 1970s from labor's pursuit of planning in the 1930s and 1940s. Whereas ideological differences cut across the organizational divide between unions and party in the earlier period, in the 1970s they tended to follow this divide. The union wing of the labor movement thus has increasingly come to embody the Social Democratic tradition that seeks to alter power relations in the corporate sector of the economy.

TWO INTERPRETATIONS OF SOCIAL DEMOCRACY

This book proceeds from a critique of both Korpi's and Przeworski's interpretations of the historical relationship between capitalism and Social Democracy. Korpi's analysis focuses on why the Swedish labor movement adopted more radical goals in the 1970s.[3] Although Korpi (1978:321) speaks of labor's strategic reorientation as a response to the "negative consequences" of postwar growth, his principal argument is that this development was a consequence of the cumulative growth of labor's power resources or, more precisely, the reduction of the "power difference" between labor and business after the war (see also Korpi 1982, 1983).

Korpi conceives the labor movement as a more or less unitary and rational actor with an inbuilt system-transformative drive: how far labor challenges capitalism at any given moment depends on the prevailing balance of power. In the 1930s the labor movement settled for the "historical compromise" because it was not powerful enough to challenge the systemic power of capital. As its power grew, labor found the terms of the compromise increasingly unacceptable. In short, the historical compromise broke down because labor outgrew it. In Korpi's account, labor's power relative to that of business grew in the postwar era for two reasons: first, capitalist development generated further proletarianization in the sense that wage-earner strata continued to expand as a percentage of the population; second, the unionization of wage earners continued to increase. Though government policy does not figure prominently in his analysis, Korpi also suggests that the reformist achievement of Social Democracy contributed to the cumulative growth of labor's power.[4]

3. In contrast to the authors cited in note 2, Korpi shares my emphasis on the reform offensive of 1968–76 as a departure from labor's postwar strategy. See Pontusson (1984a) for a more elaborate critique of his theoretical perspective.
4. This line of argument is developed more fully and consistently by Gösta Esping-Andersen (1985, 1990). See also Castles (1978), Pontusson (1987), and Rothstein (1990b).

The shortcomings of labor's reform offensive weakens Korpi's explanation of why labor turned left, for he implicitly argues that a class
does not set for itself tasks that it cannot accomplish. More generally,
the cyclical pattern that emerges so clearly if we consider the entire
period from the early 1930s through the 1980s is very much at odds
with the linear evolution Korpi posits.

It is tempting to try to rescue Korpi's schema by introducing a more
dynamic understanding of the balance of class power. Swedish developments since the mid-1970s suggest that the balance of class power is
affected far more by economic and political factors of a conjunctural
nature than Korpi allows. Though bourgeois as well as Social Democratic governments kept the lid on unemployment, the world economic
crisis of 1974–83 clearly was the context for a shift of iniative and
power from labor to business. But why did the crisis of the 1970s have
political effects opposite those of the crisis of the 1930s? This question
invites a critique of the notion that the postwar era was characterized
by the cumulative growth of labor's power relative to business. Although Korpi recognizes that business enjoys an inherent advantage
over labor in that its resources are more concentrated, his picture of
the postwar era rests entirely on evidence concerning labor's power resources.

There can be no doubt that workers became more numerous and
better organized after World War II, but it is also true that Swedish
business became more concentrated and more multinational in its operations. It is far from self-evident that the former tendencies out-
weighed the latter. Instead of trying to sort out this problem, I shall
pursue a different approach to why labor turned left, one that hinges
on the proposition that changing economic circumstances pushed the
labor movement to challenge private control of investment. Whereas
Korpi seeks to explain the goals of class actors in terms of the balance
of class power, I interpret the new reformism in terms of labor's interests and the economic conditions for their realization, and I treat the
balance of power as a constraint on what labor (or business) can
achieve.[5]

Przeworski (1985) addresses the persistent failure of reformist socialists to challenge the systemic power of business in Sweden and
elswehere, focusing on two features of electoral competition in a cap-

---

5. Bernt Schiller's (1988) study of the new labor laws of the 1970s adopts a similar
approach. Schiller argues (p. 20) that power as a motive for rational action operates only
at the upper reaches of society: "Human action to change power relations at work rather
appears to have been driven by material conditions in combination with ideological factors. It would open up [matters] for a more nuanced analysis to view power relations,
including ideological power, as decisive for what did and did *not* come of the demands
for industrial democracy."

italist setting. First, reformist socialist parties must mobilize electoral support beyond the working class to gain control of the government, for the working class does not constitute a majority in advanced capitalist societies. Second, winning future elections depends on economic performance, which in turn depends on the level of private investment. To stay in power, reformist governments must avoid reform initiatives that undermine business confidence (Block 1977; Lindblom 1977).

Przeworski correctly identifies the critical problems that reformist socialists face, but his reasoning tends to foreclose a meaningful exploration of these problems (King and Wickham-Jones 1990). While he conceives the "working class" very narrowly (as manual labor), Przeworski assumes that issues pertaining to control over capital have little or no appeal to nonworkers. Yet his own analysis shows that the steepness of the trade-off between the electoral support of workers and nonworkers varies significantly across countries and over time. Taken by itself, the proposition that reformist socialists must have support beyond the industrial working class does not tell us much about the policies they can or cannot pursue.[6]

Ultimately, Przeworski's case for the impossibility of an electoral-reformist path to socialism hinges on the constraints posed by private control of investment. Przeworski's argument must be qualified in this regard as well, for such constraints are not absolute or constant. It seems clear that capitalists' willingness to invest at any given rate of profitability is itself variable (Hodgson 1982; King and Wickham-Jones 1990). Moreover, public funds account for a significant portion of investment in all advanced capitalist countries, and quite apart from their own investments, governments influence private investment behavior. It is at least conceivable that a reformist government committed to radical reforms could sustain an adequate rate of investment through a combination of carrots to stimulate private investment, sticks to discourage capital flight and hoarding of wealth, and perhaps a partial replacement of private investment by public investment. Indeed, Przeworski (1985:217) admits that a "comprehensive, consistent system of

6. Przeworski (1985:126–27) justifies his narrow conception of the working class with reference to observed electoral behavior; that is, he treats all white-collar employees as nonworkers because they tend to vote for nonsocialist parties and because socialist parties face a trade-off between white-collar and blue-collar support (see also Przeworski and Sprague 1986). Yet his overall approach to voting behavior stresses that how far workers (and nonworkers) identify themselves as a class and vote accordingly depends on the strategies and rhetoric of political parties. From this perspective, the existence of a trade-off between lower-level white-collar votes and blue-collar votes does not necessarily tell us anything about the potential medium or long-term electoral viability of a socialist strategy appealing to the common interests of these groups as wage earners. It tells us only that established left parties have not pursued such a strategy (instead appealing to the interests of all white-collar employees as citizens, consumers, etc.).

public control over investment" opens the possibility of escaping the dilemma of reformist socialism.

Considering the actual experience of Social Democracy, there are two problems with Przeworski's approach. First, it does not lend itself well to explaining cross-national variations in the reformist achievements of Social Democracy. Second, and more important for our purposes, Przeworski's historical account completely ignores the radicalization of Social Democratic labor movements in the 1970s. In Przeworski's rendition, the history of European Social Democracy amounts to a unilinear and ultimately complete abandonment of ambitions to reform capitalist society. And so it must be, for within his theoretical framework it is incomprehensible that Social Democratic leaders should push radical reforms once they recognize the choices available.

Przeworski's schema provides an elegant explanation for the permanence of pro-capitalist investment politics as a feature of Social Democracy, but it provides no explanation at all for the occasional (perhaps cyclical) reemergence of anticapitalist investment politics. This "lopsidedness" is closely related to his focus on parties and electoral politics at the expense of union politics. As I noted above, the reform offensive of 1968–76 was initiated by the union wing of the labor movement.

In a sense Przeworski's interpretation of the Social Democratic experience is the mirror image of Korpi's. Whereas Korpi focuses on the power resources of organized labor and explains why the Swedish labor movement turned left in 1968–76, Przeworski focuses on electoral politics and explains why labor's left turn failed. It is tempting to think we might generate a more adequate interpretation of the Social Democratic experience by somehow merging Korpi's and Przeworski's analyses, but this will not do. Just as the shortcomings of labor's reform offensive require us to rethink the explanation of the new reformism proposed by Korpi, so the radicalization of the labor movement requires us to rethink the explanation of the limits of Social Democracy proposed by Przeworski.

THE LIMITS OF REFORMISM

Understanding why labor failed to democratize investment decisions calls for analyzing the balance of power between labor and business as well as strategic choices by labor. This analysis should also let us account for variations across our three cases of reformism—to address such questions as, Why were labor's codetermination initiatives more successful than its wage-earner funds initiative?

We can distinguish between arguments in terms of whether they focus on the politics of legislation or the politics of implementation. And we can distinguish between capital-centered and labor-centered arguments. Combining these overlapping criteria, we end up with four types of explanatory variables (see fig. 1 below).

Legislation versus Implementation

Arguments that focus on the politics of legislation attribute labor's failure to democratize investment decisions to limits embedded in the institutional reforms associated with its pursuit of active industrial policy, collective shareownership, and codetermination. For instance, one might argue that the wage-earner funds reform of 1983 was too limited to affect the basic structure of ownership power or that the laws governing these funds have restricted their influence. The question then becomes, Why didn't the labor movement achieve more far-reaching institutional reforms?

Alternatively, one might argue that wage-earner influence over investment is limited not so much by the legislative measures themselves as by political or institutional factors that affected the operation of the institutions created. This approach contends that such institutions provide a much greater potential for investment control than has been realized. What, then, accounts for labor's failure to realize the full potential of new institutional arrangements?

The case for focusing on legislation is very strong when we consider the potential mechanisms of wage-earner influence the labor movement introduced in the postwar period—the original AP funds and the system of investment funds. The legal rules governing the AP funds, adopted by Parliament in 1959, effectively subjected the funds to regulation by the Central Bank and precluded any leverage vis-à-vis corporate borrowers. It is more difficult to argue this case with respect to the new labor reformism of the 1970s. Although the legislative measures produced did entail important limits on the workers' influence over investment allocation, labor's failure to realize its original ambitions cannot be fully explained by legislative politics.

At the same time, the relative importance of the politics of legislation and implementation varies across our three cases. In the case of codetermination, labor reform was very successful in that Parliament passed laws that conformed to labor's expectations, but the laws did not have the effects labor had hoped for. In the case of wage-earner funds, by contrast, the gap between goals and outcomes emerges in the legislative phase. Indeed, the gap between the Meidner Plan and the wage-earner funds legislation of 1983 is much greater than the gap between the lgislation of 1983 and the practices of wage-earner funds in the second half of the 1980s. It would be a mistake, then, to focus exclusively on either the politics of legislation or the politics of implementation.

Business-Centered Explanations

We might distinguish several ways business resistance to labor's reform initiatives affected institutional outcomes. To begin with, outcomes were typically "mediated" by the deliberations of public commissions of inquiry that included representatives of organized business. The recommendations of such commissions were invariably more cautious than the reform proposals coming out of the labor movement, and they were never completely ignored by the government. Business representation on commissions of inquiry is of secondary importance in this context, however. Two other mechanisms are more important: first, the representation of business by the bourgeois parties and, second, the direct involvement of organized business in mass politics.

I do not mean that the bourgeois parties are in any sense puppets of business; but their ideological commitment to private ownership and arms-length government does correspond to business interests. There can be little doubt that the bourgeois parties' electoral advances in the 1970s, especially the formation of a bourgeois coalition government in 1976, constrained the new labor reformism. When the socialist parties have held a parliamentary majority in the past two decades, their majorities have been narrow. The Social Democrats have always had to worry about being reelected and about a reversal of government and opposition.

Direct business involvement in mass politics is particularly relevant to the limited scope of the wage-earner funds legislation enacted in 1983. As we shall see, organized business was very important in mobilizing public opinion against wage-earner funds. The previous reformist achievements of Swedish labor were possible precisely because they did not challenge the systemic interests of business. As labor began to challenge these interests, the business community coalesced and deployed power it had always had at its disposal but had previously chosen not to use.

Turning to the politics of implementation, one might cite the business representation on public pension funds and industrial bodies as an obstacle to labor's ambitions. But again, we must not exaggerate the significance of corporatist arrangements. It fades in comparison with the systemic power of business.

The simplest way to think about the systemic power of business is in terms of "exit options." Consider codetermination: even if corporate investment decisions had to be approved by the unions, capital would retain the option to exit if it deemed the outcome of codetermination bargaining unfavorable. Management might decide to locate new investment abroad, or capitalists might divest themselves of the corporation in question. As Claus Offe and Helmut Wiesenthal (1980:76) put it, the dependency relationship between labor and business is asymmetric in that "the collectivity of all workers must be . . . more concerned with the well-being and prosperity of capitalists than, inversely, the latter is [*sic*] concerned with the well-being of the working class."

The case of collective shareownership brings out the reverse side of the exit option, what we might call capital's control of entry. At some cost to themselves, existing owners could make it very expensive for collective shareholding funds to acquire shares in their corporations. Thus it becomes imperative for these funds to conform to the rules of the stock market. Finally, the experience of industrial policy brings out another source of business leverage in the politics of implementation, its control of the information public policy depends on. This consideration is also highly relevant to codetermination bargaining.

How fully the exit option and other manifestations of the systemic power of business come into play depends on the institutional reforms in question. Had the original Meidner Plan been enacted, capital's control of entry would not have applied. In this sense legislation must be considered primary and the results of reformism more contingent than Przeworski's analysis suggests, for the ability of business to mobilize its political power depends in some measure on strategic choices by labor.

As for the variations across our three cases of reformism, the business-centered explanation I propose rests on the premise that successful reformism depends on the support of at least some elements of the business community or, to use Marxist terminology, some "fractions of capital" (cf. Swenson 1991, 1992). Among labor's reform attempts in 1968–76, that of the wage-earner funds was the biggest failure because it most challenged the systemic interests of business yet provided no material incentives for business to cooperate with labor. The industrial policy initiative succeeded in that selective state intervention in industrial restructuring did indeed emerge. This success rested on an implicit alliance between labor and declining industry. By contrast, the limited but real success of codetermination was based on a confluence of interests between labor and capital in advanced industrial sectors. Over the long run, the costs of the alliance with declining industry were unacceptable to the labor movement, and the Social Democrats consequently abandoned their commitment to selective state intervention in industrial restructuring. The alliance between labor and advanced industry has proved more durable.

Labor-Centered Explanations

The legislative shortcomings of labor's reform offensive might also be explained in terms of the politics of the labor movement and the ambiguities of its approach to wage-earner influence over investment. The image of a labor movement pursuing a coherent set of goals and being constrained by external forces is indeed misleading. There are at least three labor-centered arguments that might explain the limits of reformism.

To begin with, one could argue that labor failed to institutionalize democratic control of investment because it was not really committed to this goal. According to this line of argument, the reform offensive of 1968–76 should be seen as an exercise in symbolic politics. In response to New Left criticism and rank-and-file restiveness, manifested most notably in the wildcat strikes of 1969–70, labor leaders engaged in rhetorical radicalization but never actually changed their goals or strategy. Far from being a failure, the reform offensive was a great success because it co-opted the radical currents that emerged within the labor movement in the late 1960s.

Though the reform offensive undoubtedly involved a great deal of inflated rhetoric, this argument does not adequately explain why labor turned Left. For one thing, the rank-and-file restiveness of the late 1960s remains unexplained. Why did radical rhetoric become necessary at this particular time? More important, this line of reasoning fails to account for the sustained character of labor's reform offensive. The decisions of the LO congress of 1971 (to launch a drive for codetermination legislation and to appoint a committee of experts to investigate collective profit sharing) might well be explained in terms of union officials fending off a challenge from below. But why did LO leaders endorse the Meidner Plan in 1976 and persist in advocating wage-earner funds well into the 1980s? By the onset of the world economic downturn in 1974, the challenge from above had already abated, and by the late 1970s electoral tactics militated against radical reformism.

Second, one might argue that labor abandoned its more radical ambitions because it gradually came to realize that it was neither possible nor desirable to steer the allocation of investment according to political criteria. The labor movement thus did not abandon the new reformism of the 1970s because it encountered resistance; rather, it changed its

24

mind.[7] Like the first argument, this one reflects the conventional image of Sweden as a country where labor rules, for it implies that the Swedish labor movement would have introduced economic democracy had it really wanted to.

The argument that labor came to realize that its ambitions were misguided is most readily applied to the experience of industrial policy. One would be hard put to explain labor's retreat on the wage-earner funds in these terms, since the retreat began before any funds existed. Perhaps more important, different elements of the labor movement interpreted the experience of industrial policy differently. Prominent figures in the party leadership, such as Kjell-Olof Feldt, who became minister of finance in 1982, invoked this experience to argue for a retreat from selective intervention, but LO (1981) argued for wage-earner funds as a way to turn active industrial policy in a more offensive direction and enhance organized labor's ability to influence industrial policy. Indeed, Feldt and others had always been critical of the more radical features of the reform offensive of 1968–76. The question is why their views came to prevail (again) in the 1980s, and proposing that they had been proved right is not a satisfactory answer.

This brings us to the labor-centered explanation I shall develop here. Simply put, the SAP leaders never fully shared LO's radical ambitions, and divisions between LO and SAP, regarding strategy as well as goals, weakened the reform offensive. Why, then, did the two wings of the labor movement diverge in their approaches to investment politics in the 1970s? Following Korpi (1983:34–35), Winton Higgins (1985) argues that the divisions between LO and SAP over wage-earner funds might be seen as expressing a more generic divergence between the logic of unionism and the logic of electoral competition. According to Higgins, unions project working-class interests more closely than do left parties because their activities are rooted directly in the social division of labor. In pursuing cross-class electoral support, left parties tend to compromise working-class interests (cf. Przeworski 1985).

This notion of two logics is very useful, but Higgins's formulations must be qualified (or clarified) on two counts. First, the new reform efforts that came out of LO in 1968–76 were not simply a reflection of rank-and-file demands. In part they were a response to conflicts of interest within and among LO's affiliates—a way to maintain LO's organizational cohesion. Second, radical challenges to private control of investment were not a source of divergence between LO and SAP in the 1930s and 1940s. In general the LO leadership tended to be less

7. Lewin (1967:331–32) and Sainsbury (1980:143–44) rely on a similar argument to explain labor's retreat from planning in the 1940s. See chapter 2 below.

innovative and more accommodationist than the SAP leadership in this period.[8]

Why did the logic of unionism and the logic of electoral competition diverge in the 1970s but not in the 1930s or 1940s? Two answers immediately come to mind. On one hand, LO clearly became more actively involved in politics, and took an interest in a much wider range of policy issues, as it came to encompass virtually the entire blue-collar labor force in the postwar period (Olson 1982). As Higgins (1985) himself suggests, the reform offensive of 1968–76 cannot be explained by the logic of unionism as such. Rather, it should be seen as an outgrowth of the comprehensive, class-oriented unionism that LO came to typify after World War II (which Higgins refers to as "political unionism"). On the other hand, it seems most plausible to argue that the growth of white-collar strata since the 1930s, as a percentage of the working population and of the electorate, has accentuated the potential for divergence between the logic of unionism and the logic of electoral competition. LO today represents a much smaller part of SAP's electoral constituency than it did in the 1930s.

It is common to note that TCO, the confederation of unions organizing lower- and mid-level salaried employees, has emerged as a pivotal political actor and, above all, as a pivotal electoral constituency in the past two decades. The contrast between the legislative success of labor's pursuit of codetermination and the failure of its pursuit of wage-earner funds illustrates this point most clearly. TCO joined forces with LO in demanding codetermination legislation in the early 1970s, and its position effectively forced the Center party and the Liberals to come out in favor of codetermination. By contrast, TCO leaders were less enthusiastic about wage-earner funds, and members' opinion ultimately forced them to profess neutrality. With codetermination the logic of unionism and that of electoral competition tended to converge; with wage-earner funds they tended to diverge. Bringing the white-collar unions into our analysis of labor politics makes it possible to construct a labor-centered explanation of variations in outcomes across the three reform initiatives of 1968–76.

The ambiguities of labor's pursuit of democratic control of investment cannot be entirely explained by the recalcitrance of the SAP

8. The unions were initially wary of the unemployment insurance scheme proposed by the party leaders (Rothstein 1990b) and feared that universalistic welfare reforms might undermine the self-help organizations of the labor movement (Marklund 1982). See also Therborn (1984). LO began to assume the initiative within the labor movement as early as the 1950s. As many observers have noted, LO played a major role in the political struggle surrounding the ATP reform of 1959 as well as the activation of labor market policy in the 1960s. The reform initiatives of 1968–76 stand out not because they came from LO, but rather because they were more radical than previous LO initiatives. Åmark (1988) provides a very useful historical account of relations between LO and SAP.

leaders. As we shall see, the arguments LO advanced to support its reform attempts tended to treat democratization as an end in itself and failed to specify how allocative investment decisions made under more democratic arrangements would differ from autonomous decisions by business. The failure to develop any "alternative model of economic development" may have weakened not only labor's ability to mobilize popular support for radical reforms but also its ability to wield influence through collective shareholding funds and other institutional arrangements that did emerge from its reform offensive. The absence of union efforts to establish some form of coordination among new institutions or to prescribe general guidelines for them is striking. Although LO was very active in proposing institutional reforms, and in mobilizing to get them passed, it backed off, assuming a rather passive role, once institutional reforms had been introduced. (Codetermination represents a partial exception to this generalization.)

Why did the advocates of radical reform fail to develop coherent and credible alternatives to private investment decisions? Invoking their enduring ideological commitment to free trade and Keynesian economics amounts to a reformulation of the question rather than an answer. There are two possible explanations. One is provided by mainstream economics, which holds that workers (or wage earners) simply do not have distinctive interests with respect to the allocation of investment. Within the framework of a free market economy, groups of workers may have particular interests; but considered as a class, they can only have one interest in allocating investment—to maximize efficiency— which coincides with capitalists' self-interested pursuit of maximum return on investment.

Alternatively, one might argue that labor's failure to specify the purposes of its institutional reforms reflects its lack of information, expertise, and experience concerning allocative investment decisions. For reasons I shall articulate shortly, I prefer this line of argument, which points to a strategic dilemma for labor movements engaged in radical reformism. On one hand, we cannot expect unions (or party ideologues) to develop coherent and credible alternatives to the investment decisions of private corporations without institutional arrangements that let them participate in such decisions. On the other hand, labor's ability to mobilize popular support for such arrangements may depend on its ability to propose coherent and credible alternatives.

Complementary or Alternative Explanations?

Simplifying somewhat, figure 1 sums up the preceding discussion by specifying four major factors that can be invoked to explain the limits of reformism. Each of these factors mattered, but did some matter

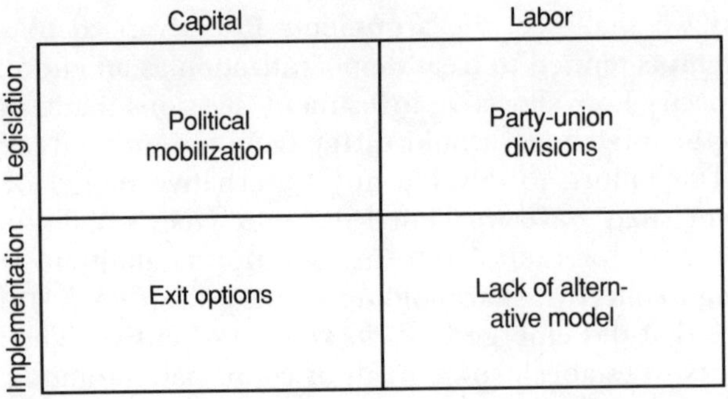

	Capital	Labor
Legislation	Political mobilization	Party-union divisions
Implementation	Exit options	Lack of alternative model

Figure 1. Explanations of the limits of reformism.

more than others? Apart from the quest for parsimony, we must ask this question for political reasons. Though business-centered and labor-centered arguments are by no means mutually exclusive, their political implications differ. Whereas business-centered arguments tend to imply that any reformist challenge to private control of investment is bound to fail, labor-centered arguments tend to imply that reforms of this kind might be significantly more successful than they have been in the Swedish case had the labor movement acted differently.

When we seek to account for variations in legislative outcomes across our three cases of reformism, business-centered and labor-centered factors complement each other in the sense that strong business resistance goes along with labor-movement divisions. The persistence of this covariation suggests a causal relation between the factors. For instance, one might argue that when business mobilized against wage-earner funds it neutralized TCO, causing political divisions within the labor movement. I shall return to this argument and the question of assigning analytical primacy to either business or labor-centered factors in the concluding chapter. My case studies do not provide the basis for any definitive, generalizable conclusions in this respect. Quite the contrary, my empirical analysis brings out the importance of attending to the interplay among the four factors identified in figure 1, for their relative significance varies across my three cases of reformism.

THE IMPETUS FOR REFORMISM

Mainstream economics posits that in the allocation of investment labor's interests coincide with the outcomes yielded by a free market economy. Przeworski's (1985) schema suggests that even if labor had an interest in democratizing investment decisions, it could not possibly achieve this goal by electoral-reformist means. From either point of view, the reform offensive of 1968–76 must be considered a big mistake. The problem with this interpretation is accentuated by the parallel between those reform attempts and labor's planning offensive of the immediate postwar period. Why did the labor movement return to a project it had previously recognized as mistaken?

Przeworski debunks the way Marxists have traditionally dealt with class collaboration as a manifestation of "false consciousness." He shows that it is possible to explain class collaboration in terms of the material interests of workers, and he argues persuasively that such an explanation is preferable, at least on methodological grounds, to one resting on the notion that workers are subject to ideological manipulation and do not know their own interests. If we are committed to an interest-based explanation of class collaboration, we should also look for an interest-based explanation of labor's radical reform initiatives rather than appealing to socialist ideology or the zeitgeist of the 1960s. We should avoid an inverted false-consciousness argument positing that labor is rational when it collaborates with business and irrational when it challenges it.

An interest-based explanation of the goals of the labor movement might be based on either the material interests of workers or wage earners or the organizational interests of unions or union officials. For reasons I have already stated, I do not think the reform offensive of 1968–76 can be adequately explained in terms of union officials fending off challenges to their authority. But like Bo Rothstein (1987, 1990a), who aptly speaks of "organized class interests," I insist on the interplay between the organizational interests of unions and the material interests of their members. Union officials must serve the interests of workers in order to maintain, let alone extend, their organizational power. Yet workers depend on unions in their struggles against employers and must take organizational interests into account. It may well be rational for workers to moderate their wage demands in order to strengthen their organizations or to avoid conflicts that would threaten them.

Organized class interests may be discerned inductively by examining the actions and programs of the labor movement. To avoid the circularity of this procedure, let me sketch some theoretical reasons why organized workers and their organizations might seek to influence the allocation of investment within the framework of a market economy. Subsequent chapters will explore how the interests posited here can explain labor's actions and programs. Since LO and its affiliates occupy center stage in my story, I will lay out these theoretical arguments in terms of the interests of "workers" (or "labor"), but I see no obvious reason they should not apply more generally to "wage earners" (to white-collar as well as blue-collar employees).[9]

1. The most fundamental interests of labor are full employment and productivity growth. While full employment strengthens labor's bargaining position, productivity growth makes it possible to reconcile full employment with price stability and thus provides the basis for real-wage growth. Full employment and productivity growth together permit the expansion of welfare-state measures that redistribute income, reduce workers' dependence on the vagaries of the labor market, or both. In addition, workers have an interest in acquiring new skills and using their skills in production. As organizations, unions have an interest in reducing discrepancies in wage and skill levels among their members. (At least they want to make sure such discrepancies do not increase.)

2. Future employment and productivity growth depend in large measure on the rate of investment. As Kevin Lancaster (1973) argued in a seminal article, it would be rational for workers to take out less in wages than the market can bear if they could be sure their restraint would translate into a higher rate of investment, but private control of investment makes this strategy risky. Thus an economic system in which workers wield significant influence over investment might be more efficient, because the rate of investment would be higher (see also Gustafsson 1981; Przeworski 1985). But would the allocation of investment be different? In an economy dominated by multinational corporations, it is hardly possible to treat the rate and the allocation of investment as separate questions.

3. The most straightforward argument for some form of economic democracy rests on the proposition that market signals are ambiguous and that market forces allow for more than one successful corporate strategy. Not only do corporations choose market strategies: as much of the literature on new working practices demonstrates, similar market strategies are compatible with different ways of organizing production, some of which produce more meaningful jobs, better working conditions, and higher wages than others (see, most notably, Piore and Sabel 1983). Similarly, corporations may have a choice among investment projects with the same expected rate of return but with different locational or environmental consequences. Whereas business is (or should be) indifferent to these choices so long as the rate of return is the same, labor may strongly prefer one option over another. In Colin Crouch's words (1980:87), "It is labour rather than capital which needs certain

9. In the concluding chapter I return to the question of the organized class interests of white-collar employees, and the reasons for the divergence between LO and TCO with respect to wage-earner funds.

kinds of investment." With respect to the geographic location of investment, Swedish labor has an obvious interest in domestic investment, and perhaps an interest in regionally balanced development within Sweden as well. (Note that this argument applies not only to corporate investment decisions, but also to the allocation of investment capital among corporations and industrial sectors: rates of profit being equal, labor has a distinctive interest in promoting high-value-added sectors relying on skilled labor.)

4. While labor has a strong interest in promoting growth and efficiency, it also has other interests and may prefer a different trade-off among these interests than business does (Himmelstrand et al. 1981). In some circumstances labor may choose to sacrifice growth in order to realize some other objective—better jobs, regional balance, less pollution, or whatever. To take a topical Swedish example, one could well argue that it would be in the interest of labor, and of society at large, to reduce the extreme dependence of the country's western regions on the auto industry, even if subsidies to promote a more diversified industrial structure reduced the rate of growth.[10]

5. For labor, investment control represents a way to achieve certain allocative outcomes. Although labor would always like to be able to influence investment decisions directly (for any of the reasons stated above), such influence may not be necessary to achieve the desired outcomes. Some combination of Keynesian demand management, restrictions on the export of capital, and active labor market policy may suffice to reconcile the logic of capitalist profitability with labor's interests. Given that business is bound to resist labor's efforts to democratize investment decisions, we would expect labor to prefer other strategies for political-strategic reasons.

According to this schema, the issue for labor is not *what* corporations should produce, but rather *how* and *where* they should produce whatever it is. Choosing products and marketing strategies becomes relevant for labor only insofar as it bears on how to organize and where to locate production. These questions are, of course, very closely related (Streeck 1985). Also, it is one thing to identify labor's interests and quite another to specify what corporate strategies would best satisfy them. This brings us back to labor's ability to formulate alternatives to private investment decisions.

The logic laid out here suggests that the problem of explaining the reform offensive of 1968–76 should be posed as follows: Under what economic conditions does it become necessary for labor to challenge

10. According to Svenska Metallindustriarbetarförbundet (1989:64), Volvo and Saab alone accounted for 25 percent of industrial employment in three western counties (Göteborg-Bohus, Älvsborg, and Skaraborg) in 1986. The figure would be significantly higher if employment by their subcontractors were included.

private control of investment? As Korpi (1978:320–21) points out, labor's reform attempts preceded the worldwide economic downturn of the mid-1970s, but this does not rule out an "economistic" explanation of labor's reform offensive. In chapter 4 I argue that the economic crisis of 1974–83 cannot be understood simply in terms of extraordinary events (oil price shocks) and ordinary business cycle fluctuations. The crisis was associated with long-term changes in the dynamics of the world economy, the structure of Swedish industry, and Sweden's relation to the world economy. These changes rendered the outcomes of private investment decisions increasingly problematic for labor from the mid-1960s onward, and they remain a source of problems for the labor movement.[11] (The miraculous recovery of the 1980s came to an end in 1989–90, and it has recently become common for Swedish observers to speak of a "new crisis.")

Labor's postwar strategy rested on the premise that the expansion of advanced (efficient and competitive) sectors of industry, promoted through solidaristic wage restraint, would generate new employment at roughly the same rate as jobs would be lost in the declining sectors. A closely related premise was that borrowed capital could readily substitute for equity capital as a source of industrial finance. To promote solidaristic wage bargaining, the Rehn-Meidner model prescribed a restrictive fiscal policy that would keep the lid on corporate profits (and thereby reduce the room for wage drift). Rehn and Meidner argued that the negative effects this policy orientation would have for business savings and investment could be offset by transforming public savings into investment. Through the mechanism of the AP funds, in the 1960s and 1970s public savings were channeled to the corporate sector in the form of low-interest loans.

For structural as well as conjunctural reasons, from the late 1960s Swedish business became increasingly unwilling to finance new investment through borrowing. At the same time, the employment effects of industrial restructuring began to diverge from the premise of labor's postwar strategy. While the "heavy," raw-materials-based industries that had been the motor of Swedish industrialization (mining, iron and steel, and forest products) now began to shed labor on a major scale, the expansion of advanced sectors (engineering and chemicals) no longer generated much employment growth—if any.

Increased export dependence and intensified international competi-

11. This may sound like a parochial explanation of why the Swedish labor movement turned to the left in 1968–76, yet I am well aware that other labor movements also underwent radicalization in this period: other advanced capitalist economies saw similar changes in the postwar era and were affected by the same changes in the world economy of the 1960s.

tion together generated renewed employer efforts to raise productivity through automation and speedups, in declining as well as advanced sectors, and many industrial workers experienced deteriorating working conditions in the course of the 1960s. (This was perhaps the major factor behind the wildcat strike movement of 1969–70.) Meanwhile, the advanced sectors of Swedish industry began to engage in direct investment abroad on an entirely new scale.

Economic developments thus made strategic innovation necessary for the labor movement. Identifying the problems labor responded to does not, of course, adequately explain its strategic reorientation. More than one response to these problems was possible. Indeed, the market-oriented policies pursued by the Social Democrats since 1982 can be seen as a response to the same problems that labor sought to resolve in the 1970s by institutional reforms with a socialist twist. In part, wage-earner funds were meant to increase the supply of risk capital to industry without redistributing income from wage earners to capitalists. Unable to achieve a major reform along these lines, the labor movement was in a sense forced to rely on private profits to increase the supply of risk capital.

To explain why labor opted for anticapitalist reforms in the 1970s and for pro-capitalist reforms in the 1980s, we must attend to politics within the labor movement as well as the balance of political power between labor and capital. But our analysis of politics must be rooted in an understanding of economic conditions and their consequences for labor's ability to realize its interests within the framework of capitalism.

CONCLUSIONS

For all their differences, Korpi and Przeworski both neglect institutional arrangements. To the extent that institutions matter to their argument, the ones that count are what we might call generic institutions of capitalism, as opposed to the institutional arrangements that distinguish capitalist states (or political economies) from each other. Korpi and Przeworski also neglect the historicity of capitalism; that is, they analyze the politics of class compromise without any reference to stages of capitalist development. By contrast, I want to emphasize that the durability of class compromise in the postwar era rested not only on rapid economic growth, but also on a particular pattern of growth, associated with the spread of Fordist mass production. This pattern of growth might be called "auto-centered" (Lipietz 1987) in the sense that domestic consumption was a major source of demand for Swedish products, and even export-oriented manufacturing corporations were organized nationally.

33

In emphasizing the variability of institutional arrangements and the importance of institutions for political processes, I draw on the neo-institutionalist tradition in political science (e.g., Evans, Rueschemeyer, and Skocpol 1985; Katzenstein 1978, 1985; Hall 1986; Zysman 1983). But I depart from this tradition in addressing the emergence of new institutions. In my account, institutional arrangements are a product of political struggles among class actors. The goals and strategies such actors pursue are determined above all by economic conditions (Gourevitch 1986). In this sense the dynamics of capitalist development "drive" class politics. But economics do not determine the outcome of political struggles.

Finally, my argument that unions have a major stake in the allocation of investment and are likely to seek direct influence over investment decisions in certain circumstances leaves open the question whether some forms of democratic control are more effective than others, or more "appropriate" from labor's point of view. I address this question in the concluding chapter.

Part I

THE RISE AND FALL OF
THE HISTORICAL COMPROMISE

CHAPTER TWO

The Politics of Planning

This chapter describes Social Democratic efforts to institutionalize planning from 1932 to 1948 and explains why so little came of these efforts. The story of planning is an important, yet often neglected, part of the formation of what Korpi (1978) so aptly refers to as the "historical compromise" between labor and capital in Sweden.

It is common to observe that the Social Democrats were able to break the stalemate that had come to characterize parliamentary politics in the 1920s and to tackle mass unemployment by striking a deal with the Agrarian party—the "cow trade" of 1933.[1] In return for increased agricultural tariffs, the Agrarian party supported SAP's policy of deficit-financed public works. The ensuing economic recovery translated into electoral gains for the Agrarians as well as the Social Democrats in the general election of 1936, and the Agrarians now entered the government as the Social Democrats' junior partner, a role they were to assume again in the 1950s.

Although the significance of the parliamentary alliance between the Social Democrats and the Agrarians can hardly be exaggerated, working-class mobilization deserves to be recognized as the other vital ingredient of the political realignment that enabled the Social Democrats to consolidate control of the government (Therborn 1984). In the local elections of 1930, the socialist parties together polled 43.4 percent of the popular vote. Their combined share increased in each successive election to reach an all-time high of 57.3 percent in the parliamentary election of 1944. Parallel to this expansion of the socialist electorate,

1. Rothstein (1990b) challenges the conventional view of the political realignment of the 1930s (e.g., Söderpalm 1975) by deemphasizing the importance of the "cow trade."

unionization among blue-collar workers increased from 45 percent in 1930 to 66 percent in 1940 and 76 percent in 1950, and LO's membership more than doubled from 1930 to 1945 (Kjellberg 1983:269–79).

The reliance on Agrarian support precluded any challenge to the principle of private ownership in the 1930s, but this caused little concern among SAP leaders. The Social Democrats had softened their commitment to socialization of the means of production in the course of the 1920s. They came to power convinced that immediate problems such as mass unemployment could be effectively addressed without changing the structure of ownership. Indeed, they were convinced that the issue of ownership had to be set aside, for political reasons, in order to solve immediate economic problems.

As Korpi (1978, 1980) argues, the political realignment of the 1930s altered the conflict strategies of both labor and business. Although business could not dislodge the Social Democrats from control of the government, the labor movement was not strong enough to take on the systemic power of capital. Some form of accommodation became imperative for both sides. Ernst Wigforss, minister of finance from 1932 to 1949, articulated the logic of the situation very clearly in a famous speech to the Gothenburg Stock Exchange Association in 1938. The business community must abandon the notion of an imminent reversal of government and opposition, he argued, and instead engage "in a discussion [with the government] based on the possibility of concessions, accommodations, and compromises." At the same time, Wigforss assured his audience that the government recognized "the necessity of maintaining favorable conditions for private enterprise in all those areas where [it is] not prepared without further ado to replace private enterprise with some form of public operations" (cited in Korpi 1983:48).

The historical compromise that emerged from this situation consisted of two distinct settlements, one pertaining to the relation between unions and employers in the industrial sphere and the other to the state's role in the economy. The first settlement was codified in the Basic Agreement signed by LO and the employers' federation, SAF, at Saltsjöbaden in 1938, which set out detailed procedures for collective bargaining and for resolving contract disputes. By signing the Basic Agreement, LO explicitly assumed responsibility for maintaining labor peace and implicitly accepted SAF's requirement that any collective bargaining agreement signed by one of its affiliates must proclaim management's prerogative to hire and fire workers and to direct them at work. In return, the employers dropped their demands for legal restrictions on union organization and the right to strike. Both LO and

SAF looked to joint regulation as a way to preempt state intervention in collective bargaining (Hadenius 1976; Söderpalm 1980; Johansson 1989).

Broadly speaking, the settlement pertaining to the role of the state in the economy can be characterized thus: while organized business and the bourgeois parties came to accept the expansion of the welfare state and the principle that the government could and should promote full employment through macroeconomic demand management, the labor movement retreated from its ambitions to introduce planning and selective state intervention in industrial restructuring. Partly because more actors and issues were involved, the terms of this settlement never were quite as clear as those of the industrial relations settlement, and hammering them out was more conflictual and protracted. It was not until the late 1940s that the ideological conflicts were finally put to rest.

Planning remained an important element of Social Democratic ideology in the postwar era, but it came to be identified with long-term economic forecasting and with public infrastructure and services rather than with industrial development. The Social Democrats in effect came to accept that strategic economic decisions should remain the purview of corporate management and that the state should primarily concern itself with the social consequences of industrial restructuring or, more positively, with society's ability to adjust.

The discussion in this chapter is essentially chronological. I first elucidate the conception of planning with which the Social Democrats came to power and their efforts to institutionalize planning in the 1930s. The second section deals with the debate over planning in the immediate postwar years. As we shall see, the institutional reforms by which the Social Democrats proposed to translate the idea of planning into practice in 1932–48 were not very radical, yet they invariably failed. In the end, the Social Democrats had virtually nothing to show for more than fifteen years of talking about planning. The reasons for this failure will be addressed in the course of the narrative and, more systematically, in the final section.

Invoking the systemic constraints of capitalism hardly constitutes an adequate explanation of labor's failure to institutionalize planning, for more far-reaching institutional reforms of this kind were introduced in other capitalist countries in the 1940s, most notably in France. Though the British Labour government of 1945 also failed to institutionalize planning, it did undertake extensive nationalization measures. Yet the proposition that the electorate rejected labor's planning ambitions is not adequate either. A marked shift to the right did occur in the parliamentary election of 1948, and this shift undoubtedly was important in labor's retreat from planning. But why did the electorate reject labor's planning efforts at this point? To explain labor's failure, we must take into account the political mobilization against planning and the ambiguities of labor's strategic outlook.

THE INTERWAR PERIOD

One of the first things the Social Democratic minority government of 1920–21 did was appoint a commission of inquiry to look into the socialization of industry (i.e., its nationalization). The Socialization Commission (Socialiseringsnämnden) deliberated on the pros and cons of socialization and the ways it might be done, but it made no apparent progress toward legislative recommendations in the course the 1920s, and it ceased its investigation altogether in the early 1930s. Rather than trying to reactivate the commission, the Social Democratic government of 1932 dismantled it. Its report, submitted in 1935, made no concrete proposals (Sainsbury 1980:29–30; Waara 1980:143–44).

Herbert Tingsten's (1973) treatise on the ideological evolution of Swedish Social Democracy, originally published in 1941, invokes the experience of the Socialization Commission as evidence for the thesis that SAP abandoned its socialist ambitions to transform society and embraced a pragmatic welfare ideology between the wars. In a polemic against this interpretation, Leif Lewin (1967, 1975) argues that the Social Democrats' failure to pursue the socialization of industry when they gained control of the government should be understood as a strategic reorientation rather than an abandonment of system-transformative goals. Lewin describes the strategic reorientation of the labor movement as a shift from a strategy of socialization to one of planning and argues that it was made possible by the assimilation of Keynesian economic theory. Whereas the Social Democrats had previously conceived public ownership as an end in itself, they now came to treat it as one of several means whereby the state could intervene in the economy to promote expansion and steer productive activity (see also Svenning 1972; Tilton 1990).

Lewin's argument captures the way the Social Democrats articulated the relation of planning to socialization when they sat down to rewrite the party program in 1943–44. But some of the statements Lewin cites from the 1930s suggest that leading Social Democrats at that time conceived of planning and socialization as necessary complements rather than subordinating socialization to planning. In part, the strategic reorientation Lewin describes might be attributed to the exigencies of government. Be that as it may, the way he identifies planning with Keynes-ianism is problematic.

Nils Unga (1976) effectively challenges the conventional view that the recovery strategy the Social Democrats pursued in the 1930s represen-ted a conscious and consistent attempt to apply the principles of Keynes-ian economics.[2] He argues that the public works policy of the time should be seen as a response to economic crisis and trade union de-mands, not as a product of new theoretical insights. Though Wigforss and other Social Democratic leaders sometimes invoked Keynesian ar-guments to justify deficit-financed public works, they conceived of defi-cit spending as necessary in an exceptional situation rather than as valuable in itself. Deficit spending was in fact restricted to the measures included in the crisis agreement of 1933. Despite an average unem-ployment rate of 12.8 percent among union members, the government made no further efforts to combat unemployment by deficit spending in 1934–39. On the contrary, it strove to repay the crisis loans of 1933, on the grounds that social reforms presupposed a balanced budget (Berg-ström 1969). As in most other countries, the "Keynesian revolution" in economic policy occurred in the context of the war.

The Social Democratic Idea of Planning

Originating in the 1920s, the Social Democratic idea of planning de-rived from a distinctly non-Keynesian logic. At this time the Social Democrats clearly subscribed to the neoclassical view that unemploy-ment meant wages were too high, but they could not advocate wage reductions as a standard defense against unemployment. Influenced by the "rationalization movement" within the business community (De Geer 1978), they looked instead to new production technologies and modern management to reduce production costs (Johansson 1989). This orientation corresponded closely to the concrete experience of unions in export industries, whose wages were almost constantly under downward pressure as a result of international competition. The fol-lowing statement to the LO congress of 1926 by a leading union official illustrates the strong belief in an "iron law of wages" within the labor movement: "Wages—I'm speaking of real wages—can be raised only insofar as improvements in production methods and economic organi-

2. Unga (1976) is the most recent substantive contribution to a long-standing debate about the origins and nature of the macroeconomic policy the Social Democrats pursued in the 1930s. See Gustafsson (1973) and Uhr (1977) for overviews and Weir and Skocpol (1985) and Gourevitch (1986) for comparative perspectives on the Swedish response to the depression.

zation create conditions therefor. . . . For us to believe that the unions' influence alone is decisive for wage increases is as much folly as it would be for the rooster to believe the sun rises because he crows" (cited in Hadenius 1976:37).

The Social Democrats linked rationalization to industrial democracy by arguing that increased employee influence in the workplace would promote measures to increase productivity and efficiency. In this vein they proposed the creation of enterprise committees (*driftsnämnder*) composed of union and management representatives in a famous parliamentary motion of 1924 (rejected by the bourgeois majority).

The planning ambitions the Social Democrats articulated in this context were closely tied to the notion of "organized capitalism" (Unga 1976:64–65). For them, cartel agreements and other forms of collaboration among producers were a natural consequence of economic concentration, itself the inevitable product of capitalist development. Concentration and collaboration contained the potential for a more rational organization of production, but they also made it possible for the capitalists to increase their profits without increasing efficiency. In the Social Democrats' view, realizing a more rational organization of production presupposed public control of producer collaboration.

The idea of firm-level cooperation to promote rationalization gained widespread acceptance in the second half of the 1920s. In 1928 LO and SAF formed a delegation to discuss matters of common interest, on the model of the Mond-Turner talks in Britain. Nothing tangible came of these discussions, but they contributed to the crystallization of what Axel Hadenius (1976) refers to as LO's "production policy."

Though the labor movement remained favorable to rationalization in principle, the onset of the Great Depression led it to adopt a more critical view of capitalist rationalization schemes (Johansson 1989). The Social Democrats' case for planning now came to rest on the notion of "misrationalization" (*felrationalisering*), articulated most consistently by Frans Severin in his reservation to the 1935 report of a commission appointed to investigate unemployment (Arbetslöshetsutredningen).[3] The empirical findings of the Unemployment Commission were that the structural (noncyclical) unemployment problem that had surfaced in the 1920s was due to the mechanization of production: in response to wage pressure, firms engaged in labor-substituting rationalization measures without expanding their capacity. The commission majority concluded that wages had to be reduced and savings increased in order for employment to increase.

3. The report of the Unemployment Commission and Severin's reservation are summarized in detail by De Geer (1978:255–65), Wickman (1980:67–72), and Johansson (1989:119–24).

In his reservation, Severin did *not* advance the Keynesian argument that demand was insufficient to sustain expansion, or claim that the commission's recommendations would simply aggravate the problem. Rather, he argued that the rationalization measures of the 1920s had been mistaken. "Misrationalization" occurred because firms' decisions were based on narrow, short-term calculations of profitability that overlooked the costs shouldered by society as a whole (most notably unemployment relief) and failed to generate expansion. For Severin, structural unemployment resulted from the misuse of savings as well as their lack. The labor movement could not agree to wage reductions and other measures to stimulate savings unless they were accompanied by the extension of public control of investment, including control over the export of capital. In a similar vein, Wigforss spoke at the 1932 SAP congress of the need for "central intervention with respect to the monetary system and with respect to the use of capital" (cited in Lewin 1967:75).

As Lewin (1967:105–7) points out, the Social Democratic conception of planning rested on the proposition that the logic of microeconomic decision making did not automatically yield macroeconomic efficiency. But it clearly went beyond macroeconomic management. To promote macroeconomic efficiency, the state had to intervene selectively in the restructuring of industry. Should pressures on or subsidies to private business prove insufficient, such intervention would have to involve public ownership.

The Practice of Planning in the 1930s

The Social Democrats considered business collaboration and broad parliamentary support necessary to effective planning. As Lewin (1967) documents, however, organized business and the bourgeois parties were deeply suspicious of even the most modest Social Democratic initiatives in matters pertaining to ownership, investment, and industrial restructuring. As the idea of planning proved to be a source of polarization, the government retreated from its more radical ambitions. In the second half of the 1930s, the Social Democrats' emphasis shifted from planning to collaboration; more precisely, their approach became less interventionist and more collaborationist.[4]

In response to a parliamentary request for an investigation of the problem of labor peace, in 1934 the government appointed a commission charged with investigating a wide range of other issues as well,

4. The following discussion draws on Lewin (1967), Söderpalm (1976, 1980), Hadenius (1976), De Geer (1978), Wickman (1980), and Johansson (1989).

including industrial democracy, employment security, incomes policy, and public control of the banks. According to the prime minister, Per Albin Hansson, legislation to curtail the right to strike presupposed that unions would be provided with other means of influencing employers. When Hansson subsequently declared that the commissions of inquiry appointed by the new government were to prepare for "a more planned ordering of the entire corporate sector" (cited in Lewin 1967:100), it was presumably this commission, commonly known as the "Mammoth Commission" (Mammututredningen), that he had foremost in mind. The bourgeois parties strongly criticized its composition and instructions.

The Mammoth Commission did not live up to the expectations or fears aroused by its appointment, however. Submitting its final report within less than a year, it opted simply to draw up some general guidelines for promoting economic growth and to provide a catalog of topics that should be investigated by more specialized commissions of inquiry. On the question of labor peace, the commission argued that it should be addressed through negotiations between LO and SAF and that legislation should be considered only if such negotiations failed.

In its wake several commissions were appointed to investigate the problems of particular industries, but no major policy initiatives resulted. Two successive commissions of inquiry appointed by the Social Democrats recommended that gasoline distribution be made a state monopoly, but the Social Democratic leaders abandoned this idea as part of the deal that led to the formation of a SAP-Agrarian coalition government in 1936. The only noteworthy extension of public ownership that occurred in the 1930s involved the takeover in 1939 of what remained of the private railroad network.

The Social Democrats' growing emphasis in the second half of the 1930s on collaboration with business might be explained in terms of the political constraints on a more radical approach to planning—in particular the constraints entailed by their continued reliance on the parliamentary support of the Agrarian party. It can also be seen as a response to new opportunities for collaboration with business.

As Sven-Anders Söderpalm (1976) has shown, the business community was deeply divided on how to deal with the new political situation. Headed by Gustaf Söderlund, managing director of SAF, the accommodationist wing argued that organized business should avoid party politics and seek to influence government policies by participating in commissions of inquiry and through other "corporatist" channels. This line was most notably opposed by the so-called Executives' Club (Direktörsklubben) consisting of the executive directors of six major engineering firms. The Executives' Club advocated using the mass media for propaganda, and it contributed generously to the electoral campaigns of the Liberals and the Conservatives in 1936.

The outcome of the 1936 election, and in particular, the Agrarian party's decision to join the government, marked a severe setback for the confrontationists. The Executives' Club continued to argue that business should engage in political opposition to the government, but the rhetoric of confrontation was toned down, and Söderlund's position within SAF was now greatly strengthened. It was against this background that SAF and LO began the consultations and negotiations that ultimately ushered in the Saltsjöbaden Agreement.

In signing the Saltzjöbaden Agreement, LO reaffirmed its commitment to collaborating with SAF in pursuit of economic expansion and rationalization. The readiness of LO to assume a more active role in enforcing labor peace, and the willingness of its affiliate unions to accept this change, must be seen at least in part as an expression of their belief that Social Democratic control of the government would ensure that economic rationalization and structural change conformed to the interests of labor.

The export-oriented character of the firms represented by the Executives' Club led Söderpalm (1976) to suggest that the political divisions within the business community in the 1930s boiled down to a divergence of interests between home-market- and export-oriented industrialists, the former being the principal beneficiaries of the government's efforts to defend, if not increase, popular consumption through public works and welfare reforms. By contrast, Peter Swenson (1991) argues that the Saltsjöbaden accommodation rested on the common interest of export-oriented employers and their unions in keeping the lid on the wages of workers in sectors that were sheltered against international competition. If we allow for several cross-class coalitions' coexisting at the same time, these interpretations are not mutually exclusive. Indeed, it is tempting to argue that it is precisely this coexistence that is the key to the historic breakthrough of Swedish Social Democracy in the 1930s.

Fearing the onset of a second depression, Wigforss announced a "reform pause" in the budget proposal that he submitted to Parliament in January 1938. According to Wigforss, further social reforms presupposed a substantial increase of state revenues, and this required broad-based parliamentary support. Apparently conceived as part of an effort to improve the government's relationship with business, the announcement of a reform pause was followed by Wigforss's speech to the Gothenburg Stock Exchange Association, in which he proposed a "collaboration conference" to let business and government representatives discuss matters of common concern, such as the export promotion, research and development (R&D) promotion, countercyclical management, and sectoral restructuring.

The government's new concern with securing favorable conditions for private business, and with eliciting its collaboration, manifested itself most concretely in the reform of corporate taxation undertaken in 1938 (Steinmo 1986:419–22). The reform encompassed five basic provisions. First, it substituted a flat-rate profits tax (of 30 percent) for a graduated one. Second, depreciation allowances for investment in machinery and buildings were liberalized so that firms could, if they wished, write off the entire cost of an investment in the same year it was made. Third, the 1938 reform let firms write off the full costs of inventory against profits. Fourth, it allowed them to set aside tax-free pension reserve funds in any amount. And finally, it exempted from taxes profits set aside as investment funds to be used at times determined by the government.

The tax breaks the 1938 legislation provided were contingent on the reinvestment of profits. At the same time, the new system of corporate taxation was designed to promote the rationalization of industry by favoring the most profitable firms, which not only benefited from the elimination of progressivity but were also more likely to take full advantage of depreciation allowances. Whereas the crisis agreement of 1933 catered to the interest of firms or sectors oriented toward the domestic market, the corporate tax reform of 1938 catered more to export-oriented industry.

Several provisions of the corporate tax reform corresponded directly to demands by organized business. The idea of investment funds was first put forth by the Federation of Industry (Sveriges Industriförbund) in a petition to the government, and on this score the 1938 legislation was a direct product of negotiations between Wigforss and the federation (Söderpalm 1976:48–49). It is noteworthy that the system of investment funds provided a tool of countercyclical management that did not involve deficit spending.

Other elements of the historical compromise were first articulated by the so-called Rationalization Commission (Rationaliseringsutredningen) appointed in 1936 and reporting in 1939. This commission of inquiry was distinguished from previous commissions appointed by Social Democrats in that it was headed by a civil servant with no direct political affiliation and was composed of two acknowledged representatives of organized business plus two union representatives. The commission self-consciously sought to reconcile the approaches to problems of rationalization and restructuring adopted by employers and unions. Its unanimous report rejected the idea, previously pushed by the unions, that individual firms should bear the social costs of rationalization. The commission recognized the right of public authorities to regulate corporate decisions, but it argued against selective state intervention in corporate decision making on the grounds that negative, short-term consequences of rationalization would overshadow its positive, long-term results. State intervention should instead address the social consequences of rationalization and promote the ability of society, and the labor force in particular, to adjust to structural changes in the economy. The Rationalization Commission thus set out the principles that were to guide the development of an active labor market policy after World War II.[5]

THE PLANNING DEBATE OF THE 1940S

The basic terms of the historical compromise had been worked out by 1939, but they had yet to be fully accepted by all relevant political actors, and the settlement pertaining to the state's role in the economy temporarily came unstuck in the immediate postwar period. At the same time as it codified the pragmatic approach to ownership the Social Democrats had adopted between the wars, the Postwar Program adopted by SAP and LO in 1944 (SAP-LO 1946) put selective nationalization measures back on the political agenda and strongly reasserted the labor movement's planning ambitions. Political conditions were more favorable to labor in the 1940s than in the 1930s, for the socialist parties now held a clear majority in both chambers of Parliament. Yet labor again failed to institutionalize planning. To understand its subsequent retreat, we must first probe the reasons for the radicalization of labor reformism immediately after the war.

Labor's Postwar Offensive

Lewin (1967:217–18) argues that the experience of wartime economic management strengthened labor's commitment to planning by demonstrating that unemployment could indeed be overcome through more systematic and selective state intervention in the economy. Deficit government spending assumed unprecedented proportions and regularity during the war, and full employment was achieved for the first time ever. To allocate scarce resources and keep the lid on inflation, the government engaged in detailed regulation of the wartime econ-

5. Working parallel to the Rationalization Commission, another commission of inquiry known as the Unemployment Commission (Arbetslöshetsutrdningen) developed more detailed policy proposals along these lines; see Rothstein (1986:117–18). The report of the Rationalization Commission is summarized in De Geer (1978:279–91).

omy, and in view of the circumstances, the system worked extremely well. According to labor's Postwar Program, the "wartime economy demonstrated the vast powers of intensive production that can be released if labor and material resources are utilized under public supervision for purposes determined by the community" (SAP-LO 1946:4).

Perhaps the most important thing about the wartime experience was that state intervention entailed intimate collaboration between the government and the business community. As in other countries, industrialists were recruited to serve on the public commissions set up to manage the allocation of resources, and business organizations themselves came to assume regulatory functions (Söderpalm 1976:96–100; Wickman 1980:75–78). Along with the formation of a national emergency government, including all the parliamentary parties except the Communists, business participation in wartime administration ensured that the state's role in the economy temporarily became a non-issue. Labor's postwar planning offensive reflected the belief that the business community would accept more state intervention as a result of the wartime experience.

The postwar offensive must also be seen as a response to rank-and-file unrest during the war and the emergence of a sizable left-wing opposition within the labor movement. The achievements of the wartime economy were in effect based on a dramatic decline of popular living standards. During the war LO was active in wage negotiations, enforcing a system that indexed wages to inflation without full compensation for price increases. While the position of the Social Democrats became increasingly vulnerable as the war continued, the Communist party benefited from the military exploits of the Soviet Union. In the parliamentary election of 1944, SAP's share of the popular vote dropped from 53.8 percent to 46.7 percent while the Communist party's share increased from 3.5 percent to 10.3 percent. The Communists also mounted a strong challenge to the Social Democrats within the unions and assumed a key role in the metalworkers' strike of 1945 (Hadenius 1976:68–70).

In response to the Communist challenge, the Social Democrats defended the need for wartime sacrifices but promised that "harvest time" would come at the end of the war. The Postwar Program adopted by SAP and LO (and endorsed by the Communist party) advanced concrete demands for increased public pensions and family allowances, comprehensive public unemployment and health insurance, improved housing for the lower classes, and a shorter workweek. These reforms were to stimulate economic growth as well as redistribute income. Advocating the systematic use of deficit spending to sustain full employment, the Postwar Program treated the tendency toward stagnation as an inherent feature of the free market economy and predicted that mass unemployment would return after the war unless the state intervened (SAP-LO 1946:42–45, 128–31).

The Postwar Program insisted that stimulating demand alone would not sustain expansion and full employment, however. Noting that "the standard of living a nation can afford is just as high as its productive capacity permits," its authors asserted that the real import of the question whether the nation could afford a certain standard of living lay in "*how* the nation uses its output, and *how* it directs its production and consumption" (SAP-LO 1946:121). Private business, they argued, passed up investments that would be profitable over the long run during periods of recession and engaged in irrational, speculative investments during periods of expansion. Moreover, higher living standards would replace population growth as the engine of economic development after the war, and one could not rely on private business to discern the investment outlets created by the new pattern of growth. A general investment plan for the entire economy was necessary in order to avoid "misguided investment," a concept akin to "misrationalization" (SAP-LO 1946:74–77).

Concretely, the Postwar Program proposed a national planning body composed of representatives of private, cooperative, and public enterprise as well as the government and organized labor. To promote investment planning, the insurance companies should be nationalized and the state should engage in commercial banking. Nationalizing the insurance companies had already been proposed in the 1930s, justified by the need to extend public control over the supply of long-term credit and to rationalize the insurance business. Without identifying any specific industries, the Postwar Program advocated considering nationalization in cases where it might improve efficiency or prevent monopolistic pricing.

Most of the social policy planks of the Postwar Program were passed by Parliament within a few years, in some cases unanimously (Bigersson et al. 1981:182–84). By contrast, its planning proposals became a source of intense political controversy right after the war, and hardly any of the institutional reforms it suggested under the general heading of planning were implemented.

The Social Democrats conceived planning as an extension and institutionalization of ongoing preparations for the return to peacetime conditions. In 1943 the government appointed a series of commissions to investigate the postwar investment plans and employment needs of various sectors of the economy, and in 1944 it set up the Commission for Postwar Economic Planning, chaired by Gunnar Myrdal, to integrate the findings and make broad policy recommendations.[6] The Myrdal Commission had more than twenty members representing various parties and interests. As with the Mammoth Commission of 1934, its instructions became a subject of heated parliamentary debate. Whereas the Social Democrats argued that the commission should explore long-term economic development, the bourgeois parties wanted to restrict its scope to immediate adjustment problems. To avoid splitting the national emergency government, the instructions were deliberately left vague, and the same controversy reappeared within the Myrdal Commission as it sought to define its tasks. The representatives of business threatened to resign when the Social Democratic majority sought to extend the commission's deliberations to the restructuring of industrial sectors, and in the end the reports of the Myrdal Commission focused almost entirely on macroeconomic policy.

Separate sector-specific commissions of inquiry were set up to investigate industrial restructuring in 1944–45. The Social Democrats initiated these commissions by passing a series of parliamentary motions submitted by backbenchers in 1944. They thus sought to set the Postwar Program in motion without splitting the national emergency government. Often quoting verbatim from the Postwar Program, the backbench motions of 1944 demanded that sectoral commissions be appointed to explore how the state might intervene to promote rationalization, and they typically invoked the possibility of nationalization.

The Retreat from Planning

The radicalization of labor politics in 1944–45 strengthened those elements of the business community that opposed participating in postwar planning. The Executives' Club called the business representatives on the Myrdal Commission hostages and argued that labor's planning offensive should be met by political countermobilization. Its views now gained support within established business organizations. In the wake of the Social Democratic motions of 1944, SAF and the Federation of Industry agreed to set aside funds to finance what ultimately became a massive propaganda campaign against planning and nationalization. After the breakup of the national emergency government and the formation of a Social Democratic minority government in May 1945, the bourgeois parties also began to attack planning, equating it with the demise of free enterprise and democracy. The parliamentary election

6. On the Myrdal Commission and the ensuing debate over planning, see Svenning (1972) and Sainsbury (1980) as well as the sources cited in note 4.

of 1948 ended the postwar debate over planning. Polling 46.1 percent of the vote, compared with 46.7 percent in 1944, the Social Democrats held their own and considered this a victory in view of the intense campaign against them. But the Communists' share of the vote dropped from 10.3 percent in 1944 to 6.3 percent in 1948. For the socialist bloc as a whole, the 1948 election marked a serious setback—the first real one since 1928. Unwilling to go it alone with the Communists, shortly after the 1948 election the Social Democrats initiated discussions with the Agrarian party about forming a new coalition government. They assured the Agrarians that they were prepared to abandon all efforts to nationalize private enterprise. Yet the Agrarian party hesitated, apparently seeking further concessions in agricultural policy, and it was not until 1951 that a new SAP-Agrarian coalition government was formed (Birgersson et al. 1981:200–201).

The significance of the 1948 election as a turning point should not be exaggerated. In a sense the election outcome simply confirmed a shift of political initiative that had already ocurred, for the Social Democrats began to retreat from the idea of planning, especially selective state intervention in industrial restructuring, well before the election. Whereas the Social Democrats had campaigned strongly for planning and economic democracy in the local elections of 1946, their 1948 election campaign downplayed such issues, emphasizing instead the need to ensure that the social reforms already enacted would not be reversed (Sainsbury 1980). Quite apart from the bourgeois campaign against planning, the Social Democrats would have been hard put to contest the 1948 election on that issue, for they could hardly point to any concrete accomplishments.

The Myrdal Commission was dismantled in 1946, and the work of the sectoral policy commissions appointed in 1944–45 was hurriedly brought to an end in the subsequent two years. The Myrdal Commission was not succeeded by any permanent planning body of the sort envisaged by the Postwar Program of the labor movement. Two advisory bodies, the Investment Council and the Trade Policy Council, were set up as forums for discussion between the government and the business community, but neither could be construed as an instrument of state intervention, and both quickly languished.

As for the sectoral policy commissions, their reports contained few policy recommendations of any significance. For the most part they concerned themselves with problems of a rather technical nature, such as the need for joint sales organizations for small firms, R&D planning, quality control, personnel training, and safety. A couple of commissions proposed creating tripartite sector councils (*branschråd*) to carry out continuing investigations of structural problems and to coordinate rationalization measures. Although LO strongly endorsed this proposal, the Federation of Industry refused even to discuss it, and the government did not persist.

Like previous commissions in the 1930s, the commission to investigate oil importation and distribution recommended nationalization, but this recommendation was never implemented: the currency crisis of 1947 made it too expensive to buy out foreign interests. None of the other sectoral commissions proposed nationalization measures. The commission to investigate the insurance business instead recommended that the boards of private insurance companies include a representative of either the state or the insurance holders. Of the various proposals to extend public control over the supply of capital put forth in the Postwar Program, only one—the creation of a state-owned commercial bank (Sveriges Kreditbank)—was realized in the second half of the 1940s.

The problems of maintaining macroeconomic stability precipitated new government efforts to elicit the collaboration of business in the late 1940s. Tripartite discussions of macroeconomic policy began shortly after the 1948 election and led to the creation of several smaller delegations that replaced the defunct investment and trade policy councils set up in 1946. One of these delegations, the "collaborative organ for the promotion of production and exports," became a regular forum for informal policy discussions among representatives of the government, the bureaucracy, and organized interests in the early 1950s, commonly known as the Thursday Club. Organized business initially was skeptical of this arrangement and objected in particular to the inclusion of union representatives. But relations between business and the government improved markedly from 1949 onward. That the Executives' Club dissolved itself in the early 1950s is perhaps the most significant indication that the era of confrontation had come to an end.[7]

7. The Thursday Club ceased to meet in 1955 and was succeeded by larger, more public, and less regular conferences between the government and organized interests at Harpsund, the official country residence of the prime minister. Like the meetings of the Thursday Club, the Harpsund conferences appear to have been strictly consultative. On the significance of "Harpsund democracy," see Lewin (1967:383–87), Elvander (1969:199-203); Svenning (1972:44-48); Hancock (1972:160–63); and Dahlkvist (1975:198–201). The Social Democratic governing elite underwent several changes in the late 1940s that might have contributed to the new climate of collaboration. Most notably, Myrdal resigned as minister of commerce in 1947, and Wigforss retired from the Ministry of Finance in 1949. Both were closely identified with planning. The new minister of finance, Per Edvin Sköld, had a reputation as a moderate, and he took it upon himself to improve relations with organized business. As a result of conflicts with the Ministry of Finance, Gustav Möller, another leading party idealogue in the 1930s and 1940s, resigned as minister of social affairs in 1951. (That Per-Albin Hansson died and Tage Erlander replaced him as party leader and prime minister in 1946 is less important in this context, for Hansson had been the major proponent of compromise and collaboration within the SAP leadership.)

Several policy initiatives helped the government improve its relations with business. Most notably, it devalued the krona by 30 percent in 1949, following Britain's lead. The devaluation boosted corporate profits and set the stage for the liberalization of trade. Also in 1949, the government appointed a commission to explore whether macroeconomic stability could be achieved through general policies rather than detailed regulations and to propose such policies. In the course of the 1950s, government regulations were phased out in all sectors of the economy other than housing and agriculture (Lewin 1967:360–65).

Labor's retreat did not mean that planning was abandoned altogether. Rather, it now came to be identified with long-term economic forecasting and, more loosely, with the expansion of the public sector. The first long-term economic survey was presented in 1948. From 1950 onward, long-term economic surveys have been produced every five years. These surveys have primarily concerned the conditions for macroeconomic stability and have analyzed economic development in terms of broadly defined aggregates (industry, housing, agriculture, etc.). They have advocated various policies to stimulate investment but have typically avoided recommendations on the allocation of capital within the corporate sector (Lönnroth 1974; Lindbeck 1974:165–69; Wickman 1980:81–97).

On both sides, the struggle over planning in the immediate postwar period was to some degree rhetorical and motivated by electoral tactics. In the industrial arena, the settlement of the late 1930s remained firmly in place. The Postwar Program of the labor movement called for introducing industrial democracy by legislative means, but the government never proposed any such legislation. Instead, LO initiated negotiations with SAF, which led to an agreement to establish joint works councils (*företagsnämnder*) in 1946. At SAF's insistence, the councils would have no decision-making powers; they would consult on workplace conditions and matters of corporate policy. In 1948 LO and SAF signed another procedural agreement, setting up standardized rules regarding time-motion studies and piece-rate systems and again affirming a shared interest in promoting rationalization and productivity increases (Söderpalm 1980; Kjellberg 1981; Johansson 1989).

CONCLUSIONS

It is commonly argued that labor's retreat from planning in the second half of the 1940s should be seen as a strategic reorientation rather than a failure (e.g., Lewin 1967:331–32; Sainsury 1980:143–44; Apple, Higgins, and Wright 1981). Labor's postwar planning offensive, so this argument runs, rested on the premise that stagnation and unemployment would again become central problems with the return to peacetime conditions, and it had to be abandoned when this premise proved false. Indeed, Sweden's gross domestic product grew by an annual rate of 4.5 percent in the second half of the 1940s (Hadenius 1985:60), and the central problem confronting the government was to contain inflationary pressures.

The Postwar Program advocated promoting industrial efficiency as well as full employment, however, and the new economic situation hardly made the notion of planning irrelevant. The objectives the Social Democrats sought to achieve through planning in 1932–43 included rationalization and productivity growth, and these concerns remained central to the anti-inflationary strategy the labor movement adopted in the 1950s. In contrast to the planning strategy of 1932–48, labor now sought to promote industrial efficiency without interfering with the autonomy of corporate management and private investors (see chap. 3). From a retrospective point of view, it seems clear that the sustained economic expansion inaugurated in the late 1940s and continuing through the 1960s made the postwar settlement concerning the state's role in the economy acceptable to the labor movement. Yet this explains the reproduction of the historical compromise over time rather than its formation.

Characterizing the retreat from planning as a strategic adjustment to new economic conditions ignores the political constraints the labor movement encountered in its efforts to institutionalize planning. The Social Democrats' reliance on the Agrarian party was the most obvious constraint on their planning ambitions in the 1930s. As for the immediate postwar period, one might be tempted to argue that the failure occurred because voters rejected planning in 1948. But why did they do so? The question is particularly pertinent since the socialist parties did very well while campaigning on the Postwar Program in the local elections of 1946 (losing less than a percentage point relative to 1944, their all-time best election performance).

The rightward electoral shift of 1948 can largely be explained in terms of the political power resources available to business in its campaign against planning, particularly its ability to influence public opinion through the mass media. This line of argument needs to be qualified on two counts: first, labor's retreat from planning began before the 1948 election; second, world events (the onset of the Cold War) and short-term economic difficulties also affected the outcome of the 1948 election.

The political power of business may have been more important to the outcome of the struggle over planning than any systemic constraints of capitalism. As I suggested at the outset, more far-reaching institutional reforms than those proposed in the Postwar Program were introduced in other capitalist countries in the 1940s.[8] Yet in the 1930s, and again in the 1940s, labor's retreat from its more radical ambitions coincided with, and appears to have been precipitated by, symptoms of economic crisis (the "second depression" of 1937–38 and the balance-of-payments crisis of 1947). At least in the collective mind of the SAP leadership, crisis conditions made accommodating business interests imperative.

The failure of the labor movement to advance toward planning and industrial policy cannot be treated as simply a result of external constraints, political or economic. It was also a failure to translate the notion of planning into concrete reforms and policies. The Social Democrats' conception of planning remained rather vague, and as we have seen, they relied heavily on public commissions of inquiry to make its meaning concrete. The experiences of these commissions in the 1930s and 1940s conform to the same pattern. Commissions with very broadly defined tasks (the Mammoth Commission and the Myrdal Commission) were first appointed, amid political controversy. These commissions set the stage for more narrowly defined commissions, typically with a sectoral focus. As attention shifted to the sectoral level, considerations of microeconomic efficiency came to dominate the investigations, and broader questions of public control and alternative paths of development receded.

As Söderpalm (1976:127–28) argues, business enjoyed a decisive advantage over labor in the context of sectoral policy commissions. Not only were there more business representatives than union representatives, but the information that provided the basis for their deliberations was furnished almost entirely by individual firms or business organizations. Organized business had in several cases already carried out its own investigations of the industry concerned, and many of the experts enlisted by the commissions were directly tied to business. Neither the government nor the unions had the "counter expertise" to challenge corporate interests in this context. At the same time as organized business mobilized politically against planning, its representatives exercised powerful influence within the supposed organs of planning. The strategies pursued by different segments of the business community complemented each other in this respect.

It is of course impossible to say what might have happened had labor

8. In a similar vein, Söderpalm (1980:59–60) notes that the works councils established by agreement between LO and SAP in 1946 represented a very modest move in the direction of industrial democracy compared with French and German codetermination reforms of that time.

pursued planning more forcefully and developed a more coherent conception of what it wanted to accomplish. In the absence of wholesale nationalization of industry, some form of accommodation with private business (at least segments of private business) was clearly necessary in the 1940s as well as the 1930s. But such an accommodation might have encompassed more active state intervention in industrial development.

CHAPTER THREE

Labor Strategy and Investment Politics in the Postwar Era

What distinguishes the Swedish labor movement, comparatively speaking, is not the vigor or success of its efforts to introduce planning but rather its ability to come up with an alternative approach to industrial restructuring. This alternative is commonly known as the "Rehn-Meidner model," so called because its principles were elaborated by Gösta Rehn and Rudolf Meidner, two economists hired by LO to head its new research department in 1945.

The Rehn-Meidner model relied on solidaristic wage policy and active labor market policy to reconcile full employment with price stability and to promote the international competitiveness of Swedish industry. I first present the Rehn-Meidner model and then explore the significance of two institutional reforms introduced by the labor movement: the system of investment funds, created in 1938 and reformed in 1955, and the huge public pension funds created as part of the pension reform of 1959.

It is common to invoke the growth of the AP funds, and the fact that the IF system was administered by the Labor Market Board (AMS), as evidence of a gradual extension of state intervention and corporatist policy bargaining into the realm of investment decisions. This line of thinking is succinctly summarized by Esping-Andersen's (1990:172) claim that "opportunities for bargains [between labor and capital] were substantially improved by the development of the (ATP) pension funds, the apparatus for active labor-market policy, and the investment reserve system, all of which incorporated the trade unions as key decision makers."

Yet, Esping-Andersen and the other proponents of this view never engage in any sustained analysis of the processes whereby pension-fund capital has been allocated and investment funds have been released. Taken by itself, the size of the AP funds tells us very little about their significance as a mechanism of public control or a site of corporatist bargaining.

What is striking about the actual investment practices of the AP funds and the practice of investment fund releases is the very limited way these institutions were ever used to influence investment patterns in a purposive and selective manner.[1] Whereas the IF system and other features of the system of corporate profits taxation introduced by the Social Democrats influenced the pattern of investment by favoring more efficient firms and sectors and by promoting more capital-intensive production, the release of investment funds was predominantly employed as a tool of countercyclical policy.

As for the AP funds, the allocation of ATP savings among aggregate economic sectors (central government, local government, housing, and business) was largely determined by the regulatory practices of the Central Bank, which required private insurance companies to allocate investment in essentially the same fashion. The tripartite boards of the AP funds made only allocative decisions of marginal significance. Critically, the lending of ATP savings to the corporate sector was exclusively indirect (the purchase of bonds and lending via intermediary credit institutions), and the funds never had any influence over the investment decisions of corporate borrowers.

My disagreement with Esping-Andersen and others may turn on what we consider to be significant degrees or forms of public influence over investment. More decisively, the following analysis casts serious doubts on the claim that trade unions have been "key decision makers" in the allocation of pension-fund capital and the release of investment funds. In any case, the limits of public investment steering, and of tripartite bargaining in these institutional settings, call for an explanation.

As we shall see, the legal-institutional framework of the AP funds severely restricted the scope of investment steering, especially the rules governing their supply of capital to the corporate sector. The obvious question is why the government adopted such restrictive rules. In part, the legal-institutional framework can be seen as an expression of the political power of labor's opponents. As we shall see, the labor movement retreated on several issues pertaining to pension-fund management in order to secure passage of its pension reform proposal. At the

1. The analysis in this chapter is restricted to the period before the economic crisis. Chapter 4 addresses the inadequacy of investment funds and public pension funds as policy tools in the face of the structural problems of the Swedish economy in the 1970s. For reasons that will emerge in chapter 4, corporations' right to set aside profits in investment funds was discontinued as part of the tax reform of 1990, and the legal-institutional framework of the AP funds is currently being reviewed.

same time, however, the legal-institutional framework of the AP funds expresses labor's strategic priorities at the time of the ATP reform.

The voluntary basis of the IF system can be viewed as a constraint on the government's ability to use investment fund releases for purposes that did not conform to corporate investment choices, but this feature of the system cannot be directly attributed to political mobilization by business. The 1955 reform of the IF system was quite uncontroversial. Also, it is not obvious why the financial incentives the system provided could not have been used to alter corporate preferences. It seems more likely that the government chose not to use investment fund releases for selective purposes. My interpretation of investment politics in the 1950s and 1069s differs from that of Esping-Andersen and others not only on what the labor movement achieved but also, and perhaps more important, on what labor sought to achieve.

LABOR'S POSTWAR STRATEGY

Contrary to the expectations of the labor movement, mass unemployment did not return at the end of the Second World War. Instead, the second half of the 1940s saw severe inflationary pressures. Unwilling to abandon an expansionary policy orientation, the government sought to control inflation as it had in the wartime economy, through administrative controls and voluntary wage restraint. Under pressure from the government, the LO unions agreed to a wage freeze in 1948 and again in 1949. This incomes-policy experiment, like similar ones in other West European countries, strained relations between the unions and the government and undermined the cohesion of the union movement, for the unions could not prevent wage increases that employers were able and willing to pay. Local wage drift undermined the authority of national union leaders and gave rise to compensatory claims by workers who did not benefit from wage drift or benefited less than others (see Hadenius 1976:111–19).

First presented in a report to the LO congress of 1951 (LO 1953), the package of policies that subsequently came to be known as the Rehn-Meidner model was conceived as an alternative strategy that would avoid the contradictions of incomes policy (Rehn 1977, 1980; Hedborg and Meidner 1984). I first consider the Rehn-Meidner model as an intellectual construct, then explore certain aspects of its implementation.[2]

---

2. On both counts, the following discussion draws heavily on the pioneering work of Andrew Martin (1975a, 1979, 1984, 1985). Rehn (1977, 1980) and Hedborg and Meidner (1984) provide crucial insights about the origins and logic of the Rehn-Meidner model. See also Tilton (1990; chap. 9).

The Rehn-Meidner Model

The Rehn-Meidner model provided two solutions to inflation; short term and long term. The short-term solution was simply that the government restrict private demand by more or less permanent budget surpluses. The government should take direct responsibility for price stability, Rehn and Meidner argued, rather than trying to pass the buck to the unions. A restrictive fiscal policy would keep the lid on corporate profits, enforcing employers' resistance to wage demands, and thus leave the unions free to press the gains of their members. But wouldn't such a policy result in unemployment? Selective measures to stimulate demand for labor in particular localities (or segments of the labor market) obviated this drawback.

The Rehn-Meidner model's long-term solution to inflation was to raise productivity by combining solidaristic wage policy with selective state intervention in the labor supply. The compression of wage differentials, Rehn and Meidner argued, would promote growth by squeezing corporate profits selectively. On the one hand, a concerted union effort to increase wages for the low paid (beyond what market forces dictate) would squeeze the profit margins of less efficient sectors or firms and force them either to rationalize production or to go out of business. And the wage restraint of the well paid implied by the principle of wage solidarity would promote the expansion of more efficient sectors or firms. The net effect would be to raise average productivity in the economy and thereby make it possible for average wages to rise without threatening macroeconomic stability.

Rehn and Meidner recognized that the unions could not possibly perform the role assigned to them unless the government intervened to compensate workers hurt by economic restructuring and to help them adjust to changes in the demand for labor. As conceived by Rehn and Meidner, "active labor market policy" encompassed selective supply-side measures to promote labor mobility (relocation and retraining programs) as well as selective demand-side measures to stimulate employment. Supply-side intervention would aid solidaristic wage policy not only be socializing the costs of industrial restructuring, but also by reducing the bargaining leverage that groups of workers might enjoy because of bottlenecks in the supply of labor.

Wage drift constituted the crux of the Rehn-Meidner model. Rehn and Meidner criticized incomes policy on the grounds that the unions could not prevent wage increases that employers were able and willing to pay; yet their alternative strategy hinged on wage restraint by well-paid workers. What, then, would prevent employers from spending the "excess profits" generated by this restraint to raise wages beyond contractual increases? For Rehn and Meidner, the solution was a fiscal policy so restrictive that even the profits of efficient firms would be somewhat squeezed. In Rehn's words, their model prescribed an "unsolidaristic profits policy . . . *within the framework of a general policy of low profits*" (Rehn 1980:46; my emphasis). But this solution contained within itself another problem: securing levels of investment in the advanced sectors of the economy adequate to offset job losses in less efficient sectors.

In an early article, Rehn (1952) suggested transforming the public savings generated by a restrictive fiscal policy into new investment. This might be done either through the expansion of the public sector or through the supply of credit to the private sector. In the latter case the state would tax away the excess profits of efficient firms, then turn around and lend them money. Low interest rates would offset whatever negative effects the combination of solidaristic wage policy and restrictive fiscal policy might have on firms' propensity to invest. Though this connection did figure explicitly in the debate over pension reform in the 1950s, the idea of using the ATP system as a mechanism of collective savings thus fit very well within the logic of the Rehn-Meidner model (Martin 1984).

Rehn's advocacy of a gradual collectivization of the "investment function" was not an attempt to steer investment allocation. The Rehn-Meidner model relied on market-determined differences in corporate profitability to allocate new investment. The compression of wage differentials was not meant to alter the direction of market-driven restructuring; rather, it was to speed up the process by reinforcing profit differentials. As Andrew Martin (1979, 1984) suggests, the Rehn-Meidner model turned traditional Keynesian economics upside down but remained true to its essential premises in leaving the allocation of investment to market forces. (Keynes also spoke of a gradual socialization of investment.) Though the composition of new investment turned out to be the key to noninflationary growth, it did not require an interventionist solution. Selective state intervention could and should be restricted to the labor market, where it would be effectively confined to adjusting the supply of labor to corporate investment decisions. In this sense, the Rehn-Meidner model accepted and operated within the terms of the postwar settlement between labor and business.

The interventionist posture of the programmatic report submitted to the LO congress of 1961 by the research department, mainly written by Rudolf Meidner (LO 1963), might be invoked against this interpretation. The report represents the labor movement's first attempt to formulate an industrial policy program since the setback of the immediate postwar period, and it can be viewed as the critical link between the planning ambitions of the 1940s and labor's industrial policy offensive of the late 1960s. At the same time, however, it represents the most articulate expression of the labor movement's ideological commitment to the free market economy in the 1950s and 1960s.[3]

Although the 1961 report proposed a series of institutional reforms that would make possible the activation and coordination of state policies to promote industrial development, it stressed that their overarching purpose should be to help business adjust to the intensification of international competition. Rather than pushing the economy "in a direction mapped out in advance," the state should seek to "strengthen the forces of competition and remove the obstacles that stand in their way" (LO 1963:57–59). It should do so through a combination of general and selective policy measures, but selective measures were to assume secondary importance in all areas other than labor market policy (LO 1963:139). In contrast to Social Democratic proponents of planning in the 1930s and 1940s, the authors of the 1961 report did not perceive any tension between the logic of the capitalist rationalization and the interests of society. The notion of "misrationalization" is entirely missing here.

The Rehn-Meidner model drew on policy ideas that the labor movement had entertained for some time. The idea that the LO unions should coordinate their wage bargaining to improve the relative position of low-paid workers was put forth by the Metalworkers Union as early as the 1920s. And in the late 1930s two commissions of inquiry that included employer as well as union representatives advocated supply-side measures to promote labor's adjustment to industrial restructuring. Following the recommendations of the Myrdal Commission for Postwar Economic Planning, in 1948 the government established a permanent state agency to administer labor-market measures, Arbetsmarknadsstyrelsen (henceforth AMS). Rehn and Meidner's contribution was to combine these policy ideas into a coherent strategy (Öhman 1973).

Solidaristic Wage Policy

By the late 1940s wage solidarity had become a widely shared ideal within the labor movement, yet very little effort had been made to

3. Meidner himself has called the report the "culmination of market-conformative thinking and unwillingness to plan or steer [*planerings- och styrningsovilligt tänkande*] within the labor movement" (Hedborg and Meidner 1984:202). For various interpretations of the report, frequently reproducing its internal ambiguities, see Lewin (1967:427–38), Svenning (1972:60–62), Elander (1978:74–78), Apple, Higgins, and Wright (1981; chap. 5), and Martin (1984:219–22).

translate this ideal into practice (see Meidner 1973; Hadenius 1976). Needless to say, it was primarily the low-wage unions within LO that were attracted to wage solidarity. The LO affiliates organizing better-paid workers, and the craft unions in particular, resisted the idea that LO should intervene in wage bargaining to reduce wage differentials. Indeed, the Metalworkers Union abandoned its advocacy of solidaristic wage policy as it moved from being a low-wage to being a high-wage union in the course of the 1940s.

The Rehn-Meidner model legitimated the redistributive demands of low-wage unions by identifying them with the long-term interests of the labor movement as a whole. It did so by using wage solidarity to promote productivity growth, and hence as an alternative to incomes policy, which all unions found unacceptable. Also, the model redefined wage solidarity to render it more acceptable to high-wage unions. Whereas solidaristic wage policy had previously been conceived simply in terms of reducing the gap between low-wage and high-wage workers, the report adopted by the LO congress of 1951 proposed that the unions coordinate their wage bargaining according to the principle of "equal pay for equal work." Thus the unions should seek to eliminate wage differentials determined by employers' ability to pay but respect wage differentials determined by the tasks different workers performed.

In retrospect, the significance of the Rehn-Meidner model as the intellectual foundation of labor's postwar strategy can hardly be exaggerated. The endorsement of the model's principles by the LO congress of 1951 was of no immediate consequence for LO's approach to wage bargaining, however. As Peter Swenson (1989) argues most persuasively, the implementation of solidaristic wage policy from the mid-1950s onward was a response to immediate pressures on LO (Hadenius 1976:81–96; Heclo and Madsen 1986; chap. 3). These pressures came from two directions. On the one hand, the employers and the government demanded that LO restrain the wage demands of its affiliates. On the other hand, the low-wage unions within LO refused to go along with restrictive LO-SAF agreements unless these agreements had a solidaristic profile. The employers' insistence on peak-level wage bargaining thus strengthened the leverage of the low-wage unions within LO.

In the absence of these pressures and their interplay, the 1951 report setting out the Rehn-Meidner model might have remained a dead letter. More important, Swenson's analysis clarifies how the practice of solidaristic wage policy has deviated from the theory of the Rehn-Meidner model. Whereas the point of the model was to free the unions from responsibility for macroeconomic stability, wage-bargaining coordination by LO always involved wage restraint as well as wage solidarity

63

(aggregate restraint as well as restraint by high-wage workers). Also, the principle of equal pay for equal work was never made fully operational. Solidaristic wage policy came to mean that LO would seek to improve the relative position of low-wage workers regardless of the tasks they performed.

Signed in 1952, the first central wage agreement between LO and SAF combined a percentage wage increase with a minimum increase specified in cash, a formula known as the "broken line." The 1952 agreement was very restrictive, however, and the redistributive effects of the cash increase were entirely offset by wage drift (due primarily to firm- or plant-level bargaining over piece rates and mainly benefiting well-paid workers). Having only reluctantly agreed to a central settlement, LO and its affiliates perceived this experiment as a setback and insisted on a return to industry-level bargaining. But LO again yielded to employer and government pressure in 1955 and 1956, and this succession of two consecutive LO-SAF agreements established a tradition of peak-level wage bargaining that continued unbroken until 1983. Like the central agreement of 1952, those of the second half of the 1950s specified a minimum cash increase or made other provisions to improve the relative position of low-wage workers. Only a modest compression of wage differentials occurred before 1965, however, and it was primarily due to the phasing out of separate wage categories for women (Meidner 1973:48–61).

The employers never abandoned the principle that market forces should determine the distribution of wage increases. In practice they were willing to compromise this principle to secure wage restraint, but their cooperation with LO's redistributive efforts was always contingent and qualified. SAF's opposition to solidaristic wage policy might be attributed to the influence of employers that would be adversely affected by above-average wage increases for the low paid. As an all-encompassing employer organization, SAF could not completely disregard the interests of such employers. But the real story is more complicated, for the employers that stood to gain from the wage restraint of well-paid workers also had an interest in using wage incentives to recruit and control labor.

Active Labor Market Policy

The government did not begin to implement the policies prescribed by the Rehn-Meidner model until the late 1950s. The coalition government of 1951–57 represented a constraint on their implementation, for the Agrarian party (SAP's junior government partner) strongly opposed increased government spending on labor market policy (Öhman

1973:82–84). But the policy recommendations Rehn and Meidner advanced initially met considerable opposition from Social Democratic ministers as well (Rehn 1977:214–222; see also Martin 1984:211–213; Rothstein 1986:87–90). In particular, the minister of finance, Per Edvin Sköld, dismissed the report to the 1951 LO congress as an intellectual scheme without practical relevance. The unions could not shirk their responsibility for preventing inflationary wage pressures, Sköld argued.

Threatening to develop into a major rift, the differences between LO and Sköld were settled at a special LO-SAP conference in 1955. At the conference, Tage Erlander, prime minister and party leader, declared his own conversion to LO's position and committed SAP to the expansion and activation of labor market policy. With the Agrarian party having split from the Social Democrats over the issue of pension reform, the Social Democratic minority government refrained from responding to the recession of 1957–58 with deficit spending and instead allocated new resources to temporary public works and other targeted labor market programs.

From the recession of 1957–58 to the late 1970s, government spending on labor market policy increased on a secular trend, in both absolute and relative terms.[4] The activation of labor market policy was initially a source of political controversy. Although organized business and the bourgeois parties went along with using selective labor market measures to combat unemployment during recessions, they objected to the expansion of supply-side measures during economic upturns. Several arguments were made against this component of the Rehn-Meidner model (Lewin 1967:412–16, 483–86, 490–91; see also Furåker 1979:136–43, 160–68).

First, the opponents of active labor market policy warned that labor might become too mobile, making it difficult for employers to hold on to their work force, and they strenuously objected to LO's proposal that relocation and retraining programs be extended to workers who were not unemployed. Secondly, they objected to the steering of economic restructuring implied by subsidizing the recruitment and training costs

4. In the second half of the 1970s (1976–80), annual spending on labor market policy averaged 7.2 percent of the central government budget and 2.7 percent of GDP. The corresponding figures for 1961–65 were 3.0 percent and 0.7 percent (Axelsson, Löfgren, and Nilsson 1983:197). The reorientation of Social Democratic policy between 1955 and 1958 was accompanied by three important leadership changes. First, Gunnar Sträng, a former trade-union official, replaced Skold as minister of finance. Second, Bertil Ohlsson became general director of the Labor Market Board. Ohlsson would subsequently distinguish himself as an advocate of active labor market policy. Third, Arne Geijer left the presidency of the Metalworkers Union to become president of LO. Having previously argued against solidaristic wage policy, Geijer now endorsed it, and tensions between high-wage and low-wage unions within LO eased under his presidency.

of certain firms or sectors, stressing the inherent difficulties of determining whether the competitive troubles of a particular firm or sector were structural or cyclical. Finally, the opponents of active labor market policy objected to the discretionary powers of AMS. Significantly, this objection figured much more prominently in the rhetoric of the bourgeois parties than in that of organized business, which was represented on the AMS board of directors.

To encourage a quick and flexible response to labor market developments, AMS had from the very beginning enjoyed wider discretion in allocating its budgetary resources than had other administrative state agencies. Since approval of the government budget is one of the principal ways Parliament can influence public administration, the opposition parties charged that the government's failure to specify the purposes of AMS spending more precisely and more strictly represented an attempt to short-circuit parliamentary democracy.

The controversy surrounding active labor market policy was resolved through a public commission of inquiry. Appointed in 1960 and reporting in 1965, the commission included representatives of all the major political parties and labor-market organizations, and its deliberations generated broad agreement on the need for a flexible administration of labor market policy, free from rigid rules and capable of responding to developments without funding delays. Its report (SOU 1965) essentially vindicated labor's approach but allayed the fears of business and the bourgeois parties on specific points. Whereas LO had proposed the AMS be empowered to restrict access to employment services for employers with high personnel turnover owing to low wages and bad working conditions, the commission reaffirmed the traditional principle that the employment services should serve all clients equally. Also, it proposed modifications of the eligibility requirements for AMS programs but did not completely sever the connection to unemployment.

The controversy surrounding active labor market policy in the early 1960s was fueled by the bourgeois parties and appears to have been motivated by tactical considerations. Representatives of organized business on previous commissions of inquiry had subscribed to the idea of selective state intervention to promote labor adjustment, and the recommendations of the commission appointed in 1960 reflected a consensus that had already emerged among employer and union representatives on the AMS board of directors.

It is common, and quite apposite, to invoke AMS as a textbook case of a corporatist state agency. Until very recently, the AMS board of directors consisted of the director general and his deputy; three representatives each for SAF and LO; three representatives of white-collar unions (two nominated by TCO and one by SACO-SR); two members appointed directly by the government to represent the interests of women and the rural population; and two nonvoting members representing the AMS staff. Although the boards of other Swedish state agencies often include representatives of organized interests, the principle of corporatist representation is nowhere as pronounced as in the case of AMS. Most important, AMS is unique in that the principle of corporatist representation at the board level has been reproduced at lower levels of the organization. The county labor boards (twenty-four) and district employment boards (eighty) are composed in basically the same way as the AMS board of directors, and within the central AMS administration, unions and employers are represented on a number of delegations or working groups that are permanently or temporarily engaged in advising and overseeing particular aspects of policy implementation.[5]

Though the unions held a formal majority on the AMS board until recently, decision making was always characterized by informal bargaining and consensus formation rather than by voting. Board members have very seldom opted to dissent formally. Writing in the late 1960s, Nils Elvander (1969:238–39) argued that conflict on the AMS board was lacking in part because the administrative staff took into account the concerns of different interest organizations in preparing board meetings; but "the major reason for the harmony within AMS is that the [interest] organizations have in fact to a very great extent agreed on the labor market policy carried out thus far."

In a somewhat different vein, the absence of conflict might be attributed to the unions' recognition that active labor market policy presupposes the cooperation of employers. For instance, AMS depends on the employers to provide information on their recruitment needs as well as advance notice of layoffs. The effectiveness of the employment services presupposes that the employers use them for their recruitment, and this imposes obvious constraints on how far access to employment services can be used as a lever to influence corporate behavior. In short, the structural position of the employers in the labor market makes it imperative for AMS to operate through consensual decision making.

On the other hand, the willingness of organized business to help for-

5. Rehn (1984) provides a comprehensive description of corporatist arrangements at AMS. Contrary to the tendency among foreign observers to treat AMS as representative of Swedish public administration in general, Rothstein (1986) and Söderlind and Petersson (1986) emphasize AMS's distinctiveness relative to other state agencies. Note that employer-union parity was established on the AMS board of directors by adding representatives for public-sector employers in the late 1980s and that in early 1990 SAF announced that it intends to withdraw from all representation on the boards of state agencies.

mulate and implement active labor market policy can be seen as an expression of the inherent limits of this type of state intervention in steering economic restructuring. For active labor market policy must be seen mainly as a matter of adjusting the supply of labor to changes in demand determined by corporate investment decisions. The corporatist structures of AMS have ensured that its activities remained within these bounds.

The Effects of Labor's Postwar Strategy

The expansion of labor market policy in the 1960s made it possible for LO to pursue solidaristic wage policy more assertively. Against this background, and as part of a more general radicalization of labor's reformist ambitions, LO renewed its commitment to wage solidarity in the second half of the decade (Hadenius 1976:98–100; Åsard 1978: 90–94). Whereas the principle of wage solidarity had previously been defined entirely in terms of redistribution among the workers represented by LO, it was now extended to encompass the reduction of wage differentials between blue-collar and white-collar workers. This new dimension strengthened the consensus behind wage solidarity within LO, for all LO unions would stand to gain if it included white-collar workers.

As figure 2 illustrates, LO's renewed commitment to wage solidarity led to a major compression of intersectoral wage differentials among blue-collar workers (see also Hibbs 1990). The timing of this development does not bear out the notion of solidaristic wage policy as the motor of economic rationalization and productivity growth, for the most rapid postwar growth of output and productivity occurred between the recessions of 1957–58 and 1967–68. Indeed, it seems plausible to attribute the compression of wage differentials to the postwar transformation of the economy rather than vice versa. The argument would be that economic restructuring increased the relative significance of more productive and hence better-paid jobs within the labor force. Also, the compression can be seen as a consequence of full employment, which strengthens the bargaining position of all workers, but especially unskilled or semiskilled ones.

This is not to say that LO's bargaining strategy was of no significance for the compression of wage differentials. The point is that economic conditions aided the implementation of solidaristic wage policy. Although there are good reasons to be skeptical about the significance of such wage policy for economic development (Erixon 1984), its political significance as a source of ideological coherence and as a mechanism to reconcile divergent interests within the labor movement can hardly be

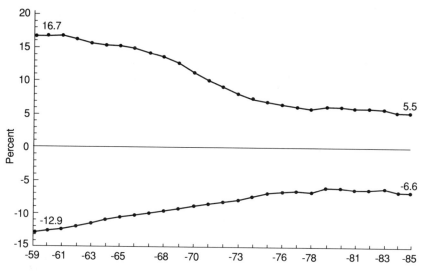

Source: Elvander (1988:36).
Note: The straight line represents the average wage of workers covered by LO-SAF agreements. The upper curve represents the average wage of the "contract areas" (typically defined by industrial sectors) that lie above the LO-SAF average in a given year, and the lower curve represents the average wage of the "contract areas" below the LO-SAF average. (All together there are 120 contract areas.)

Figure 2. Intersectoral wage differentials among private-sector workers, 1959–85.

exaggerated. Leftist critics of labor's postwar strategy commonly argue that solidaristic wage policy represents the functional equivalent of incomes policy (e.g., Dencik 1974). This argument misses the crucial point that LO was able to avoid the disintegrative effects of incomes policy by applying solidaristic principles to the voluntary exercise of wage restraint (Higgins and Apple 1983).

CORPORATE PROFITS TAXATION

The system of tax-exempt investment funds constitutes the most distinctive, and widely celebrated, feature of corporate tax policy in postwar Sweden (most notably celebrated by Shonfield 1965, but also by Przeworski 1985; chap. 6). The IF system must be seen as part of a larger system of corporate profits taxation designed by the Social Democrats.

The corporate tax legislation Wigforss introduced in 1938 articulated the basic principles of labor's postwar approach to profits taxation. Essentially, Wigforss opted to treat corporate profits taxation as a way to stimulate investment and promote efficiency rather than to redistribute income from capital to labor. The redistributive interests of labor were instead to be satisfied by progressive taxation of personal income and by public welfare. Rather than itself being a redistributive mechanism, corporate profits taxation would promote economic conditions conducive to full employment and welfare-state expansion (LO 1963:86). In effect, the Social Democratic approach distinguished between capitalists and their firms: whereas the former were to be taxed heavily on the income they receive as owners, the latter were to be encouraged to reinvest their profits through generous tax breaks.[6]

The 1938 legislation substituted a flat-rate (proportional) profits tax for a progressive tax. From 1960 to 1990, the statutory rate of profits taxation levied by the central government was 40 percent. Local government also taxed corporate profits, and the taxes paid to local governments were deductible from national taxes. The combined statutory rate of profits taxation averaged 52 percent from 1955 to 1972 and had increased to about 56 percent by the early 1980s (Taylor 1982:61; Bergström 1982:12).

Following the recommendations of a commission of inquiry, in 1955 the government undertook a comprehensive overhaul of the rules governing investment funds (government bill 100, 1955).[7] Before this reform, the effectiveness of the IF system as a tool of countercyclical management had been very limited. Regular depreciation allowances that let firms achieve similar tax reductions were more attractive, since there was no guarantee that they could use their investment funds before they again became subject to taxation (after six years).

The 1955 legislation let firms set aside up to 40 percent of their annual profits in investment funds but required them to deposit 40 percent of these funds in a blocked, interest-free account at the Central Bank. Raised to 46 percent in 1960, the deposit requirement was introduced to curtail corporate liquidity during economic booms. But three provisions of the 1955 legislation rendered the IF system more attractive to business. First, the legislation removed the limit on how long profits could remain tax exempt in an investment fund. Second, it allowed corporations to deduct from their taxable income 10 percent of any investment financed with investment funds. Third, it let corpora-

6. The system of capital gains taxation also contained "loopholes" designed to encourage wealthy people to make productive long-term investments. See Steinmo (1988, 1989).

7. SOU (1977a:242–53) provides a convenient summary of the 1955 legislation and subsequent supplementary legislation, and Petersson (1980) discusses the politics surrounding IF legislation. The legislative overhaul of the IF system enacted by the bourgeois parties in 1979 modified the system but did not alter the basic characteristics set out below. See Pontusson (1986; chap. 6) for further details.

tions draw freely, without government authorization, 30 percent of investment funds that had been set aside for more than five years.

Along with these provisions, the tightening of depreciation allowances in the second half of the 1950s and the curtailment of tax-free pension reserve funds after the public pension reform of 1959 stimulated corporate use of the IF system. From the end of 1956 to the end of 1965, the number of corporations with investment funds increased from 640 to 2,566, and their accumulated savings in these funds grew from 247 million SEK to 3,307 million SEK. The number of firms with investment funds doubled from 1965 to 1974 and again from 1974 to 1978, reaching 12,262 by the end of 1979, but the significance of accumulated IF savings declined as their release was liberalized in the 1970s. These savings averaged 2.1 percent of GDP in the 1970s, compared with 3.2 percent in the 1960s (SOU 1977b:294; AMS 1983:3).

The use of investment funds was restricted to the purchase of capital equipment and the construction or renovation of buildings until 1979, when legislation introduced by the bourgeois parties extended their use to investment in research and development and employee training. For tax purposes, an investment financed with investment funds was regarded as fully depreciated. Though tightened in the second half of the 1950s, depreciation allowances remained liberal and sometimes were as attractive as IF financing, if not more so.

Under the depreciation rules in effect from 1960 to 1990 (described by Bergström 1982:14–15 and Södersten 1977:115–17), firms could depreciate their capital equipment according to either of two schedules: they could write off 30 percent of the remaining value or 20 percent of the purchasing value each year. The purchasing value of buildings could be depreciated at approximately 4.5 percent per year. The rates at which firms could depreciate their assets for tax purposes exceeded real economic depreciation, particularly for capital equipment. According to one estimate, the real annual depreciation of capital equipment and buildings used in manufacturing averaged 7.7 percent and 2.6 percent, respectively, in the 1970s (Taylor 1982:62).

Accelerated depreciation allowances constitute a form of interest-free credit (Södersten 1977), reducing the rate at which the return on investment is taxed during an initial period. But the investment project will continue to yield a return after it has been fully depreciated for tax purposes, and the rate of taxation on this return will be higher than had the firm depreciated its assets at the rate of real depreciation. In a sense, then, the firm "repays" the loan from the government after the investment project has been fully depreciated. So long as a firm continues to expand, however, tax credits can be repaid from new tax credits. For an expanding firm, accelerated depreciation allowances reduce the overall rate of taxation. The same logic applies to investment funds, which effectively amounted to full depreciation at the time an investment was made.

Whereas the rules for depreciation allowances provided more favorable terms for investment in machinery than for investment in buildings, the terms of IF financing were the same for both. Hence the relative benefits of the IF system were considerably greater for investment in buildings (see Bergström 1982; SOU 1989:170–71). Whereas depreciation allowances were designed to promote productivity growth through investment in capital equipment, the IF system was conceived as a tool of countercyclical management. Because of the immediate employment effects of new construction, the government has sometimes restricted the release of investment funds to this type of investment. Even in the absence of such restrictions, however, construction projects accounted for 70 percent of total IF releases approved in 1975–81 (AMS 1983:15).

As figure 3 shows, the gap between statutory and real rates of profits taxation widened steadily from the mid-1950s to the early 1970s. What is most remarkable is that this development coincided with an acceleration of public sector expansion and a very major increase of the total tax burden. While the total taxes collected by local and central governments increased from 26 percent of GNP in 1955 to 41 percent in 1970 and 52 percent in 1979, corporate profit taxes as a share of total tax revenues declined from 11 percent in 1955 to 3 percent in 1970 and remained at 3 percent in 1979 (Bergström 1982:12).[8]

To repeat, the provisions that enabled firms to reduce their real rate of profits taxation were contingent on the reinvestment of profits. Also, these provisions favored certain types of firms and investment. In general they favored manufacturing capital and, within the manufacturing sector, reinforced market-determined differentials in corporate profitability. Though conceived independently, the Social Democratic approach to corporate profits taxation conformed closely to the logic of the Rehn-Meidner model in the latter respect. Corporate tax policy operated by similar mechanisms, and had (or should have had) similar structural effects. This affinity perhaps contributed to its legitimacy within the labor movement (Bergström 1982).

Beyond the structural effects built into the system of corporate

8. Deductions for the buildup of inventories became more important than either investment funds or depreciation allowances for corporations seeking to reduce their effective rate of profits taxation in the 1970s (see Södersten 1977:152). While new investment in plant and machinery slumped, the rules governing inventory valuation were liberalized to encourage firms to maintain output in the face of slack demand.

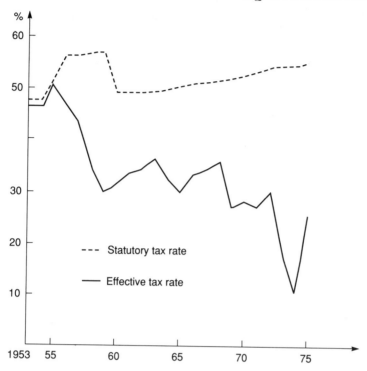

Source: Södersten (1977:152).
Note: The "effective tax rate" refers to the ratio of actual tax payments to "real" net profits —
the latter being calculated by substracting net financial costs and estimated real
depreciation of assets from gross profits, corrected for changes in the value of inventory.

Figure 3. Statutory and effective rates of profits taxation for industry, 1953–75.

profits taxation, the release of investment funds was a potential mechanism for public control of investment. Within the labor movement, the
extension of public control also served to legitimate tax breaks to business. Let us briefly consider the built-in effects the system of corporate
profits taxation had for the allocation of investment before we explore
how the government used the release of investment funds for direct
control over corporate investment decisions.

Built-in Structural Effects

The differential effects of the system of investment funds and depreciation allowances depended above all on firms' ability and willingness
to expand. Table 1 illustrates the range of variation within the engi-

Table 1. Effective rates of corporate profits taxation among fifty-one engineering firms, 1963–68

Average rate of return on own capital	Average growth of real capital			
	<5%	5–10%	>10%	All firms
<5%	73%	57%	56%	64%
5–10%	33	36	24	31
>10%	34	33	18	26
All firms	57	40	30	42

Source: Södersten (1977:180).
Note: See figure 3 for definitions.

neering industry in the mid-1960s: whereas taxes paid by corporations whose real capital expanded by more than 10 percent per year averaged 30 percent of net profits, the corresponding figure for those whose real capital expanded by less than 5 percent per year was 57 percent. The table also shows a strong negative correlation between the rate of profit and the real rate of profits taxation even when the rate of expansion is held constant. Jan Södersten (1977:179–85) explains this counterintuitive finding in terms of the need to show book profits in order to keep dividends up, which restricted corporations' ability to take full advantage of the various provisions for reducing their real tax rate. The more profitable a corporation was, the more it could benefit from such provisions.

It is commonly argued that the system of corporate profits taxation favored big corporations over smaller ones (e.g., Steinmo 1988). In a similar vein, Meidner (1980) suggests that solidaristic wage bargaining was one of the principal factors behind the concentration of capital in the postwar period. This line of argument requires qualification. Though government policy did discriminate among corporations by criteria other than profitability, the significance of such discrimination should not be exaggerated. The concentration of capital derived from the dynamics of international competition, and labor's postwar strategy contributed primarily by reinforcing market pressures.

The IF system pertained only to joint-stock companies. Family businesses and other small-scale enterprises were thus excluded from its benefits. But did it discriminate among joint-stock companies by size? According to Södersten (1977:155), corporations with more than 1,000 employees set aside an average of 11.0 percent of their annual gross profits from 1955 to 1975. The corresponding figures were 8.0 percent for corporations with 500 to 1,000 employees, 8.4 percent for those with 200 to 500 employees, and 8.5 percent for those with 50 to 200. Aside from the largest firms, corporate use of the IF system thus was already rather evenly spread across firms of different size in the 1960s.

That very large corporations set aside more of their profits in investment funds might be explained by the preferential treatment of their applications for the release of investment funds (see below). But there is another possible explanation—that these firms earned higher profits and were therefore more able to take advantage of the IF system. Presumably higher profits also let them benefit more from accelerated depreciation allowances than other firms.

During the postwar period, economies of scale operated primarily within manufacturing industry, and the very large corporations that took disproportionate advantage of the IF system were all manufacturing firms. The share of accumulated investment funds held by manufacturing firms was more than twice as large as their share of the gross domestic product of the corporate sector in the early 1970s (see Pontusson 1986:462), indicating that the system of corporate profits taxation created by the Social Democrats was heavily biased in favor of manufacturing capital. It is this bias that explains its bias in favor of big business.

In sum, the corporations that benefited most from the system of corporate profits taxation were large, capital-intensive, profitable, and rapidly growing manufacturing corporations. Reinforced by political decisions concerning the release of investment funds, the system presumably slowed down the transfer of resources from industry to services. Within the manufacturing sector, moreover, it promoted the restructuring of capital by reinforcing market-determined differentials in corporate profitability.

Being biased in favor of capital-intensive corporations and sectors, corporate tax policy encouraged firms in all sectors to become more capital intensive. In this regard the incentives provided by the IF system and, above all, the depreciation rules operated in close conjunction with the effects of solidaristic wage bargaining and the government's increasing reliance on payroll taxes to finance public expenditures.

Investment Fund Releases as a Policy Tool

The 1955 legislation gave the government wide discretion in authorizing the release of investment funds: it could restrict fund releases to investment in either buildings or machinery, and it could also restrict releases to particular firms or sectors. The legislation even empowered the government to require firms to use their investment funds, but this provision was never put into practice. The release of investment funds always took the form of the government's approving applications from firms.

In arguing for the 1955 legislation, the government stressed that the IF system was meant as a tool of macroeconomic demand management and that firm-specific fund releases would be made only in exceptional cases. To counteract fluctuations in the business cycle, the legislation stipulated that released funds had to be invested within a period specified by the government, not to exceed two years. The use of investment funds was thus restricted primarily to smaller projects that could be carried out quickly. Supplementary legislation enacted in 1959 (government bill 6, 1959) allowed the government to authorize releases for more than two years and to give preliminary authorization for firms to finance long-term investment projects with investment funds yet to be set aside. Whereas the authorization of IF releases under the original rules of the 1955 legislation, henceforth the "1955 rule," could be delegated to AMS, the government had to authorize releases under the "1959" rule directly.[9]

According to the government bill, the new legislation was meant to encourage big, export-oriented firms to undertake investment projects that would help them adjust to new competitive circumstances in the wake of the formation of the European Economic Community. The 1959 legislation thus departed from the traditional view of the IF system as strictly a tool of countercyclical management.

The 1955 rule was used to release investment funds more or less generally during the recessions of 1957–58, 1962–63, and 1967–68, and the 1959 rule was used for firm-specific releases in the 1960s. As a result, it became customary to identify the 1955 rule with general releases for countercyclical purposes and the 1959 rule with selective releases for regional and industrial policy purposes. Firms were required to submit individual investment projects for approval even under the 1955 rule, however. In principle, the 1955 rule could have been used to release investment funds selectively, and the 1959 rule came to serve as a mechanism of general IF releases in the 1970s (see chap. 4 below).

The AMS board of directors was authorized to set the terms for the first general release of investment funds in 1958, but thereafter the government assumed direct responsibility for the timing and terms of general IF releases (as well as selective releases under the 1959 rule). AMS was thus reduced to approving applications during general releases—making sure the proposed investment projects conformed to the government's specifications—and following up individual cases. The government may have decided to assume control over IF releases

9. Releases under the 1959 rule were restricted to 75 percent of a firm's total investment funds and 75 percent of the total costs of the investment project in question, and the investment was not to be eligible for the additional 10 percent investment tax deduction that accompanied regular IF releases. The following account of the release of investment funds draws on Eliasson (1965), Rudberg and Öhman (1971), Lindbeck (1974:98–102), Jones (1976; chap. 10), SOU (1977b:255–57), Johansson and Johansson (1983; chap. 2), and SOU (1989:169–75).

because the 1958 release was, by all accounts, mistimed. (Its announcement came rather late in the recession, and its stimulating effects lasted well into the recovery that began in 1969.) More generally, the government became more concerned with coordinating macroeconomic management at this time. There is another side to the story, however, for the decision to remove control over IF releases from AMS jurisdiction was made while active labor market policy and the role of AMS were subjects of political controversy. This decision appears to have encouraged political consensus around the extension of AMS's capacity to intervene selectively in the labor market and may have been motivated partly by such considerations.

The general releases of the 1960s were formulated to enhance the precision of public control over the timing of corporate investment. When it released funds for construction projects in May 1962, the government stipulated that the costs of projects financed with investment funds had to be paid between July 1962 and April 1963. In November 1962 funds for buying capital equipment were released on condition that deliveries occur during 1963. During the recession of 1967–68, IF releases were staggered over an extended period so the government could gain more accurate information on economic trends and better control the total amount of funds released. Initially, it restricted IF releases to manufacturing industry for balance-of-payments reasons.

Surveys of corporate investment suggest that the general IF releases of 1962-63 and 1967–68 provided a significant stimulus and that their "spillover effects" were limited (Eliasson 1965; Rudberg and Öhman 1971). In 1968 IF-financed investment accounted for 25 percent of total industrial investment and 12 percent of private gross capital formation. For 1956–70 as a whole, withdrawals from the IF system accounted for an average of 5.0 percent of private gross fixed capital formation in the years when general releases were in effect, compared with 2.6 percent when there were no general releases. Withdrawals averaged 75.5 percent of profits set aside in investment funds in release years and 36.3 percent in nonrelease years (AMS 1983:3; Lindbeck 1974:100; SCB, various editions).

As noted above, the 1959 rule was introduced to let firms use their investment funds to finance long-term investment projects considered of strategic importance to the international competitiveness of Swedish industry. In 1963 a government bill supported by the Center party (bill 159, 1963) extended the policy purposes of the IF system to include stimulating corporate investment in regions with structural unemployment problems, and the release of funds for investment in regions and localities targeted for government assistance became more or less automatic.

Linking the promotion of international competitiveness to regional policy objectives, "combination releases" began in 1964 and became increasingly important in the second half of the 1960s. Such releases meant that corporations willing to invest in regions or localities targeted for government assistance would be allowed to use their investment funds to finance investments elsewhere as well. Involving direct bargaining between business and the government, combination releases were restricted to a few very large corporations.[10]

According to a survey by Roger Henning (1977:76–78, 81–82), virtually all big corporations entered into negotiations with the government on the release of investment funds between 1965 and 1975. Typically there were informal discussions between corporate executives and the Ministry of Finance, which assumed responsibility for release decisions under the 1959 rule. Whatever informal contact may have occurred, organized labor was not formally represented in any of these negotiations. As the number of corporate applications for IF releases under the 1959 rule increased, AMS began to review applications and recommend the release of investment funds within regions targeted for government assistance, but in these cases approval was virtually automatic and only rarely a matter of bargaining with corporate management.

Leaving aside labor's ability to influence selective release decisions, that only about 15 percent of corporate investment financed through combination releases in the 1960s was actually made in regions targeted for government assistance (SOU 1977a:256) suggests that the government's leverage over corporate investment decisions through selective IF releases was more limited than one might suppose. But did the government use its leverage to achieve industrial policy objectives that did not hinge on the geographical location of investment? We cannot test this proposition, for it never specified any such policy objectives.

The Ministry of Finance seems to have implemented the general notion that selective IF releases should promote the international competitiveness of Swedish industry in an *ad hoc* manner that relied entirely on the corporations' own assessment of how they should adjust to new circumstances. Although regional policy purposes legitimated preferential treatment of big business through combination releases, the strings attached did not seriously impinge on the autonomy of corporate investment decisions.

In sum, the IF system appears to have been effective as an instrument of macroeconomic management in the 1960s, but its significance for public investment steering is dubious.

10. The average size of combination releases in the 1960s was 77 million SEK compared with 5 million SEK for all IF releases under the 1959 rule. All together, releases under the 1959 rule accounted for almost 40 percent of total IF releases in the 1960s, and combination releases accounted for roughly half of the total amount of investment funds released under the 1959 rule (SOU 1977a:86).

The limits of investment steering might be explained by the way the IF system was set up, for its effectiveness as a policy tool depended on voluntary business participation. In other words, firms had to be continually persuaded to set profits aside in investment funds. This structure may have reduced government leverage in negotiations with corporate management and effectively forced the government to rely on general criteria for releasing investment funds.

But do structural constraints adequately explain the limits of investment steering? After all, there were strong monetary incentives for firms to set aside profits in investment funds and to bargain with the government concerning their release. The limits of investment steering reflect at least in part that the government never tried very hard to use the IF system as a tool of industrial or regional policy. As I noted at the outset, labor's postwar strategy relied on market forces to restructure the economy. Furthermore, the policy purposes assigned to the IF system in the 1960s were somewhat incompatible. To the extent that the system was used as an instrument of industrial policy, its effectiveness in applying countercyclical policy was undermined, and vice versa. Faced with such a trade-off, the government's approach to the release of investment funds gave priority to countercyclical management.

PUBLIC PENSION FUNDS

The pensions reform of 1959 might be characterized as a second breakthrough for Swedish Social Democracy (the first being the crisis agreement of 1933). The issue polarized party politics in the 1950s and precipitated the breakup of the SAP-Agrarian government coalition in 1957, but it helped the Social Democrats mobilize new electoral support and thereby retain control of the government (see Molin 1965; Heclo 1974; chap. 5). As John Stephens (1979) and Gösta Esping-Andersen (1985) have argued, the pension reform struggle involved a shift in the class-coalitional basis of Social Democratic rule: having relied on farmers as its principal allies (a "red-green coalition"), the labor movement now came to rely on white-collar strata (a "wage-earner coalition").

The supplementary pension (ATP) system established in 1959 was conceived as a pay-as-you-go insurance scheme, as opposed to the premium-reserve principle. The fees paid by those currently employed would finance the benefits of those currently retired. Nonetheless, the Social Democrates decided that a pension fund should be built up by collecting more pension fees than necessary to meet pension payments before ATP coverage was fully extended. This fund would serve as a buffer against sudden steep increases in pension fees. More important, it would be a source of the investment capital needed to secure the economic viability of the ATP system. Financing the generous pension benefits that future generations would receive under the 1959 legislation required continued economic expansion, and productivity growth in particular. Productivity increases would make real-wage increases possible, and real-wage increases would in turn generate more pension fees at a given rate of ATP contributions. Although the level of investment had to be maintained, if not increased, the ATP reform itself would remove old-age insecurity as an incentive for individual savings and reduce business savings to the extent that employers shouldered the costs of the new pension system.

The idea of using the ATP system as a mechanism of collective savings thus fit very well within the logic of the Rehn-Meidner model, which advocated squeezing corporate profits through a combination of tight fiscal policy and wage solidarity. But the buildup of public pension funds was conceived as an interim way to increase savings and investment, *not* as a continuous collectivization of capital formation. As the number of ATP pensioners and the average size of their pensions increased, the mechanism of collective savings built into the ATP system would gradually be phased out, and the system would increasingly operate on the pay-as-you-go principle. The pace of this "maturation" would be determined by government decisions on the rate of collecting ATP contributions.

The public commission of inquiry that prepared the ATP reform put forth two schedules for increasing the rate of contributions (SOU 1957:94–96). The government opted for the more cautious of these alternatives, but the expansion of the labor force and the rapid growth of real wages in the 1960s meant this policy generated much greater savings than the commission had projected. The trend changed in the first half of the 1970s: pension payments began to grow more rapidly than pension fees, and the significance of the ATP system as a source of savings declined. After accounting for 35 percent of total credit supply at their peak in 1970–73, by 1980–81 the AP funds' share of the credit market had declined to 17 percent (SOU 1978a:165-66; SCB 1982–83:201).

The combination of economic stagnation and high inflation accelerated the decline of ATP savings in the 1970s and early 1980s, but it was destined to occur even in the most favorable economic circumstances. The ATP system thus imposed "external" constraints on the AP funds as a means of public control over investment. The legal-institutional framework of fund management severely limited the significance of the AP funds even during the two decades when they dominated the credit market.

I first lay out the legal-institutional framework of the AP funds and then consider two aspects of their investment activities: the allocation of pension-fund capital across aggregate sectors (housing, government, and business) and within the corporate sector. Having established that the law severely restricts the scope of investment steering, especially the rules governing the supply of pension-fund capital to the corporate sector, I briefly address why the Social Democrats opted for such restrictive rules in 1959.

The Legal-Institutional Framework of the AP Funds

A separate commission of inquiry appointed in 1957 prepared the legislation on the organization and investment practices of public pension funds that was passed as part of the ATP reform. Known as the Pension Committee of 1957, it was chaired by the head of the Central Bank, Per Åsbrink, and included representatives of LO and SAF plus two experts. Although successive commissions of inquiry had failed to agree on how the new pension system should be constructed, the 1957 committee quickly produced a unanimous report (SOU 1958). In all essentials, the government bill to Parliament (bill 100, 1959) followed the committee's recommendations.

The report of the 1957 committee and the government bill stressed the provisional character of the proposed legislation. In 1968 the government appointed a commission to investigate a wide range of issues pertaining to the organization and operation of capital markets. When the so-called Capital Market Commission (Kapitalmarknadsutredningen) finally submitted its report in 1978 (SOU 1978a), however, it proposed only minor changes in the legal-institutional framework of the AP funds, subsequently enacted by the bourgeois parties (government bill 165, 1978–79).

Whereas the proponents of ATP had envisaged a single pension fund, the 1959 legislation established three separate funds to administer ATP savings: one fund to invest the "excess" ATP contributions of public employers, another to invest the contributions of private employers with more than twenty employees, and a third to invest the contributions of self-employed people and employers with fewer than twenty employees. The boards of all three funds were tripartite, but the particular constellation of interest-group representatives varied, as shown in table 2.

The government opted for multiple funds to allay the fears of the business community. The 1957 committee emphasized that this construction would curtail the concentration of power and promote competition in the credit market (SOU 1958:40–41). In practice, however,

81

Table 2. Distribution of interest representation on the boards of the original AP funds

Group	First fund	Second fund	Third fund
Central government	3	1	1
Local government	3		
Unions	3	4	4
Private employers		3	1
Co-op employers		1	
Self-employed small business			3

Source: AP Funds 1–3 (1961–88).
Note: Figures are number of representatives on board.

the three funds came to function very much as a single unit, sharing an executive director and administrative staff.[11]

Although the report of the 1957 committee discussed at great length the various forms that lending by the AP funds might assume, it dismissed the idea of investment in equity capital with no discussion at all and did not even raise the possibility of real estate investment. Following the committee's recommendations, the 1959 legislation provided three channels whereby the AP funds would supply credit to corporations and public authorities. First, it entitled corporations to reborrow 50 percent of the fees paid the preceding year, provided a bank assumed the risks of such "retroverse loans" (*återlån*). Second, the law enabled the AP funds to engage in direct lending (against a promissory note) to public authorities, corporations owned by public authorities, and intermediary credit institutions. Third, the funds were free to purchase bonds issued by corporations and public authorities. By legislating against direct lending to private corporations, the government sought to eliminate the need for the AP funds to assess risk and, at the

11. From a legal point of view there exists only one pension fund (Allmänna pensions-fonden), administered by several boards. For simplicity, I shall refer to each board as if it were a separate fund. The ambition to create three funds of roughly equal size was not achieved by the formula for allocating pension fees adopted in 1959. While the second fund accounted for more than half of total pension fund assets in the 1960s, the third fund never exceeded 20 percent. At the recommendation of the Capital Market Commission, the dividing line for allocating private-employer fees between the second and the third funds was raised from twenty to fifty employees as of 1980. The funds have had three executive directors since 1960: Lennart Dahlström (1960–74), Bo Jonas Sjönander (1974–80), and Krister Wickman (1980–90). In addition to published sources, my treatment of the investment practices of the AP funds draws on interviews with Dahlström (June 1, 1983) and Wickman (June 14, 1983) as well as two long-term LO board representatives, Rudolf Meidner (March 8, 1983) and Clas-Erik Odhner (June 14, 1983). See Pontusson (1984b; 1986; chap. 7) for a more detailed analysis of the organization and investment practices of the AP funds.

same time, restricted their ability to exercise discretionary influence over private-sector borrowers.[12]

The 1957 committee and the 1959 legislation both affirmed that pension fund capital was to be administered to the greatest possible gain to those insured under the ATP system. Like private insurance companies, the AP funds should maximize return on investment within the constraints of fiduciary responsibility (investment security and the ability to meet pension payments). The 1957 committee insisted that economic and social policy should not influence the funds' investment decisions (SOU 1958:34).

Though unchallenged by the 1957 pension committee, the principle that the AP funds should operate like private insurance companies was by no means obvious. As noted above, the buildup of the AP funds was motivated by economic policy rather than by technical-administrative considerations related to the ATP system. Given that the ATP insurance is obligatory, that every person with an income is included, and that the size of insurance benefits bears no direct relation to the return on pension-fund capital, it is indeed very difficult to distinguish the "interests of the insured" from those of the general public.

Perhaps because it recognized that the principles of private pension-fund management would not be quite "natural" for the AP funds, the government imposed stricter rules on the AP funds than on private insurance companies, which were allowed limited investment in equity capital and real estate. Table 3 compares the distribution of the accu-

Table 3. Distribution of the accumulated assets of the AP funds and insurance companies by type of investment, end of 1975

Type of investment	AP funds	Insurance companies
Bonds	74%	48%
Debentures	2	1
Other securities		9
Stocks		5
Real estate		6
Promissory note loans and other direct lending	18	28
Retroverse loans	6	
Bank assets		3

Sources: AP Funds 1–3 (1975) and SOU (1978a:522).

12. Legislation enacted in 1988 allowed the funds to invest in real estate and also liberalized the rules governing their lending to private business (government bill 11, 1987–88). More recently, the Ministry of Finance has proposed a complete overhaul of the legal-institutional framework of the AP funds: see chapter 7.

mulated holdings of the AP funds and of the private insurance companies among different types of assets at the end of 1975. The differences that separate the AP funds from private insurance companies are significant on three counts. Assets that entail very little potential for direct or indirect influence over the investment decisions of marketplace actors (bonds, debentures, and retroverse loans) assume a greater share of the accumulated holdings of the AP funds. Such assets typically yield a lower average rate of return. And the heavy reliance on the bond market dictated by the legal rules has concentrated the lending of the AP funds to that segment of the credit market most directly and fully regulated by the Central Bank.

The Sectoral Allocation of ATP Savings

The annual reports of the AP funds specify the composition of their lending only in terms of four aggregate sectors: central government, local government, housing, and business. Table 4 summarizes how the allocation of pension-fund capital has evolved over time.

The finance of housing development provides the most obvious link between the lending of the AP funds and the reformist ambitions of the labor movement. By promoting the rapid and massive construction of modern, low-rent apartments, postwar Social Democratic governments sought not only to raise the living standards of the working class but also to help workers move to the urban areas of the south, where economic expansion created new jobs (Södersten 1974; Esping-Andersen 1980, 1985). As the government's housing policy grew more ambitious, the housing sector emerged as the dominant borrower of pension-fund capital in the second half of the 1960s.[13] Demand for the kind of housing built in the 1960s subsequently dropped off, and the construction industry entered a protracted period of stagnation in the first half of the 1970s. Business now replaced housing as the dominant borrower of pension-fund capital, but it was the central government that absorbed the funds made available by the decline of the housing sector's demand for credit. Its increased borrowing continued until the early 1980s, when the new Social Democratic government stressed deficit reduction and a new housing boom began.

13. This also holds true for private insurance companies. While the commercial banks played a less prominent role, the AP funds and the private insurance companies shouldered the burden of the housing program of 1965–74 more or less equally (see SOU 1978a:296). There can be no doubt that the increase of savings brought about by the ATP reform was an essential precondition for the government's housing policy, but the significance of the AP funds as an institutional mechanism is more dubious. Public control of housing development has primarily been exercised by other means (direct state loans, interest subsidies, rent subsidies, and rent control).

Table 4. Net lending to different economic sectors as a percentage of total net lending by the AP funds, 1960–88 (annual averages)

Years	Central government	Local government	Housing	Business
1960–65	10.3%	15.0%	42.4%	31.5%
1966–71	8.4	8.4	50.7	32.4
1972–77	22.0	6.9	35.1	36.1
1978–82	42.3	3.4	28.6	25.3
1983–88	23.6	−1.8	91.6	−15.8

Source: AP Funds 1–3 (1960–88).
Note: The category "foreign borrowers" has been excluded because it has rarely accounted for more than 1% of net lending. This explains why the columns do not add up to 100%. Any periodization of this kind is of course arbitrary at the margins. For example, the decline of the housing sector's share of net lending by the AP funds in the 1970s was more erratic than these averages suggest.

Table 4 demonstrates that the AP funds have helped transfer resources from business to housing and to the public sector. This is sometimes taken to mean that the AP funds have failed to promote the productive investments necessary to secure the long-term viability of the ATP system (e.g., Sjönander 1974). The labor movement, however, has traditionally argued that housing investment and public investment in infrastructure (the construction of roads, schools, hospitals, etc.) not only stimulate industrial investment but are themselves "productive" as a necessary part of economic restructuring and contribute indirectly to productivity increases (e.g., LO 1963:163). Even the proponents of the latter view agree, however, that investment by the AP funds became less productive as the central government began to borrow to finance its current expenditures in the 1970s (Wickman 1983).

The legal rules governing the investment practices of the AP funds may explain a persistent lending bias in favor of sectors that rely most heavily on the bond market as a source of credit, but what accounts for changes in the allocation of pension fund capital over time? To say the AP funds have responded to changes in the demand for credit is hardly adequate, for the credit needs of any potential borrower depend on the terms on which credit can be obtained and cannot be assumed as given. A supplier as dominant as the AP funds can be expected to affect the structure of demand inadvertently or consciously (Zysman 1983).

Until the deregulation of credit markets in the mid-1980s, the AP funds' potential for making allocative decisions of a political or discretionary nature was in large measure preempted by the Central Bank. Under the system of credit-market regulation that evolved in the 1950s, the Central Bank controlled the volume of credit and steered its allocation by three basic mechanisms: the release of bonds (*emis-*

sionskontroll); liquidity requirements for banks; and voluntary quotas under which insurance companies and, as of 1967, commercial banks as well agreed to buy bonds favored by the Central Bank.[14]

These regulatory mechanisms were created to deal with the consequences of the Social Democrats' postwar commitment to keeping interest rates as low as possible. In the 1960s, selective state intervention in the credit market was used to reconcile an active interest rate policy with labor's welfarist ambitions. To keep down the costs of housing finance despite rising interests rates, the government subsidized interest payments on housing loans. The housing sector's demand for credit thus became less sensitive to changes in interest rates, and the credit market remained overcrowded. At the same time, the Central Bank used its control of bond releases to prevent the interest rate on housing and government bonds from increasing as much as other interest rates. This differentiation enhanced the need to intervene selectively to secure credit for these purposes.

From 1960 to 1974, the AP funds enjoyed a special status among suppliers of the organized credit market in that their lending was not directly subject to quantitative regulation by the Central Bank. Although informal pressures were commonly brought to bear, the Central Bank's power to impose lending quotas on insurance companies did not encompass the AP funds, which "escaped" the system of annual agreements. The executive director of the AP funds, Lennart Dahlström, in effect used the agreements between the Central Bank and the insurance companies as a benchmark indicating roughly what quantities of housing and government bonds the AP funds would have to purchase to avoid a confrontation with the Central Bank.

In the wake of a new law on credit market regulation, the AP funds were brought into the system of annual quota agreements in 1974. Though supposedly voluntary, these agreements seldom involved any bargaining. Like other institutional investors, the AP funds simply accepted the lending quotas recommended by the Central Bank. In 1975 the bank asked the AP funds to invest 60 percent of their annual net lending in housing and government bonds. By 1979 this figure had been raised to 67 percent, and in 1980–82 the Central Bank insisted that 75 percent be invested in priority bonds.

The introduction of lending quotas may have been a formality. Relative to other lending, the amount of priority bonds the Central Bank recommended the AP funds purchase in the mid-1970s did not significantly exceed that purchased previously, and the AP funds bought

14. For futher details, see Bergström (1969); Lindbeck (1974; chap. 7); SOU (1982c; chap. 2); and Martin (1981:196–202).

more priority bonds than recommended by the Central Bank in 1975. Given the legal constraints, the large size of the AP funds has often turned out to be a source of marketplace weakness, for the funds have had little choice but to buy whatever bónds were available.

On the average, housing and government bonds given priority by the Central Bank accounted for 59.1 percent of total lending (including retroverse loans) by the AP funds in 1966–71 and 70.9 percent in 1977–83. The volume of retroverse lending averaged 4.0 percent of total lending by the AP funds in 1969–72 and 9.3 percent in 1977–80. In other words, the AP funds themselves had virtually no influence over the allocation of two-thirds to four-fifths of ATP savings.

According to what principles did the funds allocate the remaining portion of ATP savings? As far as the AP funds can be said to have pursued an investment policy in the 1960s and 1970s, it was based on the principle that their basic purpose was to promote productive investment and that priority should therefore be assigned to supplying credit to the corporate sector, and to industry in particular. Concretely, this policy manifested itself in the purchase of very large shares of corporate bond issues (sometimes 90 percent) and in an effort to supply intermediary credit institutions catering to business with as much capital as possible.

Promoted by Dahlström and his successor, Bo Jonas Sjönander, the policy of favoring industry rested on an informal and for the most part unarticulated consensus among the various interests represented on the boards of the AP funds. The shared interests of private-sector union and employer representatives on the board of the second fund, by far the largest of the three, underlay a broader consensus. In no sense did the three funds pursue separate investment policies.

The consensus on giving priority to industry presupposed that the lending capacity of the AP funds could satisfy other credit needs as well, and that both the legal rules and the regulatory policies of the Central Bank were biased in favor of these other needs. Union and government representatives took it as a matter of course that the AP funds would shoulder a major responsibility for financing the government's housing program, and the representatives of business never challenged this view. Unions and employers diverged on what resources society should devote to housing construction and public investment, but this issue did not have to be confronted within the framework of the AP funds.

The investment policy of the AP funds was never specified beyond the general principle that priority should be assigned to financing industry. The boards of the funds never engaged in any extensive discussion, let alone bargaining, concerning this principle or its translation into specific investment decisions. That task fell almost entirely to the executive director as the fund boards assumed a very passive role, typically approving his investment decisions ex post. Neither the unions nor any other interest organization can be said to have advocated a distinctive policy orientation. The allocation of credit within the corporate sector seems to have been based strictly on calculations of return, and no attempt was been made to set priorities among corporations or sectors.

The regulation of credit markets by the Central Bank constitutes the single most important instance of selective state intervention in the allocation of capital during the postwar period. Two features of this mode of state intervention seem crucial to its accommodation within the historical compromise between labor and business. First, credit policy has been formulated in a technocratic rather than a corporatist manner, and organized labor has never played an active role in this policy arena. Second, regulation of the credit market has served almost entirely to channel credit to housing and public investment, and the Central Bank has shunned selective intervention in the supply of credit to the corporate sector. Whenever the Central Bank has restricted the release of corporate bonds, the commercial banks have been allowed to issue them in rotation, and it has been up to each bank to decide which bonds to issue when its turn came (Martin 1981:203).

The Supply of ATP Savings to Business

Apart from the strategic significance of corporate investment for the development of the economy as a whole, the supply of pension-fund capital to the corporate sector is of special interest because it involves the powerful role of private banks in Social Democratic Sweden. In the course of its relatively late industrialization, Sweden developed a system of corporate finance that can be considered credit based and bank dominated (Zysman 1983). The stock market was underdeveloped, and industrial enterprise relied on commercial banks for external finance. Three large private banks emerged from the Great Depression, and two of these merged in 1972 to form Skandinaviska-Enskilda Banken (SEB), the other large private bank being Svenska Handelsbanken (SHB). Together accounting for nearly 50 percent of the combined assets of commercial banks, each of these banks constitutes the organizational nexus of a distinctive constellation of capitalist families and industrial corporations (Hermansson 1981).

The banks themselves cannot own corporate equity, but their principal owners have extensive equity stakes in their principal corporate clients, and directorships frequently overlap. Moreover, the banks control equity through their retirement funds and through investment companies closely associated with them. The supply of long-term credit provides another source of bank leverage in corporate affairs. Though formally of limited duration, much of the business lending of the commercial banks has de facto been long term. Also, the banks have traditionally mediated corporate access to the bond market, issuing bonds on behalf of their corporate clients.

Although, the legislation of 1959 prevented the AP funds from lending directly to privately owned corporations, it let them lend directly (against promissory notes) to intermediary credit institutions as well as government-owned corporations. In addition to intermediary credit institutions, the 1959 legislation provided two channels through which the AP funds would supply capital to the corporate sector: bond purchases and retroverse loans. At the end of 1980, bonds accounted for just about 40 percent of the AP funds' outstanding claims on the corporate sector, promissory notes for another 40 percent, and retroverse loans for 20 percent (AP Funds 1-3, 1980).[15]

Table 5 shows how borrowing by industry in the organized (read "regulated") credit market changed in the twenty years when the AP funds were built up. Although the bond market accounted for a stable share of industrial credit until the late 1970s, the state and intermediary credit institutions became more important and the commercial banks and insurance companies less so as sources of industrial credit. It is tempting to conclude that the growth of the AP funds undermined

Table 5. Distribution of accumulated industry borrowing in the organized credit market by source, 1966–80

Source	1966	1970	1975	1980
Commercial banks	47.5%	39.2%	36.4%	37.7%
Savings and co-op banks	3.4	2.8	3.5	3.5
Insurance companies	14.4	12.5	8.2	10.1
Intermediate credit institutions	4.2	9.7	15.2	14.9
State loans	2.5	6.3	8.2	11.7
Bond market	28.0	29.6	28.9	22.1

Source: Ministry of Industry (1981:18).

Note: The figures include short-term as well as long-term loans. Borrowing from commercial banks includes loans refinanced by the AP funds and by the Export Credit Corporation.

15. The relative significance of retroverse lending has declined since 1980, when legislation restricting the right to reborrow pension fees (government bill 165, 1978–79) took effect. Since net lending to the corporate sector has been negative for most of the 1980s, this discussion is restricted to the period before 1980.

the strategic position of the commercial banks in the system of corporate finance by promoting the growth of intermediary public or semi-public credit institutions. (According to SOU 1978a:652, the AP funds accounted for 69 percent of the long-term liability of intermediary credit institutions at the end of 1976.) What table 5 does not show, however, is that the system of retroverse lending propped up the relative significance of the commercial banks as a source of industrial credit. While intermediary credit institutions accounted for 14.9 percent, retroverse loans accounted for 10.1 percent of accumulated industry borrowing in the organized credit ·market (18 percent of the commercial banks' accumulated claims on industry) at the end of 1980 (Ministry of Industry 1981:18–19).

It should be clear that public investment cannot possibly be steered through the system of retroverse lending. Since the right to reborrow pension fees is contingent only on a bank's assuming the risks of the loan, neither the AP funds nor the Central Bank has any control over the volume of retroverse lending, let alone its specific purposes. As for the significance of corporate bonds as a way to channel ATP savings to business, corporations typically issue bonds to finance investment projects they have already undertaken. Although banks' intermediary role gives them considerable leverage, the buyer or holder of bonds wields no direct influence over corporate investment decisions. An institutional investor might steer investment by systematically buying bonds issued by certain corporations and not others, but there is absolutely no evidence that the AP funds have done so.

The significance that the growth of the AP funds has for the system of corporate finance seems to hinge on the role of intermediary credit institutions. Table 6 lists these institutions, with the years they were established, and indicates their relative importance in the mid-1970s. With but one exception, all the intermediary credit institutions created since 1960 were constituted as corporations of limited liability. Except for the Investment Bank, which is fully state owned, 50 percent of the shares of intermediary credit institutions that are constituted as corporations are owned by the state and the other 50 percent by private interests.

Intermediary credit institutions typically engage in highly specialized lending and seldom compete with on another. The Industrial Credit Corporation and the Investment Bank are the least specialized, since their lending is not restricted to any particular purpose or group of borrowers. Yet the Investment Bank has, in practice, come to concentrate on financing very large projects. A small or medium-sized industrial corporation whose loan application is turned down by the Industrial Credit Corporation is not likely to be considered by another

Table 6. Intermediary credit institutions catering to business and the volume of their new lending, 1970–76

Institution	1970–76 lending (million SEK)
AB Industrikredit/Industrial Credit Corporation	4,924
AB Företagskredit/Corporate Credit Corporation*	811
Sveriges Investeringsbank AB/ Investment Bank of Sweden	4,517
AB Svensk Exportkredit/Swedish Export Credit Corporation	4,193
Sveriges Allmänna Hypoteksbank/General Mortgage Bank of Sweden	2,409
Lanbruksnäringarnas Primärkredit AB/ Agricultural Primary Credit Corporation	1,177
Lantbruksnäringarnas Sekundärkredit AB/ Agricultural Secondary Credit Corporation*	254
Svenska Skeppshypotekskassan/Swedish Ship Mortgage Bank	890
Skeppsfarten Sekundärlånekassa/Shipping Second Mortgage Bank*	227
Företagskapital AB/Corporate Capital Corporation	31

Source: SOU (1978a:651).
Note: Asterisks denote institutions specializing in second mortgages ("sister institutions" of the immediately preceding institutions). The figures refer to "gross lending" rather than the net increase of outstanding claims.

intermediary credit institution. As the Capital Market Commission observed, the system of intermediary credit institutions has transferred decision-making power from the AP funds to a few specialized institutions rather than decentralizing lending decisions (SOU 1978a:464, 663–64). Critically, such power has gone to institutions that are, despite semipublic ownership, essentially private, in the sense that the decisions they make have not been subject to public debate or political bargaining.

Except for the Investment Bank, no provisions have been made for the direct representation of organized labor and other "societal interests" on the boards of intermediary credit institutions. Perhaps more important, the private character of intermediary credit institutions derives from and manifests itself in their institutional separation from government policy.

The intermediary credit institutions typically provide low-risk, long-term loans upon completion of an investment project. Like bonds, their loans replace the shorter term and more risky bank loans that make an investment project possible in the first place. Hence there is little direct competition between intermediary credit institutions and commercial banks, and the expansion of the former has not necessarily curtailed the latter's ability to influence corporate investment. On the contrary, one might argue that the increased availability of long-term credit from other sources strengthens the power of commercial banks or extends their reach by increasing the turnover rate on bank loans, hence increasing the "financing effect" of a given amount of bank lending (Thunholm 1981:8).

Also, the banks are important in preparing corporate loan applications to intermediary credit institutions, and they actually administer the loans of the Export Credit Corporation. In the Swedish debate, it is sometimes argued that the banks have increasingly become mediators rather than lenders, undermining an important component of the system of corporate finance by reducing their incentive to involve themselves in ongoing corporate affairs (e.g., Ministry of Industry 1981). This is another way of saying that intermediary credit institutions have failed to assume the traditional functions of the commercial banks.

The Origins of Legal-Institutional Constraints

Insofar as discretionary decisions have been made about allocating ATP savings among aggregate economic sectors, they have been made by the Central Bank. And insofar as similar decisions have been made about allocating pension-fund capital within the corporate sector, they have been made by private banks or semipublic credit institutions pursuing investment policies with no direct relation to the government's industrial policy. At both levels, investment control has gravitated toward decision-making structures in which unions have not been directly represented.

As we have seen, the use of AP funds for democratic control of investment ultimately is limited by the legal rules governing their investment practices. Why, then, were these particular rules adopted? Clearly, the task the government assigned to the Pension Committee of 1957 was precisely to come up with a set of legislative recommendations that would allay the fears of the business community and to depoliticize pension-fund management. This mandate reflected itself in the committee's composition as well as its instructions. In contrast to commissions of inquiry that prepared the ATP reform itself, the 1957 committee included no representatives of political parties. As head of the Central Bank, its chairman had distinguished himself as a someone business could trust.

The government's mandate to the 1957 committee was motivated by two sets of considerations. Most important, it was motivated by immediate political considerations. By the time the committee was appointed, the pension reform debate had become highly politicized. The Social Democrats could no longer retreat from the ATP proposal, yet they were by no means certain they would prevail. The key to victory in the pension debate was to ensure that the opposition forces did not unite behind a single alternative scheme, and "pension fund socialism" was most likely to bring about such a unification. Also, the Social Democrats believed business confidence would be essential to the AP funds' effective functioning transforming ATP savings into productive investment.

At the same time, the problems of pension-fund management were clearly secondary to the proponents of ATP. Though LO later advocated that the AP funds be allowed to hold equity assets, Rudolf Meidner, the LO representative on the 1957 committee, did not push this issue at all; nor did LO push it in the public debate surrounding the ATP reform. Significantly, the principle that the AP funds should lend in ways that made discretionary decisions concerning the allocation of credit to final borrowers unnecessary had already been articulated by the Social Democratic majority on the commission of inquiry that prepared the ATP reform itself (SOU 1957:100).

The two demands that LO pushed most strongly were that there should a single fund and that employers should have no automatic right to reborrow pension fees. Although the LO research department argued that ATP capital should be actively used to promote industrial restructuring (LO 1963:162–64), it did not present specific proposals. The lack of such proposals is perfectly intelligible within the logic of the Rehn-Meidner model, which essentially saw the market as the most efficient mechanism for allocating capital in the interests of society as a whole. When LO economists spoke of the buildup of pension funds as a way to extend public influence over capital formation, they did not conceive of "public influence" in opposition to market forces. Quite the contrary, public influence would be extended *because* markets would be more important in the allocation of capital. It was on these grounds that LO opposed retroverse lending, which would perpetuate inefficient firms (LO 1963:162–64).

In sum, there was both a strong political need and plenty of ideological room for a consensual solution to pension-fund management. Stephens (1979) correctly points out that the ATP reform was not a redistributive reform in the traditional sense, for the new pension system preserved (preretirement) income differentials. It does not follow that its purpose was to extend public control over capital, however. The way Stephens juxtaposes redistributive issues to control issues obscures labor's fundamental objective in the pension reform struggle, namely, to establish the same pension coverage for all wage earners or, in other words, to establish *equality of pension rights.* To achieve this essentially "welfarist" objective, the labor movement was willing to compromise its ambitions to extend public control over capital as well as its ambitions to redistribute income.

Democratizing investment decisions did not figure at all in labor's efforts to mobilize public opinion for the ATP reform. Those who treat this as an important motive (e.g., Lewin 1967; Stephens 1979) infer it from the arguments against "creeping socialism" advanced by opponents of the ATP reform or from the reformist ambitions labor expressed in the 1970s. Both inferences are highly problematic.

The problem with the retrospective inference is that it exaggerates the continuity of labor's strategic outlook. Meidner's (1975:95) view of the relation between the experience of the AP funds and the idea of wage-earner funds is instructive in this regard:

> The AP funds were being built up since the beginning of the 1960s, and great expectations were attached to the buildup of these funds within the trade-union movement, both regarding their character as a mechanism of collective savings under the administration and control of wage earners and regarding their role as instruments of industrial policy. Many people within the trade-union movement seem to have perceived the AP funds precisely as "wage-earner funds." . . . It would take a good decade before the trade-union movement became clearly conscious that the funds did not fulfill—*and were not meant to fulfill*—this function. But so long as the illusion existed, it was natural that one did not consider it urgent to build up wage-earner funds with similar purposes. (My emphasis)

The most obvious problem with inferring labor's motives from the opposition to the ATP reform is that organized business and the bourgeois parties quickly came to accept the AP funds as a natural component of the mixed economy. Now, there are two possible explanations of why organized business and the bourgeois parties abandoned their hostility to public pension funds. One would be that the ATP reform extended and reinforced Social Democratic hegemony and that the opposition forces accepted the buildup of the AP funds in a defeatist manner. The other explanation is that the legal-institutional framework proposed by the 1957 pension committee and adopted by the government effectively precluded the politicization of investment decisions that business had feared. The latter explanation is clearly the correct one.

CONCLUSIONS

Labor's postwar strategy hinged on the convergence of interests between labor and big, export-oriented business. Export-oriented Swedish corporations enjoyed very favorable competitive circumstances during the postwar expansion. The unions' pursuit of solidaristic wage policy benefited these corporations as high-wage workers exercised restraint and squeezed the profits of those segments of capital, often smaller corporations, that relied on less advanced production methods and operated at below-average productivity or profitability. The Social Democrats' system of corporate taxation had similar effects. Welfare reforms such as ATP and the removal of trade barriers, an integral part of labor's postwar strategy, also squeezed smaller and less efficient business. Finally, selective state intervention in the labor market subsidized the recruitment and training costs of the advanced sectors of business.

Labor's ability to strike a deal with export-oriented business may have depended on its mobilizing the political support of other, "intermediary" class actors. As we have seen, the Social Democrats consolidated control of the government by forging an alliance with the Agrarian party in the 1930s. They were forced back on this alliance option after the 1948 election, but they managed to shed their dependence on the Agrarian party by gaining new support among white-collar strata based on the ATP reform. In so doing, the Social Democrats protected their political dominance against the postwar transformation of Swedish social structure.

The coalitional realignment of the late 1950s did not, however, redefine the postwar settlement between labor and business, which rested on the labor movement's respecting the autonomy of corporate investment decisions as well as private ownership. After the war, the restructuring of labor became subject to detailed state intervention and corporatist bargaining, but the restructuring of capital remained beyond political decision making, at least in a corporatist mold. In policy arenas pertaining to investment, representatives of corporate interests either were absent or entirely lacked substantive significance, as in the case of the tripartite boards of the AP funds.

The asymmetry between a highly interventionist approach to the restructuring of labor and a market-oriented approach to the restructuring of capital might be seen as an expression of the balance of power, but the absence of selective state intervention in the supply of capital to the corporate sector was an integral part of labor's postwar strategy rather than something labor and capital continued to struggle over. To the extent that capital can be said to have "imposed" restrictions on investment steering, this occurred in the immediate postwar debate over planning (cf. chapt. 2).

Labor was able to take advantage of the available alliance options because of its internal unity, and the strategy prescribed by the Rehn-Meidner model can also be seen as a formula for reconciling different interests within the labor movement. On the one hand, unions in the advanced sectors of the economy accepted wage restraint in return for policies that promoted the expansion of these sectors and avoided protecting inefficient production. On the other hand, unions in declining sectors accepted the phase out of jobs in return for higher wages and state intervention to promote labor adjustment as well as to compensate workers for the loss of jobs. Active labor market policy might be described as the glue that held together the growth coalition within the labor movement.

The implementation of the Rehn-Meidner model was accompanied by a twofold shift in the locus of initiative and power within the labor movement: from SAP to the unions, and from local unions to national unions and to LO. Coordinated wage bargaining occupied center stage in the Rehn-Meidner strategy of promoting structural change, while this strategy introduced concerns beyond wage bargaining and led the unions to involve themselves more directly in politics. LO initiated and, to a considerable extent, pushed through the ATP reform as well as the expansion of active labor market policy (Molin 1965:129–32; Heclo 1974:238–41; Martin 1984:213–17). Through the corporatist arrangements of AMS, the unions gained direct influence over the single most important form of selective state intervention in the economy.

The pivotal role LO came to assume distinguishes the Swedish experience of Social Democratic rule from similar experiences in other countries and constitutes a major reason, perhaps *the* major reason, for the success of labor reformism in Sweden. The contrast with the British case seems particularly instructive in this respect (Martin 1975a, 1975b; Higgins and Apple 1983). Through the mediation of LO, tensions between the unions and the government were alleviated, and LO enforced the wage restraint necessary to maintain macroeconomic stability. But LO was also more sensitive to rank-and-file demands than SAP and presented these demands in ways that sustained the momentum of reformism.

CHAPTER FOUR

The Changing Economic Context of Reformism

The labor movement began to challenge private control of investment in 1968–76. It did so by seeking to institutionalize selective state intervention in industrial restructuring, union participation in corporate decisions, and collective profit sharing and shareownership. These initiatives encountered resistance from business and the bourgeois parties. They also became a source of divisions within the labor movement, especially between the unions and the party. When the Social Democrats returned to power in 1982, they effectively abandoned the radical ambitions of labor's reform offensive and opted for a profit-led strategy to promote economic growth and competitiveness, known as the "third way."

My primary concern in this chapter is to explain why labor turned left in 1968–76. Here I develop the analysis behind my claim that this strategic reorientation was a response to economic developments that undermined the viability of labor's postwar strategy and made private control of investment an increasing problem for the labor movement.[1] My analysis shows that Sweden's economic crisis in the second half of the 1970s cannot be understood simply in terms of extraordinary events (oil price shocks) and ordinary business-cycle fluctuations. The crisis was associated with long-term changes in the dynamics of the world economy, the structure of Swedish industry, and Sweden's relation to the world economy. These changes became a source of problems for the labor movement well before the crisis.

The chapter has four sections. In the first two I develop the argu-

1. Again, this approach is an alternative to Korpi's attempt to explain the radicalization of labor reformism as expressing the cumulative growth of labor's power relative to business.

ment that the allocative outcomes of private investment decisions began
to diverge from labor's interests in the second half of the 1960s, and
that this divergence increased during the 1970s. Corporations and capitalists simply did not invest enough to sustain full employment and
real-wage growth in the 1970s, but from labor's point of view the situation was more complicated, for the character of corporate investment
was changing and the payoffs of new investment for labor were not so
great. As a result, the labor movement confronted two strategic problems: how to increase the level of savings but not inequality of wealth,
and how to ensure that an increase in savings would translate into the
kinds of investment that would sustain full employment, real-wage
growth, and continued welfare-state expansion.

The new reform offensive emerged because the institutional arrangements the Social Democrats had introduced under the postwar
settlement did not give labor any means of addressing the latter problem. In the third section I develop this point with respect to the AP
funds and the system of investment funds. Not only were these institutions inadequate in the face of new problems, but as we shall see, the
economic conditions of the 1970s undermined the policy functions they
had served in the 1960s. The crisis accelerated the decline of ATP savings and greatly reduced the role of the AP funds as credit suppliers.
Meanwhile, the system of investment funds evolved into a general investment subsidy and thus lost its potency in countercyclical management.

Economic developments made strategic innovation necessary. Yet
identifying the problems labor responded to does not adequately explain its strategic reorientation. More than one response to these problems was possible. Indeed, the the Social Democrats' "neoliberal" orientation since 1982 can largely be seen as a response to the same
problems labor sought to resolve in the 1970s by institutional reforms
with a "socialist" twist.

The economic recovery of the 1980s might be taken to mean that the
problems confronting the labor movement in the 1970s were transi-
tional. Perhaps labor retreated from radical reformism because it dis-
covered it did not need to challenge private control of investment to
achieve its basic objectives? The fourth section addresses this line of
thought, arguing that the economic recovery of the 1980s was unsustainable and fueled distributive conflicts among wage earners. In certain respects the problems addressed by labor's reform efforts of 1968–
76 remain.

To explain why labor opted for anticapitalist reforms in the 1970s
and for a pro-capitalist response in the 1980s, we must attend to politics within the labor movement as well as the political balance of power

between labor and business. Subsequent chapters engage in such analysis. This chapter is not intended as a complete explanation of the strategic reorientation(s) of labor, let alone of Sweden's economic difficulties. Its purpose is to establish the new economic context of labor reformism.

We can distinguish four mechanisms whereby economic pressures associated with industrial restructuring have impinged on labor's strategic behavior. Industrial restructuring has fueled *rank-and-file demands* for better working conditions and generated *new employer demands* with respect to government policy as well as wage determination. It has also contributed to intensified *distributive conflicts among unions*. While the leadership of the labor movement has reacted to these pressures, it has also acted preemptively (or proactively), based on its own perception(s) of the long-term implications of economic developments and the advice of economic experts.

THE PROBLEMS CONFRONTING LABOR

Throughout the advanced capitalist countries, the economic crisis of the 1970s manifested itself primarily as an investment slump. In Sweden, industrial investment slowed down in the late 1960s, but the volume of industrial investment continued to increase through the first half of the 1970s. Figure 4 illustrates the subsequent sharp drop in the volume of industrial investment.

The immediate reasons for the investment slump in the second half of the 1970s are not particularly mysterious. From 1974 onward, the profitability of Swedish industry deteriorated sharply. In relation to value added, gross profits dropped from about 23 percent in 1974, a year of exceptionally high profits, to less than 5 percent in 1977–78 (Erixon 1984). The collapse of profits coincided with a veritable wage explosion. Over the duration of the two-year wage settlement of 1975–76, average hourly wages in industry increased by 18.4 percent as a result of contracts and by an additional 12.9 percent because of wage drift. If payroll taxes and other indirect labor costs are included, the total labor costs of Swedish industry increased by 39.9 percent. In this respect Sweden diverged sharply from other Organization for Economic Cooperation and Development (OECD) countries. According to widely cited estimates, the unit labor costs of industry increased by 27 percent relative to Sweden's major competitors, and Sweden's share of world trade dropped by 19 percent from 1975 to 1977 (Martin 1985).

Andrew Martin (1984, 1985) attributes the wage explosion of the mid-1970s to the contradictions of solidaristic wage bargaining. Martin

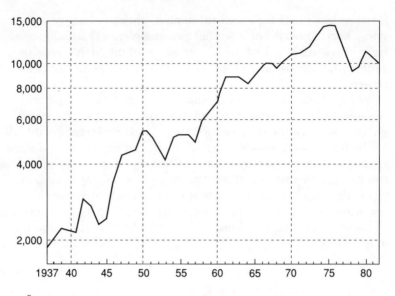

Source: Örtengren (1981:97).

Figure 4. Gross investment in mining and industry in million SEK at 1975 prices, 1937–82.

demonstrates that the fifteen to twenty years preceding the wage explosion were characterized by a secular tendency for labor's share of value added to increase at the expense of profits, and he argues that LO succeeded in raising the wages of low-wage workers in less productive sectors but failed to restrain the demands of high-wage workers in the advanced sectors of industry. Better-paid workers compensated themselves for solidaristic central agreements through wage drift, and this in turn forced LO to demand higher increases for the low-paid in the next wage round. As a result, the compression of wage differentials occurred at an average wage level that was too high to sustain the competitiveness and expansion of Swedish industry.

Martin's interpretation hinges on two propositions: that Sweden's poor export performance in the later 1970s stemmed from (relatively) high labor costs, and that high labor costs reflected the dynamics of solidaristic wage policy. Both propositions partake of conventional wisdom among Swedish economists. Indeed, bourgeois and Social Democratic governments alike have treated labor costs as the key issue in their efforts to restore (or enhance) the competiveness of Swedish industry since the mid-1970s. That Swedish industry nonetheless continues to have a competitiveness problem might be taken to mean that the problem cannot be reduced to labor costs.

Labor Costs and Wage Bargaining

In considering how labor costs affect competitiveness (Martin's first proposition), at least three other factors deserve our attention: the product and country mix of Swedish exports; energy and raw material costs; and productivity performance.

Lennart Erixon (1982a, 1982b) argues persuasively that the product mix and country composition of Swedish exports contributed greatly to the poor performance of Swedish industry relative to that of small, export-oriented countries on the Continent during the economic crisis. Within this group of countries, Sweden stands out as the most heavily concentrated on the export of raw materials, semifinished goods, and investment goods and the most heavily reliant on West European markets. Since the economic crisis manifested itself mainly as an investment slump, and since this slump was deepest in Western Europe, Swedish export industry was more severely affected by the crisis than its counterparts on the Continent. Sweden's share of world trade declined in the 1970s not only because Swedish exports became less competitive owing to increased relative costs, but also because the relative importance of Swedish export markets diminished.

Second, labor costs were not the only costs to increase immediately before the crisis: the energy and raw materials costs of Swedish industry also rose sharply. Based on mechanization and economies of scale, the "Fordist" pattern of economic development that provided the postwar paradigm for the OECD countries depended on cheap energy. The oil price shock of 1974 helps explain not only the world economic crisis, but also why Swedish industry fared particularly poorly. Traditionally, access to cheap hydroelectric power constituted a comparative advantage for Swedish industry, especially for capital-intensive, raw-materials-based export industries (iron and steel on the one hand and lumber, pulp, and paper on the other). But this advantage gradually diminished as industry continued to expand and hydroelectric capacity neared its natural limits. By the late 1960s Sweden had become one of the most oil-dependent of the OECD countries.

Third, it goes without saying that increases in wages and other costs cannot be treated in isolation from productivity. The wage explosion of 1975–76 coincided with a sharp reduction of productivity growth within Swedish industry. After averaging 6 percent in 1963–75, growth averaged only 2.5 percent in 1975–83. The slowdown of productivity can be partly explained in terms of labor hoarding and underuse of capacity during the crisis, but in retrospect it is clear that this is not the whole story, for productivity growth remained extremely sluggish during the economic recovery of the 1980s. At 2 percent, annual productivity growth in industry was even lower in 1983–88 than in 1975–83 (Ministry of Industry 1990:66). I shall return to the reasons for the enduring deceleration that occurred in the mid-1970s.

Turning now to Martin's second proposition—his contention that the wage explosion of 1975–76 was a product of the inherent contradictions of solidaristic wage bargaining—the first thing to note is that a secular tendency for capital's share of value added to decline from the early 1960s onward can be observed in other advanced capitalist countries as well. If we take into account the rate of productivity growth, the development of labor costs was considerably more favorable to business in Sweden than in any other Nordic country from 1960 to 1973 (see Erixon 1984:18–19). Yet only the Swedish and Norwegian labor movements pursued a solidaristic wage policy in this period, and intersectoral wage differentials were much more compressed in Sweden than in Norway.

The extraordinary circumstances of the wage explosion of 1975–76 must also be emphasized. As a result of the worldwide raw materials boom, corporate profits increased sharply in 1973–74, reaching their highest level since 1951. This created more room for wage increases than had been anticipated in the central agreement for 1974, and wage drift exceeded contractual increases by nearly 2 percent (6.8 percent and 5.0 percent, respectively). Because of the wide variation in corporate profitability across sectors, moreover, wage drift was highly uneven.

More generally, the uneven development of corporate profitability in the period may explain the decline of LO's ability to coordinate wage bargaining in pursuit of solidaristic wage restraint since the mid-1970s. It stands to reason that increased discrepancies in corporate profitability would fuel distributive conflicts among the LO unions. The problem here has been compounded by the growth of white-collar unions and by the instability of the world economy (Heclo and Madsen 1986, chap. 3; Elvander 1988). It was relatively easy to reconcile the two components of solidaristic wage bargaining (redistribution and restraint) in the 1960s because there were only two major actors in the wage bargaining process, LO and SAF. In a stable world economic environment, they could broadly agree on what parameters determined room for wage increases; that is, how much wages could rise without threatening the competitiveness of Swedish exports. This agreement was formalized in the so-called EFO model presented by a team of SAF, LO, and TCO economists in 1968 (Edgren, Faxén, and Odhner 1970).

"Exogenous" factors must be invoked to explain why LO failed to maintain solidaristic wage restraint in the mid-1970s. Although the growth of white-collar unions would have become a problem for LO in any economic circumstances, the wage explosion must be viewed as a consequence as well as a cause of changes in the world economy and the competitiveness of Swedish industry.

Corporate Investment Behavior and Employment Patterns

Labor's postwar acceptance of private control of investment rested on the premise that the sectors of industry that benefited from solidaristic wage bargaining would generate new employment at roughly the same rate as the sectors that were squeezed by it would shed labor. In these circumstances active labor market policy sufficed to reconcile economic restructuring with the interests of labor (at least as perceived by labor leaders). A closely related premise of postwar investment politics was that borrowed capital could readily substitute for equity capital as a source of industrial finance. Again, carrying out solidaristic wage policy required a restrictive fiscal policy, keeping the lid on corporate profits and hence reducing the room for wage drift in advanced sectors. To offset the negative effects of this policy for business savings and investment propensity, public savings had to be made available to business.

From labor's point of view, the transformation of public savings into corporate investment could well have been achieved by expanding state enterprise or the supply of equity capital to private business, but the business community was set against any solution that would extend collective ownership. The terms of the compromise struck between labor and business in the late 1940s further stipulated that transforming public savings into corporate investment must be done through indirect forms of lending that curtailed public steering of corporate investment decisions.

The ATP reform conformed to this logic and brought about a major shift in the pattern of industrial finance. Measured as the ratio of equity capital to turnover, the financial solidity of industry declined from about 44 percent in 1958 to 21 percent in 1976 (Carlsson et al. 1979: 40). While the ATP reform reduced business savings, it increased the supply of credit significantly and thus brought down interest rates. Though the return on investment tended to decline in the 1960s, it remained higher than the rate of interest. By investing borrowed capital, firms could at least partly offset the tendency for the return on their own capital to decline.

The decline of corporate self-financing occurred against the backdrop of very stable economic growth after World War II. Stability was itself an important determinant of postwar growth in Sweden and in the advanced capitalist countries more generally. As business grew accustomed to sustained and steady growth, the time horizon of corporate investment was extended, and the level of investment became less sensitive to short-term fluctuations in the return on capital. Perhaps business even came to accept a lower long-term rate of return; at any rate, it became more willing to finance investment by borrowing.

High debt-equity ratios made many corporations very vulnerable to the economic downturn of the mid-1970s. Since then, corporations have become less willing to finance investment by borrowing, and a given level of investment has come to require higher profitability. Three changes that crystallized during the economic crisis of 1974–83 seem to account for this change in corporate investment behavior. First, the world economy has become more unstable. The growing integration of the advanced capitalist economies has synchronized business cycles and made fluctuations sharper. At the same time, international integration has reduced the effectiveness of countercyclical policies.

Second, interest rates rose sharply during the crisis and, in part owing to the internationalization of capital markets, remained far higher in the 1980s than they had been in the 1960s. If borrowing still yields a positive leverage effect, it is presumably much less significant. Third, self-financing has become more important for business because of the growing importance of R&D investment relative to investment in fixed capital.[2] Because R&D investment pays off only over the long run and entails greater risks than investment in fixed capital, it is more important that firms be able to finance it on their own (Lundgren and Ståhl 1981:85–86; Wickman 1980:39–40).

Taken together, these changes made it necessary for labor either to introduce reforms involving collective ownership or to accommodate a major increase of private profits—a major redistribution of income from wage earners to capitalists. At the same time, the sectoral employment trade-off at the core of the Rehn-Meidner model became unsustainable in the 1970s. This development involves two tendencies, both traceable to the mid-1960s and thus predating the decline in the volume of investment as well as the shift in corporate preference for self-financing versus borrowing.

On the one hand, the heavy raw-materials-based industries that had been the motor of Swedish industrialization (mining, iron and steel, and forest products) and that still accounted for a considerable portion of employment as well as export earnings began to shed labor on a

2. As a percentage of total investment by industrial corporations with more than five hundred employees, "material" investment (investment in buildings and machinery) declined from 67 percent in 1978 to 45 percent in 1988, according to the Ministry of Industry (1990:30–39). The remainder includes investment in marketing as well as in R&D.

major scale as they began to decline in the second half of the 1960s. On the other hand, expansion of advanced sectors no longer generated much employment growth, if any. Employment growth in engineering turned negative in the second half of the 1960s and remained negative throughout the 1970s, even though output continued to expand. The chemical industry was the only industrial sector that generated new employment in the later 1960s, and it ceased to do so in the course of the 1970s (see SOU 1980:507).

The net result of these sectoral trends was that the total working hours industry employed declined by an annual rate of 2.2 percent from 1965 to 1981 (SOU 1982b:287–88). Government subsidies to declining sectors and increased spending on labor market policy helped keep the lid on unemployment in the 1970s, but the continued expansion of public sector employment clearly is the primary reason the decline of industrial employment never translated into mass unemployment. In terms of working hours, the public sector's share of total employment increased from 21 percent in 1970 to 27 percent in 1980 (government bill 88, 1989–90, p. 30).

Maintaining full employment by expanding the public sector quickly ran into familiar limits. Under the bourgeois tenure in government (1976–82), the central government deficit rose from less than 1 percent to more than 13 percent of GDP. It is common to say this fiscal crisis occurred because the bourgeois parties simultaneously pursued a "socialist" policy on spending and a "bourgeois" policy on taxation. But this formulation misses an important part of the story, for it appears that the overall tax burden had reached a politically defined ceiling by the late 1970s. Without a major change in voter preferences, the expansion of public expenditures thus increasingly depended on extending the revenue base through employment and productivity growth. As we have seen, the 1970s were characterized not only by employment losses, but also by a sharp slowdown of productivity in industry. The Social Democrats recognized all along that they would have to reverse these trends to safeguard their reformist achievements.

The next section explores why the continued expansion of successful export industries no longer offset the contraction of employment in declining industries in the 1970s. Labor's reform offensive of 1968–76 can be seen as an attempt to create institutional arrangements to ensure that wage restraint would translate into more domestic employment.

COMPETITIVE PRESSURES AND CORPORATE ADJUSTMENT
STRATEGIES

With its heavy emphasis on raw materials, semifinished goods, and investment goods, Sweden's industrial structure closely matched the in-

ternational demand generated by the reconstruction and modernization of the West European economies in the late 1940s and the 1950s.
Meanwhile, domestic demand for consumer durables surged. For
Swedish industry as a whole and the engineering industry in particular,
the period from the end of the war to the recession of 1957–58 is
distinguished by the balance between foreign and domestic markets.
Exports accounted for 24.0 percent of the total sales of Swedish industry in 1950 and 26.4 percent in 1960. Since the late 1950s, industrial
expansion has become increasingly export dependent. Excluding the
construction industry, exports accounted for 33 percent of sales in
1970, 39 percent in 1980, and 47 percent in 1988 (SCB, various years;
Ministry of Industry 1990:10).

The OECD-wide liberalization of trade boosted international demand and helped Swedish producers penetrate foreign markets in the
1960s. At the same time, however, trade liberalization and the growing
integration of the world economy intensified the competitive pressures
on Swedish industry. The competitive position of Swedish raw materials and raw-materials-based industries now began to deteriorate, but
the pressures on advanced sectors (engineering and chemical products)
also intensified. As I have already suggested, the nature of corporate
adjustment strategies in advanced sectors made the decline of basic industries a greater problem for the labor movement.

Restructuring and Rationalization in the 1960s

New competitors enjoying decisive advantages over Swedish producers emerged in timber as well as iron ore while shipping costs
dropped dramatically in the 1960s.[3] Although Sweden was the world's
largest exporter of iron ore in 1967, by 1976 both Brazil and Australia
exported more than four times as much.

The increased relative costs of Swedish timber and iron ore in turn
affected the competitive standing of the paper and pulp industry and
the steel industry. Basic steel had become very closely linked to shipbuilding, and both industries came under intense pressure from Japanese producers in the 1960s. Japanese steel makers and shipbuilders
not only enjoyed a decisive wage-cost advantage over Swedish and
other West European producers but were also able to increase economies of scale through rapid expansion and standardization. (Japan's
share of world trade in steel increased from 2 percent to 20 percent,
and its share of world shipbuilding increased from 20 percent to 50

3. My treatment of the decline of basic industries draws primarily on the Boston Consulting Group (1978) and Carlsson et al. (1979).

percent during the 1960s.) Because of its industrial structure, Sweden was particularly affected by the first phase of Japan's penetration of West European markets.

Swedish industry in general, and declining sectors in particular, responded to growing international competition in the 1960s by rationalizing the existing structure of production rather than moving into new product areas. The "rationalization movement" took several forms, all contributing to the exceptional productivity growth of this period. First, corporations increased their productivity by substituting machines for labor power, that is, by increasing their capital intensity. Defined as the ratio of fixed capital to the total input of man-hours, the average capital intensity of Swedish industry increased by an annual rate of 4.8 percent in 1950–60, 5.3 percent in 1960–65, and 7.2 percent in 1965–70 (SOU 1970:92). This accelerated increase in capital intensity is all the more remarkable because it was offset by the growing importance of the engineering industry, which has always been less capital intensive than basic industries.

Second, and related to the first point, corporations increased their productivity by installing more advanced capital equipment. This modernization was a particularly important source of productivity increases during the investment boom of the late 1950s and early 1960s. Third, the shutdown of inefficient plants constituted a major source of productivity growth in the 1960s. The number of corporations going out of business each year increased markedly during this decade, and so did the number of mergers. According to the study by Bengt Rydén (1971), the mergers of the 1960s were almost entirely between corporations in the same industrial sector, and merger activity was particularly intense in mining, iron and steel, and paper and pulp. Most mergers in these sectors were "defensive" in that corporations with competitive difficulties and sagging profitability sought to rationalize their production by acquiring other corporations in the same line of business.

Mergers enabled corporations not only to shut down inefficient plants, but also to take advantage of economies of scale, and this constituted a fourth source of productivity increases. As a result of smaller corporations' going out of business as well as mergers, the concentration of capital accelerated. From 1960 to 1965 the number of corporations with more than one thousand employees increased from 91 to 135, and their share of industrial employment increased from 54 percent to 59 percent. By 1975 the number with more than one thousand employees had dropped to 117, but their share of employment had increased to 60 percent (Erixon 1984).

Bo Carlsson et al. (1979) argue that the pattern of productivity growth changed in the 1960s (cf. also Kuuse 1986). Put somewhat crudely, the emphasis of rationalization shifted from introducing new technology to substituting machines for labor and eliminating old capital equipment. These rationalization measures brought significant productivity increases and let corporations maintain their competitive position over the short run, but the potential for further rationalization of existing production was gradually exhausted. At the same time, the rationalization measures of the 1960s were largely financed through borrowing, which again left many corporations in declining sectors very vulnerable to the economic downturn of the mid-1970s.

Though mergers continued at a high level, the productivity gains they brought diminished in the 1970s (Erixon 1984). The diminishing potential for rationalization within existing structures might thus explain the long-term deceleration of productivity that occurred then. In a somewhat different vein, this deceleration might also be explained by workers' resistance to further parceling and machine pacing of the labor process. Labor turnover, absenteeism, and wildcat strikes increased throughout the advanced capitalist countries in the late 1960s and early 1970s, and Sweden was certainly no exception. Quite the contrary, one might argue that the reformist achievements of the Swedish labor movement in the postwar era made it more difficult for Swedish employers to realize productivity growth through traditional Fordist methods. Be that as it may, the "crisis of Fordism" on the shop floor constitutes an important part of the slowdown of productivity (Mjöset et al. 1986: 173–80).

Competitive Adjustment Strategies in Advanced Sectors

In addition to renewed efforts at product specialization and production rationalization, the advanced sectors of industry responded to international competition in the 1960s by increased investment abroad. Measured in terms of fixed capital (buildings and machines), direct investment abroad corresponded to 16 percent of domestic industrial investment in 1965–69, 18 percent in 1970–74, and 23 percent in 1975–79 (Carlsson 1981:44). The internationalization of corporate investment accelerated further in the 1980s. In relation to domestic industrial employment, the employment of foreign subsidiaries increased from 12 percent in 1960 to 26 percent in 1978, and 37 percent in 1987. The engineering industry alone accounted for 68 percent of total foreign employment by Swedish industry in 1987 (Ministry of Industry 1990:105, 107).

Reducing labor costs does not appear to have been a primary motive behind expanded foreign production. Typically, corporations that invest abroad are more profitable than those that do not, and solidaristic wage policy has favored these firms. Moreover, the bulk of foreign investment has been made in other high-wage countries (in Western Europe and North America). Most observers agree that corporations invest abroad primarily to circumvent tariff barriers and to strengthen their marketing position in the countries where they have established plants. Establishing a presence inside the European Community appears to have been a particularly important motive. Direct investment has frequently meant buying foreign competitors so as to use their sales organizations. Also, local production reduces transport costs and delivery times and helps firms meet customers' demands (Carlsson et al. 1979; SOU 1982c:192–99; SOU 1983:97–109).

Product specialization and direct investment abroad enabled the big engineering firms to defend and, indeed, extend their shares of the world market for their main products. As Swedish multinationals have thus increased their ability to influence world prices, competition in these markets has come to revolve around factors other than pricing, such as product development, systems sales, marketing, and service. Erixon (1982a, 1982b, 1985) argues that the combination of these two developments has encouraged firms to mark up prices to counteract declining profitability. He sees this practice as part of a broader reorientation of corporate strategies since the late 1960s. Whereas the big export corporations traditionally sought to increase profits by expanding production, their strategies now focus more on increasing profit at a given level of production.

Corporate efforts to improve financial solidity are a critical component of this reorientation. As Erixon demonstrates, Swedish export firms used the devaluations of 1976–77 and 1981 primarily to increase their profit margins. Had they instead tried to increase their market shares by reducing prices, they would have had to finance the necessary expansion of capacity through borrowing. The desire to improve solidity and liquidity also appears to be the primary motive behind the increase in financial engagements by industrial firms, including the purchase of equity capital in other firms. The share of the total capital of Swedish industry devoted to such engagements increased from 22 percent in 1970 to 30 percent in 1980 and exceeded 40 percent by 1988 (Carlsson 1981:44; Erixon 1985:44–45; Ministry of Industry 1990: 49).

I have already alluded to the principal reasons corporations not only became more reluctant to finance investment through further borrowing but actively sought to reverse the decline of self-financing. To reiterate, market conditions grew more unstable, interest rates rose while the return on investment declined, and R&D investment became critical to competitiveness. One more factor should be added: as a result of their internationalization, advanced sector firms have become more and more dependent on foreign borrowing, and the solidity requirements of foreign creditors are more stringent than those of domestic creditors (Erixon 1985; SOU 1978a:270–271).

These considerations are important to the more intransigent wage-bargaining posture SAF adopted in the late 1970s. Arguing explicitly that it could no longer accept the EFO model's neutrality on whether investment would be financed by borrowing from the AP funds or by raising equity capital in the stock market, SAF now rejected the way room for wage increases had previously been defined as a function of productivity in those sectors of the economy that are exposed to international competition. Raising capital in the stock market required larger profit margins, and larger profit margins in turn meant the room for wage increases had to be based on increased productivity in the entire economy (Martin 1984:298–328; see also Martin 1985).

The change in SAF's view of wage bargaining was closely related to its growing criticism of public spending, for the public sector is by far the largest segment of the protected part of the economy, and productivity growth (as conventionally conceived) there is typically much lower than in the corporate sector. SAF's new posture might also mean that increased export dependence has reduced the significance of the gains to big business from stimulating the domestic market through public spending.

In the wage negotiations of 1980, SAF took the position that any increase in wages presupposed public sector cutbacks. Its intransigence precipitated a generalized work stoppage, mainly a lockout, that paralyzed the entire economy for ten days. In the end the government prevailed on SAF and the negotiating agency for public employers to accept one-year settlements that entailed significant wage increases (Broström 1981). The immediate outcome thus marked a setback for the employers. Retrospectively, however, the conflict assumes a different meaning. The resolve the employers demonstrated clearly affected the outlook of the bourgeois parties, whose economic policy became markedly more neoliberal in fall 1980 (Erixon 1985). Furthermore, the employers began to insist on more decentralized forms of wage bargaining in the aftermath of the 1980 conflict.

The conventional view among Swedish policymakers is that foreign investment has improved the competitiveness of Swedish industry and thereby secured domestic jobs (e.g., SOU 1983:128–37). The (untested) premise of this view is that competitiveness could not have been improved as much through alternative domestic investments. Whether or not direct investment abroad is a necessary feature of international competition does not alter the fact that it reduces the demand for domestic labor, however. Also, the exports of Swedish subsidiaries abroad increased more than Swedish exports in 1974–78 (Erixon 1985). In part, Swedish corporations "lost" world market shares to their own subsidiaries.

One final aspect of the restructuring of Swedish industry since the mid-1960s is that the sectors that have grown in importance have a much higher import content in their products than those that have declined. In the mid-1970s, imported inputs accounted for 5 percent of total inputs in iron mining, 15 percent in forestry industries, and some 40 to 50 percent in the engineering and chemical industries (Boston Consulting Group 1978:35–37). The average import content of Swedish exports has risen not only because the relative importance of engineering and chemical products has increased, but also because of the restructuring of the engineering industry (the decline of shipbuilding and other steel-based sectors) and the internationalization of the big engineering corporations. Whereas imported inputs accounted for 24 percent of total inputs in the engineering industry in 1957, they accounted for 44 percent in 1980 (Carlsson 1981:69). This means that any given increase of exports now yields a considerably smaller rise in net export value and domestic employment.

THE INADEQUACY OF EXISTING POLICY TOOLS

It is sometimes suggested that the policies the labor movement pursued in the postwar era made Swedish industry less able to adjust to the new competitive pressures that emerged in the later 1960s. By favoring large, export-oriented businesses, union and government policies contributed to market-driven tendencies toward greater concentration and capital intensity, perhaps creating a more rigid industrial structure (Schön 1982).

More specifically, the structural effects built into the system of profits taxation might have hindered industrial adjustment by discriminating among corporations based on capital intensity and past profitability, and they certainly encouraged corporations to substitute capital for labor rather than pursuing more "flexible" adjustment strategies (Södersten 1977:188; Bergström 1982:20). Taxing profits as both corporate and personal income can also be said to have promoted conservatism by encouraging owners to plow profits back into their corporations (Lundgren and Ståhl 1981:94–96).

The following discussion of the IF system and the AP funds revolves around two rather different claims: that the economic crisis undermined their traditional policy functions, and that neither set of institutions gave labor any means of addressing the new problems it confronted in the 1970s. But let me first make one point with respect to the economic consequences of policy bias: insofar as a conservative bias existed, it was because labor's postwar strategy avoided selective state intervention and instead relied on reinforcing corporate profit differentials to promote productivity. As we saw in chapter 3, business helped shape labor's postwar strategy.

The AP Funds

The ATP system did increase savings without aggravating inequalities of wealth in the 1960s, but it gradually ceased to perform this function. By 1982, annual pension payments exceeded the fees paid into the system, and by the late 1980s, the AP funds had to cover huge annual fee deficits. The combination of economic stagnation and high inflation in 1974–82 accelerated ATP's evolution into a pay-as-you-go system of insurance—a process ultimately driven by the gradual increase in the number of ATP pensioners and the size of their pensions.[4]

The average rate of interest realized by the AP funds kept up with inflation in only three of the twelve years between 1970 and 1982, and in real terms the funds' assets contracted in the early 1980s. As interest rates were adjusted upward and loans at precrisis rates expired, however, the rate of return improved significantly in the 1980s. In 1989 the funds made 36.3 billion SEK, of which 11.6 billion SEK went to cover the fee deficit (AP Funds 1–3, 1989). Still, the relative significance of the AP funds as a source of credit continued to decline during the credit boom of the 1980s. By 1986 they accounted for only 6 percent of all credit provided to Swedish borrowers (SCB 1989:287), compared with 35 percent during their peak in the early 1970s.

While the relative significance of the AP funds declined sharply, the central government absorbed an increasing proportion of their lending as deficit spending skyrocketed during the bourgeois tenure in government (1976–82). Seeking to finance the government deficit outside the banking sector and thereby to curtail its consequences for liquidity growth, the Central Bank tightened the lending quotas imposed on the

4. At a given rate of contributions, the revenues of the ATP system are determined by the total income of the economically active population. Since benefits are indexed to consumer prices, pension payments are determined by the rate of inflation as well as by the number of pensioners and their income before retirement. If the last two factors are held constant, pension fees grow faster than pension payments when wage increases exceed price increases. Along with the rapid expansion of the labor force, this contributed to the rapid growth of the AP funds in the 1960s and early 1970s. The reverse effect operated as real wages declined and employment growth slowed in the second half of the 1970s.

AP funds (see chap. 3). Far from compensating for the shortfall of private investment in industry, an increasing proportion of pension fund capital was thus used for current government spending. Investment by the AP funds became less rather than more productive during the economic crisis.

When the Central Bank raised the quota to be invested in priority bonds to 75 percent in 1980, the boards of the AP funds protested in a joint statement. Promising to do their best to meet the quota, they affirmed that in the event of a shortage of capital for the corporate sector, "the boards consider it their obligation to finance such productive investment in order to assure future pension payments" (cited in Martin 1981:202; see AP Funds 1–3, 1980). In the end this conflict petered out because corporate demand for capital, at least in the forms or on the terms the AP funds could offer, was so low that the funds had few alternatives but to comply with the quota (Sjönander 1981).

While the Social Democrats eliminated the government deficit, industrial investment boomed in the 1980s. Nonetheless, business borrowing from the AP funds turned negative in this period: the sum of new borrowing by private business was less than loan repayments (see table 4 above). Enabling businesses to finance new investment out of savings, the profit-led recovery strategy pursued by the Social Democrats in the 1980s effectively rendered the AP funds irrelevant to business.

The decline of ATP savings could, of course, have been counteracted by raising the rate of contributions, but this would have entailed either an increase in (indirect) labor costs for employers or a reduction in purchasing power for wage earners. Faced with such a trade-off, Social Democratic as well as bourgeois governments opted to make the AP funds bear some of the burden of pension payments. With the Social Democrats, this choice perhaps reflected a growing recognition within the labor movement of the inadequacy of the AP funds for influencing industrial restructuring. For reasons spelled out in chapter 3, any use of the AP funds for industrial policy purposes would have required major changes in their legal-institutional framework. In the 1970s the labor movement sought instead to influence investment decisions by creating entirely new institutions, including a fourth pension fund, perhaps to preserve the political consensus established around the ATP system.

Investment Funds

Following the recommendations of a public commission of inquiry appointed by the Social Democrats, in 1979 the bourgeois parties enacted a legislative package that removed some of the biases of corporate profits taxation (government bill 210, 1978–79, p. 210). The new legislation extended the range of investment projects that could be financed with investment funds to include R&D investment and employee training, and it also made the IF system even more attractive to business by increasing from 40 percent to 50 percent the share of annual profits that could be set aside in investment funds.

In contrast to the debate over establishing the IF system in the 1950s, in the controversy surrounding the 1979 legislation organized business and the bourgeois parties defended the system while spokesmen for labor were more critical. This reversal of roles reflects the evolution of the IF system as well as the radicalizing of labor's reformist ambitions. As LO and TCO both pointed out in their official commentaries (*remissvar*) on the report of the corporate tax policy commission, the IF system ceased to serve macroeconomic management in the course of the 1970s and instead evolved into a mechanism of subsidizing corporate profits and investment in general (government bill 210, 1978–79, p. 252; Petersson 1980).

Two separate procedures for the release of investment funds were established in the 1950s. Under the initial legislation of 1955, the funds had to be invested within two years of their release. Supplementary legislation in 1959 made it possible for the government to release investment funds for a longer period, but such releases would not entitle corporations to the 10 percent investment tax deduction provided under the 1955 law. Instead of authorizing a general release under the 1955 rule, the government responded to the 1971 recession by announcing that firms should apply for IF releases under the 1959 rule, but this procedural change was *not* accompanied by a more selective approach during the recession.[5] Just as in the 1960s, investment funds were released for any investment project that conformed to general criteria established by the government. By the same token, the bourgeois parties' decision (in 1977) to revert to general releases under the 1955 law can hardly be described as a dramatic reorientation of the government's approach to investment funds. By introducing a single release procedure that could be used for selective as well as general purposes, the 1979 legislation simply recognized that the distinction between the 1955 and 1959 rules had lost its practical significance.

From 1972 until 1987, industrial firms could effectively use their investment funds at any time to finance construction projects throughout the country. For investment in capital equipment, the release announced in June 1975 was extended until March 1985. The government made no attempt to restrict the release of investment funds dur-

5. This account of IF release policies since 1971 is based on SOU (1977a:255–57), Johansson and Johansson (1983, chap. 2), AMS (1983), and SOU (1989:169–75).

ing the economic recovery of 1979. Since the funds were released generally throughout the country, the practice of "combination releases" ceased during this period.

The government's increasing reliance on investment fund releases to counteract the decline of corporate investment not only ruled out their use for investment steering, but also undermined their use for countercyclical management. Based on aggregate data for 1961–75 and 1966–78, Taylor's (1982) econometric analysis shows that the corporate investment in buildings tended to be countercyclical in the first period and pro-cyclical in the second. This finding suggests that the effectiveness of the IF system in countercyclical management began to decline before the bourgeois parties assumed control of the government in 1976.

Both Social Democratic and bourgeois governments could, of course, have chosen not to rely on the IF system as a permanent investment stimulus, but they clearly had to do something to counteract the slump in corporate investment. The effectiveness of the IF system as a policy tool was undermined not only by the more or less permanent release of investment funds, but also by the introduction of a variety of other measures to stimulate investment (investment allowances, direct subsidies, etc.). Such measures reduced the leverage the government could exercise through the IF system by making firms less dependent on IF releases to reduce tax payments and investment costs.

The Social Democrats ended the permanent release of investment funds for capital equipment in 1985 and subsequently restricted their release for construction purposes to projects outside big cities. These measures did not mark a durable return to traditional practices, however. On the contrary, the Social Democrats abolished the entire IF system as part of the tax reform of 1989–90 (government bill 50, 1989–90). Seeking to eliminate sectoral biases and promote capital mobility, the reform reduced the rate of profits taxation to 30 percent while eliminating various tax expenditures. The commission of inquiry that prepared the reform argued that the IF system did not provide a very effective way to influence corporate investment and that the reduction of the statutory tax rate would make the system even less effective as a policy tool (SOU 1989:175, 208).

THE RECOVERY OF THE 1980S

When the Social Democrats returned to power in 1982, they adopted a recovery strategy that came to be known as the "third way" to indicate its creators' ambition to stake out a path between the reflationary approach of traditional Keynesianism (as practiced, at the time, by the French Socialists) and the deflationary approach of neoliberalism (as practiced by the British Tories). The centerpiece of this strategy was a 16 percent devaluation, which the new government undertook on its first day in office, and came on top of a 10 percent devaluation by the bourgeois parties in 1981. By devaluing the currency, the Social Democrats hoped to reduce the relative costs of Swedish exports, to encourage Swedish consumers to buy domestic goods rather than imports, and to promote new industrial investment by boosting corporate profits.

Although the economic policy program endorsed by the LO congress of 1981 (LO 1981) recognized the need for wage restraint, it explicitly rejected devaluation and argued that aggregate demand should be stimulated in a selective manner, notably through increased investment in public transportation and infrastructure. The LO program also insisted that wage restraint be linked to wage-earner funds. By comparison, the program adopted by the Social Democratic party conference of the same year (SAP 1981) placed much less emphasis on wage-earner funds. Moreover, the party program diverged from the LO program in that it stated explicitly that economic recovery required public sector cutbacks as well as wage restraint. Public sector cutbacks became the subject of a rather heated debate among Social Democratic economists in the year before the 1982 election, essentially pitting the economists of the LO research department against academic economists who would subsequently become advisers to Kjell-Olof Feldt, the new minister of finance.

While LO accommodated the devaluation of 1982 by demanding average wage increases of 2.5 percent in the ensuing wage-bargaining round, the Social Democrats reaffirmed their election promise to restore welfare entitlements cut by the bourgeois parties and introduced legislation that would spread the burden of austerity by increasing the taxation of wealth, inheritance, gifts, and stock market transactions. Also, the new government quickly launched a public investment program and ultimately introduced wage-earner funds. The actual recovery strategy the new government pursued might thus be seen as a compromise between the policies advocated by LO and SAP before the election. But the overall thrust of government policy after 1982 conformed closely to the prescriptions of Feldt and his advisers, and it must be considered a defeat for LO and its allies within the SAP leadership. The public investment program of 1982 was financed by cutting other public expenditures, especially state subsidies to industry, and the scope of the wage-earner funds legislation of 1983 was very limited.[6]

6. Bergström (1987) provides a detailed account of policy deliberations within the Social Democratic governing elite before the resumption of power in 1982. On the preelec-

As Peter Walters (1985:368) points out, the critical feature of the third way was "its insistence on the renewal of the private sector as the engine of economic recovery." In their efforts to reduce the government deficit and thereby counteract the inflationary potential of devaluation, the Social Democrats relied primarily on expenditure cuts. As a share of GDP, government revenues fell from an all-time high of 67 percent in 1982 to 60 percent in 1988, and as a share of total employment, public sector employment remained constant in this period (28 percent of working hours). Feldt and his advisers clearly accepted the neoliberal argument that the sluggishness of the economy was largely due to the public sector's "crowding out" the private sector.

Coinciding with the beginning of the world economic boom of the 1980s, the devaluation of 1982 contributed to a dramatic reversal in economic performance. Corporate profits soared in 1982–84, and industrial investment (gross investment as a percentage of value added) increased from an all-time low of 12.5 percent in 1983 to 18 percent in 1989. The output of Swedish industry grew by slightly more than 3 percent a year from 1982 to 1988, and a considerable balance-of-payments surplus had emerged by 1986 (compared with a deficit corresponding to 4 percent of GDP in 1982). By the end of 1987 Swedish industry had regained two-thirds of the world trade it had lost in 1975–82 (Ministry of Industry 1990).

Although industry's share continued to decline, total employment (measured in terms of working hours) grew at an average annual rate of 1 percent in 1981–88, compared with a negative annual rate of 0.5 percent in the 1970s, and in absolute terms industrial employment declined only slightly (government bill 88, 1989–90, p. 30; Ministry of Industry 1990:73). Unemployment fell below 2 percent in 1987. Finally, rapid growth helped reduce the budget deficit, and by fiscal year 1988–89 the government had achieved a balanced budget.

The successes of the third way did not endure, however. Throughout the 1980s, the Swedish rate of inflation was higher than the OECD average. By 1988 domestic inflation had "eaten up" the effects of the devaluation of 1982, and Swedish industry again began to lose world market shares. At the same time, the rate of inflation accelerated and the discrepancy between the Swedish rate and the OECD average increased. (In 1989 the Swedish rate of inflation was 6.6 percent, compared with 4 percent in 1986–87 and 4.5 percent for the OECD as a whole in 1989.) By 1989 the balance-of-payments deficit exceeded that of 1982.

---

tion debate between LO and SAP, see also Åmark (1988) and Heclo and Madsen (1986, chap. 2). More generally on the conception and policies of the third way, see Walters (1985), Martin (1987), Erixon (1985, 1988), and Feldt (1991).

Having handily won the elections of 1985 and 1988, in 1990 the Social Democrats suddenly found themselves in a political crisis. The course of this as yet unresolved crisis need not concern us here (see Bergström 1991 and Sainsbury 1991), but we must attend to the deterioration of competitiveness in 1989–90 to appreciate the nature of the economic recovery of the 1980s. The growing discrepancy between Sweden's inflation rate and that of other OECD countries corresponded to a rise in relative labor costs, and consistent with its basic policy orientation since 1982, the government's efforts to reverse the deterioration of competitiveness focused on wage restraint. Once again, however, it seems superficial to consider "excessive" inflation simply in terms of labor costs. Other factors contributed to inflationary pressures in the 1980s: most notably, the deregulation of financial markets stimulated an unprecedented credit boom. Also, wage drift accounted for nearly as much of the increase of relative labor costs as did contractual wage increases in the second half of the 1980s (Söderström 1990:115–18).

The profits boom of the 1980s made the need for wage restraint less compelling to export-oriented employers and stimulated wage drift through plant-level bargaining over piece rates, productivity bonuses, and the like. The government's policy orientation thus made it more difficult for LO, and the peak organizations of white-collar unions as well, to exercise wage restraint, and it played into the hands of those employer groups that began to push for more decentralized forms of wage bargaining in the early 1980s.[7]

Within the private sector, peak-level wage bargaining broke down completely in 1983–84. In 1983 the Metalworkers Union and the engineering employers struck a separate deal apart from the central LO-SAF agreement, and in 1984 the employers successfully insisted on industry-level negotiations with all the LO unions. Under pressure from the government, SAF agreed to peak-level negotiations in the second half of the 1980s, but such negotiations left far more room for industry- and firm-level negotiations than in the past. The downward shift in the locus of bargaining is shown in that central agreements no longer preempt the right to strike (or lock out) in the course of industry-level negotiations.

The experience of the 1980s confirms the crucial insight of the Rehn-Meidner model: over the long run, it is impossible to combine full employment, wage restraint, and high corporate profits. Committed to full employment and unwilling to challenge private control of

7. English-language accounts of wage-bargaining developments in the 1980s include Lash (1985), Martin (1987, 1991), Ahlén (1989), and Swenson (1992). My treatment also draws on Elvander (1988).

investment, the government depended on union-organized wage restraint to secure the level of profitability necessary to regain competitiveness; yet soaring profits in turn undermined the unions' ability to organize wage restraint.

To appreciate how this generic problem of full-employment capitalism worked itself out in the 1980s, we must consider two additional factors. First, employers' efforts to decentralize wage bargaining must be linked to changing production strategies. The engineering employers led the "employer offensive" of the 1980s. Though the big engineering firms enjoyed soaring profits, they came under increasing marketplace pressure to improve quality and productivity and to become more "flexible" in the sense of producing a wider product range or more customized products. These firms came to view more differentiated wage systems as a necessary component of competitive adjustment (Elvander 1991).

Second, the government's efforts to "decouple" private and public sector wages made wage restraint by labor's peak organizations even more difficult. As part of its effort to cut public expenditures, the government began to put the squeeze on public sector unions in 1985–86, specifying wage ceilings for public sector contracts in advance of private sector settlements and insisting that public sector employees would no longer be automatically compensated for private sector wage drift. Meanwhile, the government sought to address recruitment bottlenecks and to promote productivity improvements by decentralizing wage determination in the public sector (by allowing more room for variations in wages according to localities and individual effort). Both aspects of the government's incomes policy for the public sector challenged the principle of "equal pay for equal work" and may have contributed to the erosion of the normative consensus that underpinned centralized wage bargaining in the 1960s and 1970s.

Following the logic of the Rehn-Meidner model, the problem of inflation might be conceived in terms of inadequate productivity growth rather than excessive wage demands. At 2 percent, the annual growth rate of labor productivity in industry was lower in 1983–88 than in 1975–83, and considerably lower than the corresponding figures for Sweden's principal competitors (see Ministry of Industry 1990:66). That there was no trend toward more rapid productivity growth from 1983 through 1989 suggests that this is not simply a question of productivity growth lagging behind investment growth.

What, then, might account for the continued sluggishness in productivity? As Erixon (1989) argues, the government's own recovery strategy alleviated some of the pressure on business to rationalize production and encouraged it to compete based on labor costs. Consistent with this argument, the research department of the Metalworkers Union has shown that, for all the talk about new technology and upgrading industrial work, the proportion of blue-collar engineering jobs requiring few skills and involving physically hard work actually increased in the 1980s. Machine tools and other engineering industries competing based on worker skills lost ground both to mass-producers of consumer durables and to "high-tech" engineering sectors, distinguished by their disproportionate employment of relatively unskilled blue-collar labor in addition to well-educated white-collar labor (Svenska Metallindustriarbetarförbundet 1989:60–73). Insofar as government policy encouraged this pattern of restructuring, it can be said to have created problems for the unions' efforts to promote solidaristic "work humanization" as well as to exercise solidaristic wage restraint.

As figure 5 illustrates, foreign direct investment by Swedish corporations accelerated markedly in the 1980s. It is hard to avoid the conclusion that in part the profits boom did not translate into sufficient productivity growth because profits were invested abroad. As many observers have noted, the ongoing internationalization of Swedish business entered a qualitatively new phase in the 1980s. Starting out as

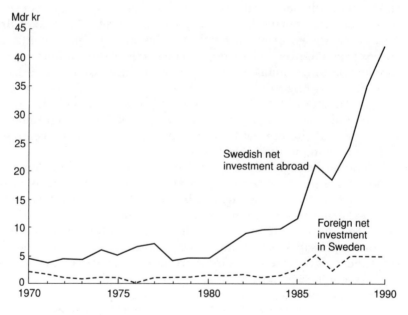

Source: Söderström (1991:50).

Figure 5. Swedish net investment abroad and foreign net investment in Sweden, billion SEK at 1985 prices, 1970–90.

Swedish export-oriented businesses with assembly plants and sales organizations abroad, the corporations in question have become truly multinational, drawing on research and development and other corporate resources in several countries (Ministry of Industry 1990:133–34). Recent decisions by several large corporations to move their headquarters abroad represent the most dramatic manifestation of multinationalization.

The elimination of exchange controls may have contributed to the marked increase in investment abroad in the later 1980s, but there is little doubt that the European Community's efforts to forge a single market constitute the primary motive for this development. Indeed, the government responded to the outflow of capital by announcing its intention to apply for EC membership. In a very real sense, Swedish business has already joined the Community, and this has left the government with little option in the matter.

Since 1988, LO and several of its affiliates have demanded that the AP funds be allowed to purchase corporate equity (e.g., LO 1988, 1991), and the Ministry of Finance presented a reform proposal along these lines in spring 1991 (see chap. 7). Arguably, the multinationalization of business and Sweden's growing integration into a European-wide economy has forced the labor movement to raise the issue of investment control again. The connection here emerges explicitly in the programmatic report to the 1989 congress of the Metalworkers Union (Svenska Metallindustriarbetarförbundet 1989), which argues that it is no longer possible to prevent private capital from operating internationally and that the government should instead seek to promote domestic investment and employment by lifting the legal restrictions on the "national capital" that exists in the form of private insurance savings and tax-subsidized individual savings in share certificates (*allemansfonder*) as well as the AP funds.

CONCLUSIONS

Under the favorable world economic conditions of the postwar era, the combination of macroeconomic management, active labor market policy, and restrictions on the international mobility of capital ensured that the allocative outcomes of private investment decisions served labor's immediate material interests. We can identify four new developments from the mid-1960s through the 1970s that made private control of investment an increasing problem for labor.

1. The emergence of new suppliers undermined the competitiveness

of Swedish iron ore and timber and weakened the position of the industries that relied on these raw materials. As a result, the Swedish economy became increasingly dependent on industrial sectors with a higher import content of value added and a greater potential for multinationalization.

2. Increased rationalization meant that new investment in advanced sectors no longer generated much new employment—certainly not enough to offset the accelerated decline of employment in basic industries.

3. The concentration and internationalization of capital in the advanced sectors of industry made the link between profits and new investment more precarious. The previous barriers to the mobility of capital were primarily technological and organizational. At the same time as market conditions drove export-oriented corporations to invest abroad, changes in transportation and communications during the 1960s helped remove such barriers. (At least in the first instance, the deregulation of capital movements in the 1980s must be seen as a consequence rather than a cause of the internationalization of capital.)

4. As a result of world economic instability, higher interest rates, and the growing importance of R&D, Swedish business developed a strong preference for self-financing or equity capital over borrowed capital.

Along with the decline of the ATP system as a mechanism of collective savings, this last development exacerbated a problem the labor movement had previously been able to fudge: to sustain an adequate level of investment, labor would have to accommodate a major increase of private profits or introduce reforms that involved collective ownership. Naturally labor preferred the latter course. While avoiding a transfer of income from wage earners to capitalists and a further concentration of wealth, introducing some form of collective ownership spoke to the other strategic problem confronting the labor movement—how to construct institutions that would ensure that wage restraint translated into productive investment in Sweden.

Against the background of the intense debate over wage-earner funds, the Social Democratic government of 1982 chose to ignore the issue of investment control and opted to stimulate investment by boosting private profits. In doing so, however, the government fueled inflationary pressures and undermined the cohesion of the labor movement. In terms of promoting sustained growth, the recovery strategy the Social Democrats adopted would probably have been successful had the government undertaken to create unemployment; but such a policy would of course have led to a direct conflict with the unions. This is really the crux of the current crisis of Swedish Social Democracy: How could the third way possibly be restored without compromising the commitment to full employment? Again, the current crisis lies beyond the limits of this book. Suffice it to note here that the reform intiatives of 1967–76 were meant to preempt the dilemma in which labor now finds itself. The following chapters explore their fate.

Part II

INVESTMENT POLITICS
IN THE 1970s AND 1980s

CHAPTER FIVE

Active Industrial Policy

In Sweden, postwar state intervention in the economy assumed a predominantly macroeconomic character. The labor movement failed to institutionalize planning and industrial policy after the war and quickly retreated from these ambitions. Labor's postwar strategy was greatly concerned with industrial restructuring, but it relied on policies designed to enhance market-determined differences in corporate profitability rather than directly steering the allocation of investment. Except for promoting nuclear and military technology, the government did not in any active sense pursue an "industrial policy" before the late 1960s.

The expansion of active labor market policy in the 1960s spearheaded a more general shift toward selective state intervention. Seeking to extend their success with selective state intervention in the labor market, from 1968 to 1973 the Social Democrats introduced institutional reforms designed to increase the state's capacity to plan the transfer of resources from declining to expanding industrial sectors and to impinge on the investment decisions of private business. The government also began to promote the expansion of state enterprise and created a holding company to coordinate the activities of state-owned corporations.

These initiatives did indeed inaugurate a new era of selective state intervention in the restructuring of capital at the level of firms and industrial sectors. But labor's industrial policy offensive nonetheless failed. First, industrial policy became entirely defensive as declining sectors absorbed an increasing share of industrial policy spending in the course of the 1970s. Second, industrial policy came to be dominated by ad hoc measures, and its early identification with planning proved illusory. Third, several of the institutions set up to carry out an active, forward-looking industrial policy were never really integrated into policy-making. Finally, tripartite bargaining was never institutionalized in the arena of industrial policy, and organized labor played a much more marginal role than in labor market policy.

These characteristics of industrial policy became particularly pronounced under the bourgeois governments of 1976–82, but they predate the bourgeois tenure in government. When the Social Democrats returned to power in 1982, they did not launch another quest for an "active industrial policy." Rather, their industrial policy efforts add up to a retreat from selective state intervention in the restructuring of capital.

The first part of my analysis explores the development of industrial policy from the late 1960s to the present. The second part seeks to explain labor's failure by contrasting the experience of industrial policy with that of labor market policy. I argue that the defensive orientation of industrial policy reflects the absence of an institutionalized state capacity to intervene in capital markets and that organized labor's marginal role in industrial policy-making reflects its subordinate position in an economy that remains essentially capitalist.

THE DEVELOPMENT OF INDUSTRIAL POLICY

Industrial policy since the late 1960s falls into three distinct periods: the initial period of Social Democratic government; the bourgeois tenure in power (1976 to 1982); and the second period of Social Democratic government (1982–91). Within each period, my treatment of industrial policy under the Social Democrats is split into two sections, one dealing specifically with state enterprise. But let me first address the origins of labor's industrial policy offensive and the motives behind it.

The Origins of Labor's Offensive

The Social Democrats launched their industrial policy offensive in the wake of a major electoral setback. Polling only 42.2 percent of the popular vote, SAP did worse in the municipal elections of 1966 than in any election since 1934. The party interpreted this setback to mean that it needed to reassert its distinctive ideological profile and to address more directly the problems associated with rapid industrial restructuring. This interpretation reflected the drift of debate within the labor movement since the early 1960s as well as the specifics of the 1966 election outcome.

In a sense labor's offensive can be traced back to the programmatic report submitted to the LO congress of 1961 by the LO research department (LO 1963). Titled *Coordinated Industrial Policy* (Samordnad näringspolitik), this report argued that the ongoing liberalization of world trade would increase pressures for change within Swedish industry and that future industrial adjustment called for a concerted response by business, labor, and the state. While emphasizing the need for a more active labor market policy, it broached the idea of more direct government involvement in industrial investment.

The differences between the general approach of the 1961 report and the industrial policy program adopted by the SAP congress of 1968 (SAP 1968) are also noteworthy.[1] The authors of the 1961 report conceived industrial policy strictly in terms of market-conformative measures. Their argument proceeded from an analysis that focused on institutional obstacles to the mobility of the factors of production and assumed that corporate decisions aimed at maximizing profits would yield macroeconomic efficiency under perfect market conditions. By contrast, the industrial policy program of 1968 emphasized the narrowness of private profitability as a criterion of economic decision making. Drafted by a joint SAP-LO committee, this "action program" argued that, while it may be rational for a corporation to shut down on unprofitable plant, a shutdown might reduce rather than increase macroeconomic efficiency if the manpower and other resources released cannot be put to more productive use elsewhere in the economy. In other words, maximizing macroeconomic efficiency requires state intervention in economic restructuring (SAP 1968:17–19, 38–39).

Though it typically identified "societal interests" with "macroeconomic efficiency," the industrial policy program of 1968 also suggested that planning or industrial policy should reconcile economic efficiency, however defined, with social need. This theme represents a clear departure from the separation of economic and social policy in *Coordinated Industrial Policy*, which conceived of economic policy in terms of stimulating (capitalist) growth and of social policy in terms of correcting the inequalities generated by growth.

The question whether the state should rely on general or selective means to influence industrial development provides a related dimen-

1. At the initiative of rank-and-file delegates, the SAP congress of 1964 instructed the party leaders to appoint a committee to draft an industrial policy program, but the committee did not begin to meet until after the municipal elections of 1966. Its preliminary report to the extraordinary SAP congress of 1967 (SAP 1967) anticipated virtually all the arguments and proposals of the 1968 program. My account of labor's industrial policy offensive draws on Lewin (1967:499–501); Svenning (1972, chaps. 7–8); Henning (1974:31–38); Martin (1984:230–35); and an interview with Krister Wickman (June 14, 1983).

sion for contrasting the ideas advanced in the late 1960s with those of
the 1961 report. Though not explicitly articulated by the 1968 program, labor's industrial policy was informed by the idea that the selective approach of active labor market policy could and should be extended to investment control.

Finally, the 1968 program is distinguished from the 1961 report by
its criticism of the concentration of economic power and, in particular,
of the dominant role of a few banks and capitalist groupings. Whereas
the 1961 report treated industrial policy essentially as a matter of labor
and business jointly responding to adjustment problems generated by
changes in the international environment, the proponents of industrial
policy in the late 1960s emphasized the need to curtail the power of
business and to democratize economic decision making (SAP 1967:18–
20; 1968:25–30).

The first real steps toward selective state intervention in industrial
restructuring were motivated by regional policy objectives. In 1963–64
Parliament passed legislation that let the government use selective investment fund releases to encourage industrial firms to locate new investment in economically depressed regions, and it approved the government's proposal for a five-year program of selective investment
subsidies (grants and subsidized loans) for the same purpose. The
thrust of these measures ran directly counter to *Coordinated Industrial
Policy*, which had insisted (LO 1963:126–134) on the need to concentrate industry in the urban regions of southern Sweden.

The problems of regional decline grew massive in the 1960s. From
1960 to 1965, the net population loss of the "forested counties"
(*skogslänen*), mostly in the North, averaged 13,350 per year, and the
corresponding figure for 1966–70 was 8,600 (Elander 1978:93–94).
While the workers who moved to urban areas in the South frequently
had trouble adjusting, the deindustrialization of the North eroded the
economic base of social services as well as the marketplace power of the
workers who stayed. Especially since the regions most adversely affected were bastions of Social Democratic strength, it became politically
necessary for the government to stimulate their economic growth.

For the leaders of the labor movement, regional development aid
was meant not to promote a different pattern of economic development, but rather to address the immediate employment problems of
declining regions and thereby attenuate the political resistance to
industrial restructuring (Elander 1978). All three bourgeois parties
agreed that the state should provide some regional development aid.
Indeed, the Center party advocated a much more ambitious regional
development program than that proposed by the government. While
defending the interests of its traditional base of support in rural areas,

the Center party used the regional policy debate of the 1960s to project itself as the party of decentralization and environmental protection and thereby extend its support among urban white-collar strata. Regional decline also gave the Communist party an opportunity to criticize the government for failing to favor human needs over corporate profits. Many Social Democratic supporters were clearly receptive to this line of criticism, for most of SAP's losses in the municipal elections of 1966 translated into gains for the Center party and the Communists (see Korpi 1983:270–71).

The electoral setback of 1966 added urgency to rank-and-file pressures on labor leaders to address the negative effects of restructuring and shifted the policy debate within the labor movement in favor of a more interventionist posture, previously advocated by left-leaning intellectuals. Shortly after the municipal elections, the SAP leaders announced that an extraordinary party congress would be held in 1967 (only the second one ever) to launch a new reform offensive, and they instructed the previously appointed SAP-LO committee on industrial policy to prepare a preliminary report for the congress. At the same time, the government itself began to prepare legislation that would create an institutional framework for industrial policy.

Compared with subsequent reform initiatives (codetermination and wage-earner funds), the industrial policy initiatives of the late 1960s were introduced in a great hurry. They also stand out for the importance of electoral considerations and the active role assumed by the SAP leaders. But again, electoral pressures were closely linked to economic pressures. As the SAP leaders lost interest in using active industrial policy to assert the party's distinctive ideological profile, LO emerged as its advocate within the labor movement in the 1970s.

Institutional Reforms, 1968–73

Among the first institutional results of labor's industrial policy offensive was the creation in 1968 of a separate Ministry of Industry and a tripartite Industrial Policy Council (Näringspolitiska Rådet) to serve the new ministry. The new minister of industry, Krister Wickman, had previously distinguished himself as an advocate of active industrial policy within the party leadership. Together with the Ministry of Industry, the Industrial Policy Council commissioned a series of investigations of the problems of particular industrial sectors in the late 1960s and early 1970s. Several of these investigations led to the establishment of sector programs and tripartite sector councils to promote innovation and competitiveness.

The Board of Industry (Statens Industriverk, SIND) was established

THE LIMITS OF SOCIAL DEMOCRACY

in 1973 to administer sector programs as well as to gather information and carry out research on behalf of the Ministry of Industry. Though SIND was apparently modeled on AMS, the administration of industrial policy remained dispersed among a number of public agencies and corporations, and SIND never gained an autonomous policy-making role like that of AMS. SIND's sector programs and other activities came to concentrate on sectors dominated by small business and to account for only a rather small portion of total industrial expenditures in the 1970s.[2]

Labor's industrial policy offensive resulted in four other noteworthy institutions: the state-owned Investment Bank, *Investeringsbanken*, created by Parliament in 1967; the Board for Technological Development, *Styrelsen för Teknisk Utveckling* (STU), created in 1968; the State Enterprise Corporation *Statsföretag AB*, a holding company for state-owned industrial enterprise created in 1970; and the Fourth AP Fund, created in 1973 to invest ATP savings in the stock market. For our purposes, the legislation that created the Investment Bank and the State Enterprise Corporation will illustrate how the government sought to translate labor's policy goals into practice.[3]

The bill proposing the creation of the Investment Bank (government bill 56, 1967) proceeded from the observation that large investment projects of a long-term, and hence risky, character had become more important to maintaining the competitiveness of Swedish industry as a result of increasing economies of scale and the accelerated technological innovation that accompanied growing international competition. At the same time, business was less able to finance such projects out of savings, and the government's redistributive ambitions militated against policies designed to promote self-financing.

More of the industrial investment needed to sustain competitiveness would have to be financed with external capital. Because of the *kind* of investment needed, however, the existing system of corporate finance would not be adequate. The lending practices of the commercial banks were biased against innovative strategic investment projects because of

2. See tables 8 and 9 below. See SIND (1981) on the organization of SIND and its sector programs (which cover textiles and apparel, furs, shoes, glass, furniture, carpentry, wooden houses, foundries, and metal manufacturing). In Ministry of Industry (1982b, 1982c) there is an overview of the institutional framework of industrial policy; see also Jacobsson (1989, chap. 3).

3. The Fourth AP Fund will be discussed in chapter 7. On the legislation creating the Investment Bank, see Svenning (1972:75–80), Ministry of Industry (1978:4–6), Waara (1980:160–61), and Wickman (1980:105–6); and on the legislation creating the State Enterprise Corporation, see SOU (1978c:42–45), Waara (1980:166–67), and Eliasson and Ysander (1983:167–76).

the narrow or shortsighted profit criteria the banks used and their preferential treatment of long-standing corporate clients. The basic purpose of the Investment Bank, then, was to finance strategic investment projects that the private banks were either unable or unwilling to finance. In addition to long-term lending, the bank would be able to assume ownership stakes for this purpose. Being constituted as a banking corporation, the new institution could raise capital in the bond market and thereby draw on the resources of the AP funds. Though it shunned any attempt to specify in advance what kind of projects the bank should promote, the government expected that it would focus on two broad objectives: promoting innovation and development in technologically advanced sectors, and creating large, competitive firms in basic industries.

Although Tage Erlander, the prime minister, stressed that the Investment Bank was not intended as an instrument for steering private investment decisions in the parliamentary debate, at the SAP congress of 1967 Wickman hailed the legislation as a "decisive alteration of the distribution of power in our credit market," to be followed by further reforms that would enhance public control over the system of corporate finance (Svenning 1972:85–87). Still, Wickman joined other party leaders in opposing rank-and-file proposals to nationalize the commercial banks. Proposals to this effect were again rejected by the SAP congresses of 1968 and 1969. Instead of nationalization, the party leadership advocated government representation on the boards of the commercial banks, and Parliament subsequently passed legislation instituting it.

The industrial policy program adopted by the SAP congress of 1968 advocated actively promoting the expansion of state enterprise, arguing that "new state-owned corporations should be established and existing corporations expanded, especially in sectors with strong future prospects and in areas with employment problems" (SAP 1968:41). In his speech to the SAP congress of 1969, Wickman emphasized that though state enterprise should seek to maximize efficiency according to commercial criteria, it was by no means sufficient for state-owned corporations to emulate private business. State enterprise should be a tool of regional policy as well as addressing structural problems in particular sectors, Wickman argued; it should also play "a special role in the development of advanced and therefore risky technology." More generally, the expansion of state enterprise would strengthen the capacity of "society" to intervene in industrial restructuring using the detailed knowledge of specific sectors and the administrative-technical competence built up in state-owned firms. Alongside these industrial policy functions, the state enterprise sector should also lead in developing industrial democracy (Svenning 1972:93–95; Henning 1974:77–87).

As constituted in 1970, the State Enterprise Corporation consisted of twenty-two subsidiaries with combined sales of 3.6 billion SEK and a work force of some 34,000, and it ranked as the eighth largest corporation in Sweden by either of these criteria (Henning 1974:28). The government bill (bill 121, 1969) assigned this holding company two basic roles: to plan and coordinate various functions common to its subsidiaries, and to be the institutional link between these firms and the Ministry of Industry. While affirming that state-owned corporations have "a special responsibility to consider the interests of society" in making decisions concerning production and its location, the legislation creating the State Enterprise Corporation held that this responsibility must not entail constraints that would place state-owned corporations at a disadvantage relative to private firms and thereby inhibit their expansion. Insofar as it was burdened by policy tasks that could not be justified by commercial criteria, the State Enterprise Corporation should be compensated out of the state budget (government bill 121, 1969, pp. 30–37).

As Roger Henning (1974) has pointed out, the legislation deliberately defined the goals of the State Enterprise Corporation in vague and very general terms. No attempt was made to specify the profitability requirement, and the problem of setting priorities among partly contradictory goals ("profitability," "expansion," and "societal considerations") in concrete situations was left to be settled by its executive management, its board of directors (with representatives of organized labor and business as well as the government), and the Ministry of Industry. From the very beginning the management of the State Enterprise Corporation assigned priority to profitability, defined in the conventional terms of private business.

The Expansion of State Enterprise

Broadly conceived, the state enterprise sector in Sweden consists of three components: first, "commercial state agencies" (affärsverk) that administer services the state provides to the general public for a charge or that provide goods or services to the state for a charge; second, "fiscal corporations" that operate monopolies granted by the state (lotteries and sports betting as well as the importing, production, and distribution of wine and liquor); and third, corporations that operate in a competitive environment. Whereas corporations owned by the state are governed by the same corporate law as corporations owned by private individuals or institutions, the commercial state agencies fall within the legal framework of public administration.[4]

When the issue of creating a holding company for state enterprise came up in the late 1960s, LO advocated including all forms of state enterprise under the same roof. The special delegation appointed by the minister of industry to investigate proposed an organizational formula that excluded the commercial state agencies, but critics within the government and the business community charged that even this formula was too broad. In the end, the legislation that set up the State Enterprise Corporation also excluded the fiscal corporations, the Investment Bank and other intermediary credit institutions, and state-owned corporations engaged in nuclear research and development.

Table 7. Major subsidiaries of the State Enterprise Corporation as of 1976, ranked according to their employment at the time of their acquisition (1970 unless otherwise noted in parentheses)

Subsidiary	Employment at acquisition	Sales at acquisition (million SEK)
LKAB	7,145	1,624
SARA (restaurants)	6,905	357
ASSI	4,280	570
NJA	3,423	339
Uddevalla Shipyards	2,841	257
Swedish Tobacco Corporation	2,115	405
Rockwool (1975)	1,943	201
Karlskrona Shipyards	1,633	53
Kalmar Engineering	1,077	81
AB Kabi	1,015	118
Essbo (1975)	968	143
Liber Grafiska (1973)	860	167
SMT Machine Company	743	54
Berol Kemi (1973)	659	247
Svetab	638	28
Other subsidiaries in 1970	2,281	242

Source: SOU (1978b:64–65).

4. Many of the functions of commercial state agencies are carried out by corporations they own, and this has become increasingly so in the 1980s. One of the commercial state agencies, the National Industries Board, which produces materiel for the armed forces, was transformed into a state-owned corporation in 1990. This leaves six commercial state agencies: the Post Office, the Board of Telecommunications, the State Railways, the Board of Civil Aviation, the Hydro-electric Power Board, and the Public Domains Authority. See Waara (1980, chap. 4) and Söderlind and Petersson (1986, chap. 2) on the structure of the state enterprise sector and the legal status of different forms of state enterprise.

Table 7 lists the major subsidiaries of the State Enterprise Corporation as of 1976. By far the largest was LKAB (Luossavaara-Kirunavaara AB), which operates the iron ore fields of Norrbotten and today accounts for roughly 85 percent of total iron ore production in Sweden. In terms of sales, the other subsidiaries in the top five were ASSI (AB Statens Skogsindustrier), a forest-products firm; the Swedish Tobacco Corporation, a de facto monopoly; SARA, a restaurant chain; and NJA (Norbottens Järnverk AB), a steel mill established in 1939 to process LKAB iron ore into crude steel. All of these corporations had been state-owned since their inception, and all but one (SARA) predated the end of World War II.

The creation of the State Enterprise Corporation formed part of a broader effort to promote the expansion of state enterprise. Whereas that sector had hardly grown at all in the previous twenty-five years, the state acquired and created a number of industrial firms from 1960 to 1975, especially in the latter half of this period. The expansion of state enterprise began before labor's industrial policy offensive, in response to various concrete and quite specific problems. Simplifying somewhat, government measures that resulted in the formation of new state-owned firms from 1960 to 1975 can be grouped into four basic categories (Henning 1974:55–63; SOU 1978c:35–40; Waara 1980: 154–76).

First, a number of state-owned firms were formed in response to local employment problems. Most notably, employment was the primary motive for the state's assuming 50 percent ownership in the Uddevalla Shipyards in 1963 and acquiring 50 percent of the Eiser Corporation, one of the country's largest textile firms, in 1973. Second, a number of state-owned firms were formed in the mid-1960s through the reorganization and "commercialization" of state functions, such as inspecting cars, providing security, and publishing schoolbooks and informational materials.

Third, and most closely related to labor's industrial policy offensive, a few state-owned corporations were acquired or created in the late 1960s to promote industrial innovation. In addition to the Investment Bank and the development corporation mentioned earlier, the state acquired AB Kabi, a research-intensive pharmaceutical firm, and engaged in two major joint ventures with private business, Uddcomb Sweden AB and ASEA-Atom, both in nuclear energy. These "high-tech" firms were tiny compared with LKAB, NJA, and ASSI, however, and the state enterprise sector remained heavily concentrated to basic industries. Finally, we have two cases in which the extension of public control itself was the primary motive for forming state-owned firms: the 1971 nationalization of pharmacies and their consolidation in a single state-owned firm (Apoteksbolaget), and the 1975 acquisition of a controlling interest in Pripps Breweries.

Most of the formation of new state enterprise in the first half of the 1970s occurred outside the State Enterprise Corporation. The government avoided burdening the corporation with new ownership engagements motivated by regional employment considerations, but profitable firms such as the Pharmacy Corporation and the Pripps Breweries were also left outside. Nonetheless, the State Enterprise Corporation expanded much faster than Swedish industry as a whole in the first half of the 1970s. From 1970 to 1976, its total sales increased from 3.6 billion SEK to 9.8 billion SEK, and its work force grew from 34,100 to 47,700. The annual fixed capital formation per thousand employees averaged 28.8 million SEK for the State Enterprise Corporation, in 1971–76 compared with 12.2 million SEK for all mining and manufacturing industry (SOU 1978c:73). While this marked difference is largely attributable to the concentration of state ownership in capital-intensive industrial sectors, there can be little doubt that it also reflects a greater commitment to expansion.

The expansion of the State Enterprise Corporation in 1971–75 was financed out of savings and borrowing. Direct capital infusions by the state accounted for only 7 percent of total capital expenditures (SOU 1978c:85). Except in one case, the government does not appear to have intervened systematically in the investment decisions of the State Enterprise Corporation. The exception was the disastrous "Steel Plant 80" project (see Henning 1980a). In its initial version, put forth and approved by Parliament in 1973, the first phase of this massive investment project would have increased NJA's crude steel capacity from 2.8 million to 6.8 million tons by 1980. According to one estimate, the project would have accounted for 6 percent of industrial investment in Sweden over a five-year period.

The motives behind the Steel Plant 80 project were essentially the same as those that led the government to create NJA in the first place: some 90 percent of the iron ore LKAB produced was still being exported without any further value added, and the employment situation of Norrbotten continued to deteriorate. In the two years following Parliament's appropriation of initial funding for the Steel Plant 80 project, however, the cost estimates for the project soared while world demand for steel turned sharply downward. The project was much revised and eventually abandoned after the bourgeois parties came to power.

Within the labor movement, the Steel Plant 80 project came to epitomize active industrial policy in 1973–75. In a sense its failure marks the end of labor's industrial policy offensive. But that active industrial policy came to be so closely identified with a single investment project in the state enterprise sector suggests that labor's industrial policy offensive had already petered out.

Industrial Policy under Bourgeois Governments

Organized business and the bourgeois parties opposed the interventionist thrust of labor's industrial policy offensive, especially the creation of the Investment Bank, the State Enterprise Corporation, and the Fourth AP Fund. As usual, however, the bourgeois parties failed to mount a unified opposition to Social Democratic initiatives. In contrast to the others, the Center party criticized particular aspects of the government's legislative proposals but did not challenge the principle of creating public institutions to supply the private sector with risk capital. Whereas the Conservatives opposed the creation of the State Enterprise Corporation, the Center party and the Liberals criticized what they perceived as the government's policy of expanding state enterprise regardless of profitability and argued that the goals of the new holding company should be defined strictly in terms of the commercial criteria used by private business (Henning 1974:28–29, 40–46, 73–75).

As table 8 illustrates, government spending on industrial policy measures nonetheless continued to increase in relative as well as absolute terms after the bourgeois parties came to power in 1976. Annual spending on such measures averaged 6.1 percent of the state budget from fiscal year 1970–71 through FY 1975–76 and 9.3 percent from FY 1976–77 through FY 1979–80. By comparison, the AMS budget (excluding regional policy measures) averaged 6.2 percent of the state budget in the first period and 7.6 percent in the second.[5]

The increase of government spending on industrial policy after 1976 occurred entirely through the expansion of "extraordinary measures"—essentially rescue operations to bail out and reconstruct corporations on the verge of bankruptcy. Encompassing ownership engagements as well as direct subsidies, subsidized loans, and loan guarantees, such measures accounted for 43.8 percent of industrial policy expenditures in 1976–77 through 1979–80, compared with 11.3 percent in 1970–71 through 1975–76. They were almost wholly concentrated in textiles, shipbuilding, steel, iron ore, and forest products; indeed, these five sectors together accounted for more than 95 percent of combined spending on extraordinary measures and other forms of sectoral aid from FY 1971–72 through FY 1980–81 (Lundgren and Ståhl 1981: 158–61).

5. These figures have been calculated from data in SOU (1981a:51) and in Axelsson, Löfgren, and Nilsson (1983:197) as well as table 8.

Table 8. Industrial policy expenditures in billion SEK at 1980 prices, disaggregated by type of policy measures, 1970–80

Fiscal year	Regional aid	Small business aid	Sector programs	R&D support	Export credits	Extra-ordinary aid
1970–71	0.3	1.6	1.4	0.4	1.0	0.3
1971–72	1.1	1.6	1.4	0.4	1.4	0.9
1972–73	0.8	1.5	1.1	0.5	2.3	0.5
1973–74	1.2	2.0	1.0	0.5	1.2	0.5
1974–75	1.5	1.8	1.5	1.2	1.9	0.9
1975–76	1.1	2.0	1.9	1.2	2.1	1.9
1976–77	1.1	2.4	1.4	1.3	2.2	5.1
1977–78	1.1	2.5	2.6	1.4	2.2	5.0
1978–79	0.3	3.1	1.5	1.4	1.1	3.3
1979–80	1.1	2.7	1.3	2.1	1.6	8.1
Total	10.5	21.1	15.0	10.3	16.9	31.9

Source: SOU (1981a:53).

The sectoral crisis measures undertaken by the bourgeois parties in the first half of the 1970s were often a direct continuation of Social Democratic policy.[6] In the case of textiles, the government established a sector program to promote mergers and other forms of rationalization in 1970 and provided special subsidies to sustain employment in the mid-1970s. In 1977 the government acquired the production facilities of a bankrupt textile firm (Algots), bought out the remaining private owners of Eiser, and consolidated all state-owned textile firms under the auspices of Eiser, reconstituted as a subsidiary of the State Enterprise Corporation. (In 1979 the new Eiser Corporation accounted for 15.3 percent of the total employment of the textiles and apparel industry.)

In shipbuilding, state intervention at the firm level dates back to the 1960s. Having acquired 50 percent of the Uddevalla Shipyard in 1963, the state helped finance its modernization in 1965–67 and bought out the remaining private owners in 1971. Also in 1971, the government provided loans to aid the financial reconstruction of one of the major Gothenburg shipyards, Götaverken. The financial situation of most shipyards became untenable in 1975–76. The government was now forced to bail out Eriksbergs Mekaniska Verkstad at Gothenburg. While Götaverken acquired Eriksbergs, the state acquired 51 percent of Götaverken shortly before the 1976 election. The bourgeois parties completed the takeover of Götaverken and in 1977 consolidated all state-owned shipyards (Karlskrona, Uddevalla, Eriksbergs, and Götaverken

6. The following account draws primarily on Ericsson (1979), SOU (1981a), and Lundgren and Ståhl (1981). See also Lundmark (1983) and Henning (1984).

into a single corporation, Swedyard (Svenska Varv AB). The one sizable shipbuilding firm that remained in private hands, Kockums, had to be bailed out in 1978 and was finally acquired by Swedyard in 1979. Because of the massive aid that would be required to keep it afloat, Swedyard was constituted as an entity separate from the State Enterprise Corporation.

Much like the shipbuilders, Swedish steel producers enjoyed favorable market conditions and expanded their productive capacity in the first half of the 1970s. This investment boom contributed to subsequent problems of overcapacity, while the reliance on borrowed capital eroded their financial ability to cope with such problems. By the time the bourgeois parties came to power, NJA was on the verge of bankruptcy, and the other basic steel producers, Gränges and Stora Kopparberg, were also in serious trouble. In 1978 Parliament approved the allocation of some 1.2 billion SEK to finance the formation of Swedish Steel Corporation (Svenskt Stål AB; SSAB). The State Enterprise Corporation assumed 50 percent ownership of the new corporation, and the other 50 percent was divided equally between Gränges and Stora Kopparberg. Most of the state's financial contribution was used to compensate these corporate conglomerates for the plants they passed on to SSAB and thereby to improve their financial situation. In 1981 Stora Kopparberg exercised its option to sell out, and the state's share in SSAB increase to 75 percent. In specialty steels, the government sought to avoid a comprehensive solution along the lines of the SSAB formula. Instead it set up a tripartite delegation (strukturdelegationen) to administer the allocation of some 700 million SEK in subsidized loan guarantees to specialty steel producers so as to improve short-term liquidity as well as promote rationalization.

The crisis of the European steel industry in the mid-1970s completely reversed the fortunes of LKAB, the mining company that had previously been one of the most profitable subsidiaries of the State Enterprise Corporation, and huge state contributions became necessary to keep LKAB afloat from 1978 onward. In forest products, the bourgeois parties introduced loan guarantees to help corporations maintain liquidity and provided the state-owned ASSI with 550 million SEK for an investment program to sustain employment at its Karlsborg plant. Also, it intervened to bail out two forest-product firms owned cooperatively by forest owners, Norrlands Skogsägares Cellulosa AB (NCB) and Södra Skogsägarna AB (Södra), acquiring 75 percent of NCB and 40 percent of Södra.

Finally, in 1979 the government also took over Luxor, a family-owned electronics firm. All told, the bourgeois parties nationalized more industry during their first three years in power than the Social

Democrats had in the previous forty-four years! The reasons for this apparent paradox are not so mysterious. The sectoral crisis measures undertaken by the bourgeois parties certainly did not represent an ideological conversion to planning and the extension of public ownership. For these parties, the crisis of Swedish industry in the 1970s was above all a cost crisis, and general measures to restore the cost competitiveness of Swedish exports, such as devaluation and reducing payroll taxes, constituted the key to recovery (Martin 1981; Walters 1983; Heclo and Madsen 1986, chap. 2). Selective state intervention was meant essentially to ensure that industrial restructuring occurred in "socially acceptable forms."

The bourgeois parties' commitment to a gradual phase-out of overcapacity and employment in the crisis sectors was reinforced by their fear that allowing unemployment to increase would cause an electoral backlash. The regional concentration of employment problems made it more difficult for the government, and the Center party in particular, to resist political pressures for state intervention (Henning 1984). Had the government simply wanted to maintain employment, however, it would have been much cheaper to let firms go bankrupt, then take over their plants. Quite clearly, sectoral crisis measures were motivated by other considerations as well. In several instances the owners of failing corporations were bought out on terms that improved their overall financial situation. Perhaps more important, bailing firms out before bankruptcy shielded the financial system against the effects of sectoral crises and sustained the ability of Swedish business to borrow abroad (SOU 1981a:122–27).

Catering to the interests of both labor and business, the sectoral crises measures of the late 1970s can be seen as a continuation of the politics of class compromise. The compromise embedded in these measures was essentially defensive, however. In contrast to the compromise implicit in labor's postwar strategy, there was no trade-off between the growth of advanced sectors and the phase-out of declining ones. In response to mounting criticism, in 1979–82 the bourgeois parties made some effort to adopt a more coherent, long-term approach to industrial policy and to increase state aid to advanced sectors. Among other things, they extended subsidized export credits and increased R&D support. They also established the Industrial Fund (Industrifonden) and several development corporations to promote the commercial application of new technologies, and they set up a planning bureau (struktursekretariatet) within the Ministry of Industry to coordinate investigations and pursue questions relevant to the long-term development of industry.

The significance of these innovations was limited, however. The planning bureau within the Ministry of Industry was assigned no policy-making functions, and its staff consisted of only four persons by the time the government changed hands in 1982. Though expenditures for export promotion more than quadrupled and expenditures for R&D promotion increased by nearly 50 percent from 1979–80 to 1981–82, these two items still accounted for only 15.7 percent of total government spending on industrial policy in 1981–82 (Ministry of Industry 1982a:15).

The New Social Democratic Policy Orientation

The Social Democratic government of 1982 moved swiftly to undertake a major restructuring of the state enterprise sector (government bill 68, 1982–83). This initiative involved the infusion of new capital and other forms of direct financial aid. The government indicated very clearly, however, that it would not provide any further subsidies for maintaining production and employment in the state enterprise sector. Henceforth the fate of state-owned corporations would depend on their ability to compete in the marketplace and, by implication, private

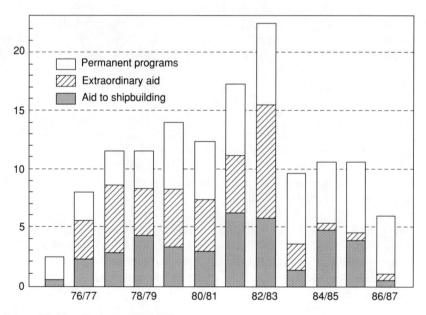

Source: Ministry of Industry (1988: 10).

Figure 6. Net costs of state aid to industry in billion SEK (at 1987 prices), FY 1975–76 through 1986–87.

Table 9. Net industrial policy expenditures by type of policy measures, FY 1981–82 and FY 1987–88 (current prices)

Policy measure	1981–82		1987–88	
	Million SEK	% of total	Million SEK	% of total
Extraordinary aid	8,323	68	974	19
Sectoral aid	314	3	204	4
R&D support	611	5	405	8
Regional aid	302	2	1,367	27
Export aid	1,060	9	1,117	22
Small business aid	60	0	146	3
Energy measures	1,022	8	224	4
Other measures	507	4	707	14
Total	12,199		5,144	

Source: Ministry of Industry (1982a:15, 1989:11).

corporations on the verge of bankruptcy would no longer be acquired by the state.

As figure 6 indicates, the Social Democrats almost completely eliminated government spending on extraordinary aid to industry during their first five years in power, and total government spending on industrial policy declined significantly. Table 9 presents a more disaggregated view of how the composition of industrial policy spending changed during the first five years of the new Social Democratic tenure in government. As the relative importance of extraordinary crisis measures declined, the importance of more "offensive" policy measures—designed to promote international competitiveness—increased. Yet since 1982 there has been more of a retreat from selective industrial policy than a reorientation of it. Figure 7 illustrates this point: in real terms, government spending on offensive industrial policy measures, such as export credits and R&D promotion, hardly increased at all from the early 1980s to FY 1986–87.[7]

The Social Democrats opted to use the savings from cutting industrial subsidies to balance the budget rather than to finance new industrial policy initiatives. But there is more to the retreat from selective industrial policy than budgetary considerations. Reflecting on the experience of the previous decade, the Social Democrats returned to power convinced that firms, workers, and local communities had become accustomed to the idea that the government would protect them against market forces and that the only way to resist such pressures was to restrict state intervention in industrial restructuring. Again, the recov-

7. Note that figures 6 and 7 and table 9 (but not table 8 above) refer to the *net costs* of industrial policy. "Net costs" are calculated by subtracting interest payments and loan repayments received by the government from new spending in a given fiscal year.

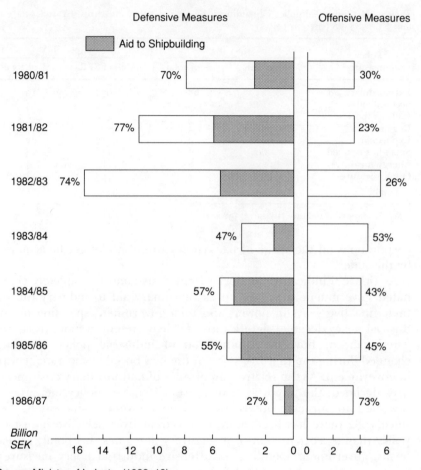

Source: Ministry of Industry (1988: 13).

Figure 7. Net costs of state aid to industry divided between defensive and offensive measures, FY 1980–81 through 1986–87 (1987 prices).

ery strategy the Social Democrats adopted in 1982 avoided selective incentives and instead relied on devaluation to boost corporate profits in general. In a 1983 interview the new minister of finance, Kjell-Olof Feldt, explicitly debunked what he called "the industrial policy model of 1968" (Feldt 1984:15–16, 82).

The turn to a more market-oriented approach does not mean the Social Democrats completely withdrew from state involvement in industrial restructuring. Rather, they sought to restrict the nature and purposes of this involvement. As articulated by the government itself, a fundamental principle of the new industrial policy was that solutions to firm crises and sectoral decline should target individuals and communities rather than corporations.[8] Such measures seemed preferable to firm-level intervention because they do not retard necessary changes in the structure of production, at least not to the same extent. This policy orientation can be seen as a return to the Rehn-Meidner model. Indeed, the industrial policy bill the government submitted in 1987 made this connection explicit by invoking the industrial policy report to the LO congress of 1961 as the intellectual source of the policy pursued since 1982(government bill 74, 1986–87, p. 19).

The new approach diverged from that of the 1961 report in devoting considerable resources to regional development aid (the only form of industrial policy for which the government provided new budgetary resources after 1982), but the approach to regional development problems the Social Democrats adopted in the 1980s differed from the initiatives of 1965–75. The old regional policy focused largely on attracting major investment projects to depressed regions and often relied on state enterprise to achieve this, as with the infamous Steel Plant 80 project. By contrast, the new regional policy emphasized promoting diversified regional economies along with government investment in infrastructure and other improvements in the general business climate. Specifically, the government sought to promote the establishment of new firms and the expansion of small and medium-sized firms indigenous to the region.

Providing services and loans to small and medium-sized business, the regional development funds (*regionala utvecklingsfonder*) set up in 1978 were given additional budgetary resources by the government and expanded their activities after 1982. In several instances these funds have helped establish regionally oriented venture capital and development corporations. In 1984 the new Social Democratic government also set up a Small Business Fund (Småföretagsfonden) to invest ATP savings in investment and development corporations that financed small business.

In a similar vein, the government encouraged both state-owned and private industry to establish development corporations to promote small business in localities where plants were closing down or laying off workers (Jacobsson 1989, chap. 4). The specialty steel merger of 1983–84 exemplifies the distinctive features of industrial policy-making in the 1980s. The merger involved a complicated deal whereby the steel operations of four conglomerates (essentially all of the remaining pri-

8. This discussion of the government's approach to industrial policy draws primarily on two omnibus bills (bill 135, 1983–84, and bill 74, 1986–87) submitted to Parliament by the minister of industry. The annual reports published by the Ministry of Industry since 1982 (Ministry of Industry 1982a, 1983–89) have also been used.

vate steel industry) were reorganized into two new firms. This solution to the industry's structural problems was quite similar to the earlier government-financed consolidation of shipbuilding and basic steel, but this time the government stayed away from new financial commitments. Its contribution took the form of writing off 405 million SEK of loans to the firms involved in the merger. In return the firms agreed to put up 100 million SEK to establish a development corporation targeted to steel-producing communities (Ministry of Industry 1985:14–17; *Dagens Nyheter*, July 1, 1983).

The way the government dealt with the consequences of Swedyard's decision to close the Uddevalla Shipyard is another example of the new emphasis on collaborating with private business. When the government launched a program to encourage small business development in Uddevalla, it looked around for a big firm that might locate a new plant there. A deal was negotiated whereby Volvo acquired the bankrupt shipyard and agreed to convert it into an assembly plant employing at least one thousand people. In return, Volvo was allowed to write off the yard's past losses and to use its accumulated investment funds to modernize its plant in Gothenburg. The government also paid Volvo a regional employment subsidy and promised to build a freeway between Gothenburg and Uddevalla ahead of schedule. (The tax concessions alone exceeded the costs of building the Uddevalla plant.)

Finally, the Social Democrats undertook a series of new initiatives in research and development in the 1980s. Within a year of taking office they began a "national program" to promote research and general competence in microelectronics, and they subsequently started several other programs of this sort. A serious assessment of R&D policy obviously lies beyond the scope of this book. Let me simply make a few observations. To begin with, direct spending by the Ministry of Industry on R&D promotion actually *decreased*, even measured in current prices, from FY 1981–82 to FY 1987–88 (see table 9 above), and overall government spending on R&D in Sweden is heavily concentrated in basic research. R&D, especially basic research, is an area where the interests of labor and business tend to converge. Government promotion of R&D can hardly be interpreted as a threat to the power and prerogatives of private business, and it is not surprising that it has become such a prominent feature of industrial policy debate in a new era of class compromise. Also, the new emphasis on R&D represents a reorientation that actually began under the bourgeois parties in 1979–82.

When the interests of labor and business diverge with respect to new technology, such conflicts pertain not to the development of new products and processes, but to the way firms use them and the changes in skill requirements and work organization they entail. In the Swedish case, such issues have been left to codetermination bargaining at the firm level (see chap. 7). In no sense have they shaped the government's R&D policy. Similarly, the aid package the government put together to encourage Volvo to build a new plant in Uddevalla did not stipulate production methods or work organization.

The Social Democrats' abandonment of their earlier identification of industrial policy with selective intervention in strategic investment projects is exemplified by the way the government in 1989 bestowed ownership of the Investment Bank on the Postal and Credit Bank (PK-Banken), a commercial bank owned predominantly by the state but entirely insulated from industrial policy-making. (Previously the Ministry of Industry had exercised ownership of the Investment Bank on behalf of the government.)

Restructuring and Privatization of State Enterprise

The Social Democrats' retreat from their ambitions of 1968–76 is most apparent with respect to the organization and role of state enterprise. As part of a broader effort to restore the commercial viability of the state enterprise sector, in 1983 the government scaled down the State Enterprise Corporation by taking over the assets of its principal loss-making subsidiaries: LKAB (iron mining), ASSI (forestry), and SSAB (basic steel). Its sales thus dropped from 15.4 billion SEK in 1981 to 11.5 billions SEK in 1983, and its work force fell from 46,080 to 25,719. The government also explicitly specified efficiency and profitability as the criteria for judging its performance. Whereas the initial legislation setting up the State Enterprise Corporation defined its overarching purpose as achieving "the greatest possible expansion while maintaining profitability," the new legislation charged it with "increasing the efficiency and competitiveness of state enterprise, and thereby enhancing its capacity to expand" (government bill 68, 1982–83, cited in Ministry of Industry 1984:65).

The 1983 reorganization served two purposes. First, it distinguished more clearly between, on the one hand, commercially viable corporations that would no longer be expected to assume responsibility for regional employment or other aspects of public policy and, on the other hand, corporations that would continue to carry some responsibility in this respect and hence would not be judged simply by efficiency and profitability. Second, the reorganization transformed the State Enterprise Corporation (which renamed itself Procordia in 1984) from an institutional link between the Ministry of Industry and state-owned corporations into a corporate concern with a distinctive set of operations (primarily concentrated in food processing, food services, and pharmaceuticals). Procordia was made more coherent by selling some subsidiaries and acquiring others in the following years.

The state enterprise sector thus came to be organized into several industrial concerns, with no holding company at the center. While it relieved the State Enterprise Corporation of LKAB, ASSI, and SSAB, the government reconstructed these corporations financially so they could embark on new investment programs to rationalize production.

The reorganization of state enterprise in 1983 set the stage for a series of privatization measures. We must distinguish here between two types of privatization: the sale of state assets and new share issues by state-owned corporations. In Sweden, privatization has almost entirely taken the latter form. Indeed, there are only two major cases where state assets have been sold, and one is exceptional: the repurchase of the government's stake in Södra Skogsägarna AB by the original owners. The other case is the sale of Luxor, the consumer electronics firm acquired in 1979, to a Finnish corporation.[9]

The first issue of new shares to private investors was undertaken by the Postal and Credit Bank in 1984 (at the time, fully owned by the state). After another share issue, at the end of 1989 the government held 70 percent of the shares in PK—Banken. In late 1987 the government went public with Procordia by issuing new shares corresponding to 20 percent of its equity capital, sold for a total of 1 billion SEK (compared with 512 million SEK raised by PK-Banken in 1984). Only 38 percent of the new Procordia shares were issued to the general public, however; 20 percent were reserved for Procordia employees and 42 percent for four institutional investors (a private insurance company, two private pension funds, and the Fourth AP Fund).

In 1986 the remaining private partner in SSAB (Gränges) exercised its option to sell out to the government. Meanwhile the government sold one-third of the shares in SSAB to a consortium consisting of one private insurance company, four private pension funds, and the Fourth AP Fund. In 1989 SSAB was listed on the stock exchange, and a new share issue reduced the government's stake to 50.2 percent of the shareholder votes (40 percent of equity). Moreover, the government reduced its stake in NCB (the other cooperative forestry firm bailed out in 1979) from 71 percent to 51 percent through a new share issue in 1989. As with the Procordia issue of 1987, the bulk of new shares issued by SSAB and NCB were reserved for institutional investors.

9. The unique (and rather minor) case of UV Shipping represents a hybrid of the two types of privatization identified above: in the first instance, the government sold its shares in the company to three wage-earner funds; in the second instance, the company issued new shares to private investors (reducing the wage earner funds' combined stake to 25 percent). My treatment of recent privatization measures draws primarily on Ministry of Industry (1987–89); Olsson (1989); government bill 88, 1989–90; Veckans Affärer, February 2, 1989; and Financial Times of London, April 6, 1990. See also Pontusson (1988).

To complete this picture of privatization, in a deal struck in 1989 Procordia acquired two of Volvo's subsidiaries and Volvo acquired 40 percent of the new Procordia. The government retains 40 percent of shareholder votes (33 percent of equity).

Although the Social Democrats have privatized corporations operating competitively, they have eschewed that option for social services and public utilities. The tendency for commercial state agencies to organize their activities into subsidiary corporations has been accentuated since 1982 (see Olsson (1989:22–24), but the government has not taken the bourgeois parties' suggestion that the nonregulatory functions of commercial state agencies be privatized. Moreover, three major corporations—LKAB, ASSI, and Celsius Industries (the successor of Swedyard)—remain fully state owned. Together these three corporations accounted for 34 percent of sales of state-owned corporations (not including the subsidiaries of commercial state agencies) in 1988.

Privatization has also been only partial. The government has stated clearly that it intends to retain a major stake in PK-Banken, Procordia, SSAB, and NCB. Perhaps the most distinctive feature of Swedish privatization is that it has primarily involved new share issues to private corporations or institutional investors—including collective shareholding funds such as the Fourth AP Fund. The government has sought out new owners or partners likely to look on their investment as a long-term commitment. Furthermore, Swedish privatization has not involved any of the media hype of privatization measures carried out in the name of "popular capitalism" in Britain and elsewhere.

Significantly, the budget deficit was brought under control before the government seriously began to consider privatization as a policy option. What has perhaps been the major pragmatic motive for privatization in other countries—to raise revenues without raising taxes—does not seem to explain recent privatization measures in Sweden. The government conceived privatization primarily as a way to raise new capital for state-owned corporations. Two general considerations attracted the government to that option: on the one hand, the imperatives of fiscal management made it reluctant to finance capital infusions through the budget, and on the other, a buoyant stock market made share issues a relatively cheap way to raise new capital.

Beyond these considerations, recent privatization measures express a basic change in the Social Democratic attitude to state enterprise. Although the government accepts that it must support state-owned corporations with poor profitability, its conception of successful state enterprise does not appear to be any different from its conception of successful private enterprise. Given this outlook, the question confronting the government is not so much Why privatize? but rather, Why not? The Social Democrats' new attitude to state enterprise is in turn part of a broader retreat from selective industrial policy. According to Bengt Jacobsson (1989:97), the partial privatization of state-owned corporations is part of a conscious effort to insulate these corporations from political pressures while relieving politicians of responsibility for corporate decisions.

As table 10 illustrates, restructuring state enterprise in the 1980s caused some major employment losses. As Jan Olsson (1989:59) puts it, "The regional responsibility of state-owned corporations for employment has diminished during the 1980s." Surveying the major firms, Olsson concludes that state-owned corporations "have been able to close down and sell off activities in localities with a weak labor market" and that "with a couple of exceptions, they have not located themselves [their new plants] in regions where the need for new employment is greatest."

Although LO supported the government's policy of partial privatization, the union wing of the labor movement began to criticize its lack of commitment to industrial policy in the late 1980s. Most notably, the programmatic report to the Metalworkers congress of 1989 (Svenska Metallindustriarbetarförbundet 1989) pointed out that cuts in subsidies had not translated into increased resources for more offensive measures and argued that the industrial policy measures undertaken were not adequately coordinated. A more active industrial policy was necessary to counteract the tendency for the third way to promote the expansion of industrial sectors competing based on low wages rather than on skills and quality (cf. chap. 4).

Apparently in response to this criticism, Prime Minister Ingvar Carlsson appointed Rune Molin, vice president of LO, minister of industry in January 1990. Molin's appointment coincided with two changes in the organization of the cabinet: first, the Ministry of Energy and Environment was broken up and responsibility for energy policy was transferred to the Ministry of Industry; second, the cabinet was organized into four groups, with Molin being head of the one responsible for

Table 10. Employment in state enterprise, 1982 and 1988

	1982	1988
State Enterprise Corporation/Procordia	27,701	24,840
LKAB	6,806	4,081
SSAB	14,709	14,352
SVAB/Celsius	22,545	12,309
ASSI	8,529	3,425
Total	80,289	59,007

Source: Ministry of Industry (1984:63–64, 1989:15).

policies relating to economic development and a member of the "inner cabinet."

The cabinet reshuffle of 1990 marked a victory for LO's "pragmatic" position on the phase-out of nuclear power (a defeat for the opponents of nuclear power) and boosted the position of the Ministry of Industry in institutional terms. It is far less clear that it represented a reorientation of industrial policy. The omnibus bill Molin submitted to Parliament in March 1990 (government bill 88, 1989–90) contained only one major new initiative: a new corporation to manage corporate shares owned by the state. This corporation was established under the name Fortia in January 1991. Its assets include the remaining state shares in SSAB, NCB, and Celsius Industries as well as the corporations that were part of the original State Enterprise Corporation. The ambitions behind this institutional innovation were clearly very different from those that motivated the creation of the State Enterprise Corporation in 1970, however. Whereas the State Enterprise Corporation was supposed to serve as a link between state-owned corporations and the Ministry of Industry, Fortia seems to be meant as a buffer. In particular, its creation means that further privatization of the corporations in question will not require parliamentary approval.

INDUSTRIAL POLICY VERSUS LABOR MARKET POLICY

The labor movement's industrial policy offensive was intended to extend the principles of active labor market policy to corporate investment decisions, but practice in the 1970s diverged sharply from this model. The contrast between these two arenas applies to policy orientation and specific outcomes as well as policy-making itself.[10]

Policy Orientation

In both theory and practice, active labor market policy undertakes offensive adjustment, catering to the recruitment and training needs of the advanced sectors of the economy, and it involves extensive planning and continual state intervention in labor markets. Industrial policy before 1982 was defensive not only in focusing on declining sectors, but also in being reactive. Except for the Steel Plant 80 project, the major industrial policies of the 1970s were invariably responses to firm crises, initiated by corporate requests for state aid. In no case did the government anticipate or actively seek to preempt firm crises.

10. See Pontusson (1991) for an abbreviated version of the following discussion.

It has also been argued that the industrial policy measures of the 1970s were defensive in that they subsidized inefficient production (e.g., IUI 1984), but this argument requires some qualification. The extraordinary measures of the late 1970s were intended to subsidize inefficient production *temporarily*, giving firms, workers, and state agencies more time for the adjustments necessitated by long-term changes in world market conditions. A very substantial reduction of employment in declining sectors did occur from 1974 to 1982: employment dropped by 13.2 percent in mining, by 36.1 percent in the steel industry and by 44.4 percent in shipbuilding (Erixon 1984).

Economic circumstances, and the bourgeois tenure in government, provide the most obvious explanation for the defensive orientation of industrial policy. Selective state intervention was clearly necessary to prevent sectoral crises from translating into mass unemployment, but this line of argument does not explain the absence of state intervention in the restructuring of advanced sectors. As I noted above, the bourgeois parties conceived of selective state intervention as a way to ensure that industrial restructuring occurred in "socially acceptable forms" and saw little need to intervene in fundamentally "healthy" sectors of the economy. The significance of the change of government should not be exaggerated, however, for the industrial policies of the bourgeois parties in most cases were an extension of previous Social Democratic initiatives, and except for the Steel Plant 80 project, one would be hard put to name any significant Social Democratic initiatives that the bourgeois parties discontinued.

According to the Boston Consulting Group (1978, exhibit 31), in Sweden declining sectors accounted for 73 percent of state aid to industry in 1970–77, compared with 27 percent for West Germany, 32 percent for France, and 37 percent for the United Kingdom. Clearly, the defensiveness of industrial policy cannot be explained simply in terms of the ideological preferences of the bourgeois parties. Following John Zysman (1983), I suggest that it also expresses the lack of an institutionalized state capacity to intervene in capital markets. In other words, it reflects the legacy of class compromise embedded in the organization of the AP funds and other institutional arrangements.

Contrasting postwar French and Japanese industrial policies to the "arms-length government" of Britain and the United States, Zysman argues that for the state to intervene at the firm level, institutional arrangements must let it manipulate capital markets. By manipulating the allocation and terms of long-term credit, the state influences the marketplace choices of individual firms and thus becomes a "market player." Zysman identifies two features of postwar French and Japanese financial systems that lent themselves to selective state intervention—indeed, made it imperative. First, securities markets were under-developed, and firms depended heavily on credit for external finance. This dependence gave banks or other credit institutions leverage on corporate management. In addition to forcing banks to take a direct interest in the affairs of their corporate clients, long-term lending made them dependent on the state to regulate interest rates and refinance loans. Second, interest rates were administratively determined and systematically kept down. As a result, corporate borrowers queued for credit, and banks queued at the Central Bank or other refinancing institutions.

Swedish corporations have also been dependent on credit for external finance, and in the postwar period interest rates were often kept below the market-clearing level. But the big private banks effectively resisted selective state intervention in their lending practices and retained their strategic position within the system of corporate finance. Using Zysman's terminology, the Swedish system of corporate finance must be described as bank dominated rather than state dominated.

Labor did seek to enhance the state's ability to intervene in capital markets. The Investment Bank and the Fourth AP Fund are its principal achievements in this regard. The significance of these institutional reforms was limited, however. To begin with, it was limited in strictly quantitative terms. At its peak (in 1976), the volume of the Investment Bank's accumulated lending to industry was 7.9 percent of that of the commercial banks (SOU 1978a:557, 657), and the assets of the Fourth AP Fund still account for less than 3 percent of corporate shares registered on the stock exchange. More important, though, these institutions were never used systematically to carry out an offensive industrial policy. This is clearest for the Fourth AP Fund (see chap. 7 below).

The lack of an institutionalized capacity to manipulate capital markets restricted the government's ability to influence corporate adjustment strategies in the advanced sectors and forced it to rely on direct subsidies and ownership to cope with declining sectors. A striking feature of the Swedish experience is that none of the policy initiatives described above have had any direct bearing on foreign investment by Swedish firms. By and large, multinational corporations have remained outside the orbit of industrial policy. Although the engineering industry accounted for 42 percent of the Investment Bank's outstanding loans in 1977, only two of the largest twenty engineering firms figured among its clients (Ministry of Industry 1978:40).

The bourgeois parties and the Social Democrats alike saw state ownership as means of ensuring that corporations subsidized by the state would undertake the adjustment measures they considered necessary. In a somewhat different vein, the reliance on state ownership can be seen as an expression of the severity of the firm crises that triggered state intervention. In almost all cases, the firms could be reconstructed only through a major increase of their equity capital, and the prospects that they would become profitable again were simply not good enough for private capitalists to be interested in ownership.

The latter point raises the question why the government failed to anticipate firm crises. Here too Zysman's (1983) comparative discussion is apposite. According to Zysman, banks in France and Japan have served not only as levels whereby state policymakers can influence corporate marketplace decisions, but also as sources of information on corporate affairs. Many observers have pointed out that the formulation of Swedish industrial policy has depended heavily on information furnished by corporations requesting state aid (see, e.g., LO 1981:311–18; SOU 1981a, chap. 7; Henning 1980b, 1984). This was particularly true of the sectoral crisis measures of the late 1970s because they were so urgent. Only in a couple of cases—basic steel and specialty steels—did the government commission independent investigations of sectoral problems before committing itself to a course of action, and even these investigations relied primarily on information from the firms in question. By and large, corporate management defined the problems to be addressed by state intervention.

The Social Democratic proponents of an active industrial policy in the late 1960s envisioned the state enterprise sector as a source of detailed knowledge and technical-administrative competence for the government. But the relations between state-owned corporations and the Ministry of Industry do not appear to have been very different from those between private corporations and the ministry. Although ownership engagements have served as a tool of industrial policy, state-owned corporations, once established, have operated independently of the Ministry of Industry so long as they have been commercially successful and have largely conformed to conventional business practices. Though intended to implement industrial policy, the State Enterprise Corporation in effect acted as a buffer between the government and state-owned firms (Henning 1974). The organizational reforms the Social Democrats introduced in the 1980s reinforced the autonomy of the management in state-owned corporations.

The lack of an institutionalized state capacity to intervene in capital markets had important implications not only for the relations between corporate management and government officials but also for the politics of industrial policy in a broader sense. Two points are crucial here. First, the restrictions on the state's ability to influence the adjustment strategies of "healthy" corporations precluded any explicit package deal whereby labor would accept layoffs in crisis sectors in return for job-creating investments in other sectors, and the absence of such a deal made it more difficult for the national union leadership to resist protectionist pressures from below. Despite their commitment to industrial restructuring, the unions had little choice but to defend existing jobs in the late 1970s and early 1980s.

Second, the state's inability to intervene in capital markets meant that sectoral crisis measures had to be financed directly through the state budget and hence approved by Parliament case by case. Considering the very narrow electoral majorities of 1973–82, this procedure appears to have strengthened the claims of local constituencies and thus reinforced the defensiveness of industrial policy (cf. SOU 1981a, chap. 7; Henning 1984).

The Social Democratic election victory of 1982 was hardly a landslide, but it was enough to give the party a parliamentary majority so long as the Communists did not vote with a unified bourgeois opposition. Along with the world economic recovery of the mid-1980s, this new parliamentary situation let the Social Democrats reorient industrial policy. But the successful mobilization of public opinion against wage-earner funds in the early 1980s precluded any radical new efforts to institutionalize state intervention in capital markets (see chap. 7).

POLICY-MAKING AND INTEREST REPRESENTATION

The starkest contrast between industrial policy and labor market policy has to do with organized labor's role in policy-making. As we saw in chapter 3, active labor market policy was a product of demands emanating from LO, and the unions came to have an integral part in policy formulation and implementation through the corporatist structure of AMS. Corporatist arrangements never assumed the same prominence in the industrial policy arena, and labor's influence there has been much more limited. The question of organized labor appears to be closely related to another contrast between labor market policy and industrial policy—the way the implementation of industrial policy came to involve a plethora of public agencies and corporations whereas for labor market policy it was concentrated in a single agency.

The relative weakness of organized labor can be documented most readily in terms of direct representation on the boards of bodies responsible for carrying out industrial policy. Whereas the unions until recently held a clear majority on district and county labor market boards as well as on the AMS board of directors, according to a report by TCO (1981:122), business organizations have three times as many representatives on the boards of industrial policy bodies as LO and

TCO combined. The boards of the bodies responsible for implementing industrial policy are distinguished from that of AMS not only by the "underrepresentation" of the unions but also, and more importantly, by the marginal role of bargaining between the representatives of labor and business. In contrast to AMS, moreover, corporatist interest representation has not been reproduced at their lower organizational levels.[11]

Elevating key industrial policy decisions to the ministerial level curtailed the direct influence of organized labor. Like labor market policy, industrial policy in Sweden diverged from the traditional division of labor between ministries and administrative agencies, but the two diverged in opposite directions: whereas AMS tended to assume responsibility for formulating as well as implementing labor market policy, the Ministry of Industry generally took responsibility for both implementing and formulating industrial policy.[12] A tripartite Industrial Policy Council was set up in 1968 to advise the Ministry of Industry, and several tripartite sector councils were organized under the ministry's auspices in the 1970s. These bodies never undertook any real policymaking, however. They had no resources for this, and they do not appear to have played any significant role in policy-making within the Ministry of Industry. According to TCO (1981:122), most of the sector councils were "sleeping" in the early 1980s (Jacobsson 1989:48–50).

The delegation for specialty steels (*strukturdelegationen*) set up in 1978 was the only tripartite sectoral body with the authority and financial resources to implement industrial policy. Its activities were restricted in advance to a two-year period, however. The government also defined the delegation's assignment in a way that effectively precluded the approach advocated by the Metalworkers Union—that the delegation would develop a plan for restructuring the specialty steels industry and allocate financial support accordingly.[13]

The sectoral crisis measures of the 1970s and early 1980s were typically formulated through direct negotiations between the Ministry of Industry and the corporate management of the firms in question. Owners and creditors often became directly involved in these negotiations as well. Representatives of the Metalworkers Union participated

11. That AMS actively recruited administrative personnel from the unions in the postwar period undoubtedly reinforced the influence that corporatist representation provided to organized labor; see Rothstein (1986), who aptly refers to AMS as a "Social Democratic reform bureaucracy." Though I have not pursued this line of analysis, I would expect the recruitment and administrative practices of SIND and other industrial policy agencies to be very different from the AMS practices described by Rothstein.

12. Note that the Ministry of Labor was not established until 1973. Before then, AMS served under the Ministry of Domestic Affairs (Civildepartementet), which was responsible for a wide range of duties, and this undoubtedly contributed to its autonomy.

13. Interview with Lars Starrell, Ministry of Industry, June 21, 1983.

in the negotiations that led to the formation of Swedyard and SSAB, but in most other sectoral policy decisions labor was represented by union locals that lobbied for "their" firms. Even in shipbuilding and steel the role of organized labor was rather marginal, and the unions' ability to influence policy appears to have been almost entirely restricted to narrow employment issues (Ericsson 1979).

Economic circumstances may well be the primary explanation for the defensiveness of industrial policy, but they hardly explain the marginal role of organized labor in industrial policy-making. Similarly, the change of government in 1976 seems rather unimportant in this context, since the institutional features distinguishing industrial policy from labor market policy clearly predate this change. One would be hard put to argue that the bourgeois parties actively tried to exclude organized labor from industrial policy-making. Quite the contrary, they created several new sector councils and reactivated the Industrial Policy Council, which had hardly met at all during the last years of Social Democratic rule.[14]

In the early 1980s both LO and TCO proposed institutional reforms designed to enhance organized labor's part in policy-making as well as the state's ability to pursue an offensive industrial policy. The industrial policy report to the LO congress of 1981 (LO 1981) argued that strategic investment decisions by big firms should be subject to regularized negotiations and formal agreements with the state. The report suggested that such negotiations might be carried out by a tripartite industrial policy board (*näringspolitisk nämnd*) rather than by the Ministry of Industry. Similarly, a TCO report (TCO 1981) proposed a tripartite structural commission (*strukturkommission*) to coordinate industrial policy and argued that all state aid to industry should be administered by tripartite sector boards or regional investment funds. On their return to power, the Social Democrats established three new sector councils but did not pursue the more comprehensive reforms proposed by LO and TCO.[15]

Several factors help to explain the marginal role of organized labor in industrial policy-making. For one thing, organized labor lacked a coherent overall conception of the kinds of industrial changes it wanted to promote. Even more so than government officials, it lacked inde-

14. Interview with Torsten Löfgren, Ministry of Industry, June 16, 1983.
15. When Rune Molin became minister of industry in 1990, he also reactivated the Industrial Policy Council (Dagens Nyheter, March 19, 1990). The council seems to be the sort of body that each new minister sets out to reactivate. Currently there exist nine sector councils: three dating back to the first half of the 1970s (construction, forestry, and steel), another three dating to the late 1970s (textiles and apparel, shipbuilding, and autos), and the last three dating to 1984 (pharmaceuticals, aerospace, and retail and distribution).

pendent information and relevant expertise. Furthermore, the interests of different segments of the labor force diverged sharply with respect to specific industrial policy measures.

Such considerations might be subsumed under a more basic explanation of the contrast between labor market policy and industrial policy. Arguably, organized labor was able to dominate the debate about labor market policy and to influence policy outcomes because of the close relation between labor market policy and labor's marketplace power. By contrast, the implementation of industrial policy does not depend directly on trade-union cooperation, and it is more difficult for labor to bring its marketplace power to bear on the specifics of industrial policy-making. To put it somewhat crudely, labor does not have the bargaining chips it needs to participate as an independent actor in negotiations between firms and government officials. While it was less necessary for business or government to integrate organized labor, the business community resisted the institutionalization of tripartite bargaining over industrial policy more than over labor market policy.

I do not mean labor had no influence over industrial policy in the 1970s, but its influence was essentially indirect and negative. The bourgeois parties' concern with ensuring that sectoral decline would assume "socially acceptable forms" was motivated by their desire to avoid a confrontation with the unions and to secure the wage restraint necessary to make devaluation work. The power of organized labor in Sweden thus shaped the parameters of industrial policy, but the unions had very little direct influence over policy choices within these parameters.

CONCLUSIONS

In conjunction with the economic crisis, labor's industrial policy efforts did indeed yield a significant extension of selective state intervention in industrial restructuring. But again, the experience of industrial policy evolved in ways the labor movement had not expected. Whereas it wanted to institutionalize tripartite bargaining about the terms of competitive adjustment, industrial policy came to be dominated by defensive, ad hoc measures elaborated through political bargaining, with national unions playing a marginal part. The extension of selective state intervention rested on an implicit alliance between labor and declining industry. Over the long run, such an alliance was not desirable from labor's point of view. Apart from the economic costs of maintaining inefficient production, the policy orientation that came to prevail in the 1970s threatened the cohesion of the labor movement by politicizing firm-based or sectoral conflicts of interest among wage earners. In the 1980s the Social Democrats responded to these problems by re-treating to a less interventionist posture.

It is tempting to argue that labor's industrial policy offensive failed because labor abandoned it, and that labor did so because it recognized the inherent difficulties that arise when the state becomes involved in microeconomic decision making in a market economy. Social Democratic leaders, and bureaucrats in the Ministry of Industry tended to construe the story of industrial policy thus in the 1980s. For instance, the omnibus bill submitted by the minister of industry in 1987 (government bill 74, 1986–87) affirmed that "the experience of the 1970s has led us to modify our view of the possibilities of planning." Yet can one really say anything about the possibilities of planning based on the Swedish experience in the 1970s? After all, the outstanding feature of this experience is the absence of planning. As Jacobsson (1989:137–39) argues, the government's new industrial policy rhetoric reconstructed the experience of the 1970s in accord with the dominant ideological currents in the 1980s; indeed, it rested on "the memory of what did not happen."

Following TCO (1981) one might conclude that corporations are not interested in sharing information and engaging in negotiations with state agencies unless they are grappling with acute financial problems. But this conclusion is contingent on the institutional arrangements of the financial system. The defensive orientation of Swedish industrial policy reflects the lack of an institutionalized state capacity to intervene in capital markets. The efforts the labor movement made to create such a capacity through institutional reforms were of limited significance. The failure to undertake more radical reforms along these lines might be attributed to the electoral decline of Social Democracy in the 1970s, but again, the change of government in 1976 does not represent a turning point in the development of industrial policy. Also, organized business, though critical of the industrial policy efforts of the labor movement in 1968–73, never mobilized politically against labor's offensive. Of the three cases treated in this study, industrial policy is clearly the one where resistance to labor reformism was weakest and least coherent.

The failure of labor's industrial policy offensive was mainly due to a lack of commitment by the government. From the very beginning, elements within the Social Democratic leadership resisted the more interventionist approach to industrial policy adopted in the late 1960s. Although it is difficult to gauge the depth and nature of these differences, it seems clear that the minister of finance, Gunnar Sträng, and his advisers, including Kjell-Olof Feldt, were skeptical, if not openly critical, of the ideas pushed by Wickman and others. The government embraced the idea of active industrial policy in response to the electoral setback of 1966, and its commitment to far-reaching industrial policy reforms appears to have waned in the aftermath of the landslide election victory of 1968.

This brings us to the most obvious flaw in the theory that in the 1980s labor came to recognize its earlier ambitions as mistaken: at least in the first instance, different elements of the labor movement drew different lessons from the experience of the 1970s. Whereas Feldt and others invoked this experience to argue for a retreat from selective intervention, LO (1981) argued for wage-earner funds as a way to turn active industrial policy in a more offensive direction and to enhance organized labor's influence over policy-making. The political failure of LO's wage-earner funds settled this debate over the role and orientation of industrial policy for the time being. Having failed to impose its own solution, LO had to accept—and indeed welcomed—the retreat from selective state intervention organized by the Social Democrats.

I have argued that the power resources of business are far better suited to effect particular outcomes in industrial policy than are the resources of labor. The failure of labor's offensive cannot be explained entirely in terms of institutional and political constraints, however. It was also in part a failure by the labor movement to develop a coherent conception of what kind of industrial development the state should promote, and this failure can in turn be related to labor's traditional ideological commitment to Keynesian economics. Most important, this line of reasoning seems to explain why institutions such as the State Enterprise Corporation and the Fourth AP Fund were from the beginning left to determine their own investment strategies.

As Anna Hedborg and Rudolf Meidner (1984:202) have pointed out, the industrial policy programs of the labor movement have concerned themselves primarily with creating the instruments for a possible industrial policy and have been much less concerned with how such a policy could be carried out and what its goals should be. The industrial policy report submitted to the LO congress of 1981 was far more explicit than previous programmatic statements in these respects, but it proved to be a nonstarter in the new political context of the 1980s. As we have seen, however, the debate over the role and orientation of industrial policy resurfaced within the labor movement in the late 1980s.

CHAPTER SIX

Codetermination

Thus far, I have focused on the ability of Swedish unions to influence the allocation of investment capital within the corporate sector through their influence over government policy or the actions of state institutions such as public pension funds. In this chapter, I turn to the exercise of labor's influence "from below," that is, union participation in corporate decision making at the level of the plant and the firm. Such participation may or may not involve investment decisions, and its significance as a mechanism of union influence is inherently limited, for unions still cannot influence the interfirm allocation of investment. But it is certainly conceivable that labor could significantly influence corporate investment through this channel.

The labor movement's acceptance of the authority of management was an essential component of the politics of class compromise in postwar Sweden, dating back to the "December Compromise" of 1906. In return for employers' recognition of their right to organize workers and bargain on their behalf, at this time the LO unions recognized the principle of managerial prerogatives. As stipulated by the SAF statutes (paragraph 23, later renumbered 32), all collective bargaining agreements signed by an employer affiliated with SAF would henceforth include a statement affirming that the employer has "the right to lead and allocate work and to hire and fire workers freely, irrespective of whether they are organized" (Schiller 1973:304). In other words, the December Compromise confined collective bargaining to the terms of employment—wages, working hours, and benefits. The Saltsjöbaden Agreement of 1938 somewhat restricted employers' right to fire employees freely but otherwise respected managerial prerogatives, and the works councils SAF agreed to in 1946 were strictly consultative.

The continued confinement of collective bargaining to the terms of employment reflected not only the power of the employers, but also the ideology of the labor movement. On the one hand, LO and its affiliated unions (at least their national leaders) adopted a very positive view of management's efforts to raise productivity through mechanization and more "scientific" management methods (Sundgren 1978). On the other hand, they wanted to retain their autonomy vis-à-vis management by avoiding any responsibility for managerial decisions.

For reasons we shall explore, LO's posture changed dramatically in 1969–71, and the need to democratize working life emerged as the central theme of the LO congress of 1971. LO's industrial democracy offensive resulted in a whole series of legislative measures in 1972–77 pertaining to the rights of employees and unions (see Edlund and Nyström 1988 for an overview). Following Klas Åmark (1988), we can distinguish two types of legislative measures: measures designed to strengthen the position of labor in the labor market (e.g., by requiring advanced notification of layoffs) and measures designed to give labor direct influence in corporate decision making. Since it is the latter objective that concerns us here, the following discussion will focus on two of the industrial relations reforms of the 1970s: union representation on corporate boards of directors, and the extension of collective bargaining through the Codetermination Act of 1976.

At the time it passed, Olof Palme hailed the Codetermination Act as the greatest reform since universal suffrage. In practice, the act clearly did not empower labor as much as such statements led union activists to expect; yet it did contribute to major changes in the relationship between unions and management at the firm level.

A comprehensive assessment of codetermination practices in the corporate sector—let alone the economy as a whole—would require an entire book, for codetermination encompasses a wide range of issues and its forms vary across sectors, corporations, and plants. My ambitions in this chapter are more limited: I use the case of Volvo to illustrate the limits of codetermination as a way for unions to influence corporate investment decisions. Needless to say, I did not choose this case at random: Volvo is Sweden's largest corporation and has been in the vanguard in developing new forms of work organization as well as codetermination practices in the past two decades. Just as Sweden might be seen as a limiting case of the achievements of Social Democracy in general, so Volvo might be seen as a limiting case of what Swedish unions have achieved through codetermination within the corporate sector.

Although the Volvo unions have come to wield some influence over the development of work organization and the design of new plants, they have made no significant inroads in decision making that pertains to Volvo's overall strategy as a multinational corporation. Other research strongly suggests that at least the latter part of this assessment applies more generally to large manufacturing corporations (e.g., Sandkull 1982; Berggren 1986; Levinson 1990). It is tempting to conclude that codetermination reform has not yielded much union influence over corporate investment decisions, but such a conclusion rests on a rather narrow conception of what constitutes "investment decisions." Insofar as workplace innovations entail a long-term commitment of resources, they fall into the realm of investment politics. And many workplace innovations clearly do involve a long-term commitment of resources—not only in new plants, but also in equipment and "human capital."

My discussion of the practice of codetermination at Volvo is supplemented by an analysis of the system of renewal funds (RF) introduced by the Social Democrats in 1984. Modeled on the investment funds discussed earlier, this scheme required corporations to set aside a portion of their profits in funds earmarked for employee training and R&D. Though its scope was limited, the RF scheme gave local unions veto power over the use of the funds. In stipulating that management had to share decision-making authority equally with labor, the scheme went beyond the Codetermination Act.

Before turning to the Volvo case, and then to the experience of renewal funds, I explore the origins and course of labor's efforts to reform industrial relations through legislation and collective bargaining at the national level.

THE POLITICS OF CODETERMINATION REFORM

The first part of this section establishes that the industrial democracy program adopted by the LO congress of 1971 represented a radical departure from LO's traditional posture and sets out the reasons for this reorientation. The second part describes the politics of codetermination legislation in 1972–76 and its basic provisions. The third part describes the Development Agreement signed by SAF, LO, and PTK (the bargaining cartel of private sector white-collar unions) in 1982 and the renewal funds legislation the Social Democrats introduced in 1984.

The Origins of Labor's Legislative Offensive

LO's traditional posture on managerial authority and union participation in corporate decision making was articulated most consistently in a report to the 1961 congress.[1] On the grounds that unions must avoid any "dual loyalty," so as to be able to defend employees' interests vis-à-vis management, this report rejected the idea of assigning decision-making authority to works councils as well as the idea of union representation on corporate boards of directors. At the same time, it strongly criticized the employers for failing to live up to the spirit of the Works Council Agreement of 1946, pointing out, among other things, that it was common for works councils to meet less frequently than prescribed by the agreement (four times a year) and for management to raise issues only after they had been decided (to use works council meetings to inform rather than consult with the unions).

The report to the 1961 congress argued that LO should seek to reinforce union rights of access to information and strengthen the advisory role of works councils through negotiations with SAF. Such negotiations ushered in a new works council agreement, signed in 1966. Although SAF committed itself to activating works councils, it successfully resisted LO's demands for access to information as well as direct influence in personnel policy. In retrospect, however, the most striking thing about the negotiations that led to the Works Council Agreement is how limited LO's ambitions were at this time.

Written by a committee appointed in June 1969, the report on industrial democracy endorsed by the LO congress of 1971 (LO 1971) demanded union representation on corporate boards of directors but downplayed its significance. Essentially, the report treated board representation as a means of gaining information about and insight into corporate decision making rather than as a means of influencing decisions, and it argued that influence should be exercised by extending collective bargaining to corporate policy. For gaining information and insight, minority representation on the board of directors would be sufficient.

Thus LO rejected the goal of parity representation, which had figured so prominently in the German labor movement's quest for codetermination. It also rejected the German model of works councils with directly elected employee representatives. This model threatened to undermine the position of local unions as the representatives of the labor force. Although LO would seek to exercise influence through the existing system of works councils, based on union representation rather than direct elections, it now proposed that local unions be able to demand regular collective bargaining over issues that could not be resolved consensually. In contrast to the German model, this way of organizing codetermination would preserve the right to strike as well as the representational monopoly of the unions.

1. LO (1961). The following discussion of when, how, and why LO's outlook changed draws on Schiller (1973), Martin (1977), Kjellberg (1981), Hadenius (1983), and Simonson (1988).

Two additional features of the industrial democracy program of 1971 must be noted if we are to appreciate its novelty. To begin with, LO now aspired to influence a much wider range of corporate decisions. Through the 1960s, LO looked to the system of works councils primarily as a way to influence personnel policy—decisions about hiring, firing, layoffs, promotions, and intrafirm reallocation of labor. The LO unions obviously remained concerned with such issues, but the codetermination offensive of the early 1970s involved a twofold shift of attention: "downward" to work organization and shop-floor conditions, and "upward" to corporate strategy and investment decisions. According to the 1971 report, the ultimate goal was to establish "parity between employees and owners of capital" on all issues affecting employees (LO, 1971:59).

Also, the 1971 report broke with LO's traditional posture by advocating legislation as the way to achieve codetermination. This change of strategy was a logical consequence of LO's new goals, for extending collective bargaining to work organization and corporate policy would obviously run up against paragraph 32 of the SAF statutes, and the employers were unlikely to budge on the principle of managerial prerogatives. At the same time, however, the report considered collective bargaining a necessary complement to legislation in the development of codetermination.

Why then did LO suddenly opt for a frontal assault on paragraph 32? Several developments must be invoked to explain LO's strategic reorientation. Most immediately, the industrial democracy program of 1971 was a response to the wildcat strike movement of 1969–70 and, in particular, the highly publicized strike in the LKAB mines. The wildcat strike movement might in turn be seen as a reaction to solidaristic wage policy: for the most part, the strikers were LO members whose wages had been held back in recent years (Fulcher 1976; Swenson 1989). But the wildcat strikes also featured new, "qualitative" demands and were widely interpreted as expressing growing worker discontent with the working conditions and managerial practices characteristic of Fordist-style mass production. In this respect the strikes, and their public reception, conformed to general trends throughout Western Europe at the time.

The new militancy might be seen as the result of either an objective deterioration of working conditions (owing to management efforts to speed up and further rationalize production to meet growing international competition) or a decline of workers' tolerance for conditions they had previously accepted (owing to some combination of postwar educational reforms, full employment, rising standards of living, and the antiauthoritarian values of the 1960s). These interpretations are by no means mutually exclusive, and determining the relative weight to be assigned to each lies well beyond our current concerns. Suffice it to note that there is at least some evidence that working conditions in mass-production industries did deteriorate in the 1960s (e.g., payment by piece rates increased markedly), and a great deal of evidence that union activists saw this as true (e.g., LO 1967).

A very important aspect of the wildcat strike movement of 1967–70 is that it took LO by surprise and revealed a major "communication gap" between the rank and file and national union officials. As Martin (1977) suggests, LO appears to have attributed this gap to the weakening of union locals (*verkstadsklubbar*) in the wake of the centralization of wage bargaining. Thus conceived, the organizational problem confronting LO was how to revitalize union locals without abandoning the centralized wage bargaining solidaristic wage policy depended on. At least in principle, extending collective bargaining to nonwage issues provided a solution. In other words, LO's codetermination offensive not only reflected new rank-and-file demands, but also solved organizational problems associated with rank-and-file militancy.

The wildcat strike movement does not adequately explain LO's codetermination efforts, however, for the LO leaders had already begun to rethink their traditional posture when the LKAB strike erupted (Simonson 1988, chap. 3). Two political considerations that predated the wildcat strikes pushed LO toward codetermination reform. First, the Liberals and the Center party both presented themselves as advocates of industrial democracy in the second half of the 1960s (Hadenius 1983). Emphasizing the need to promote individual employees' ability to participate in immediate decisions affecting them, but also proposing minority employee representation on boards of directors, these parties pictured firm-level participation as a democratic alternative to the centralized (corporatist) collaboration between labor and business promoted by the Social Democrats. Second, the TCO unions became increasingly interested in codetermination in the late 1960s. The programmatic report by the TCO congress of 1970 looked to collective bargaining rather than legislation to achieve codetermination rights, but it clearly showed that there was great potential for collaboration between LO and TCO in this area. In part labor's codetermination offensive was intended to preempt the bourgeois parties' efforts to "outflank" the Social Democrats and to bring TCO closer to Social Democracy. Against this backdrop, the wildcat strike movement added urgency to the offensive and radicalized LO's ambitions.

From a more retrospective point of view, finally, labor's codetermination offensive might also be seen as a response to employers' efforts to reorganize work on a more participatory basis. Several corporations began to experiment with teamwork in the second half of the 1960s, but it was not until the 1970s that management-initiated innovations along these lines became widespread, and new corporate strategies were hardly a major impetus behind LO's reorientation in 1970–71.[2] The unions' pursuit of codetermination and the employers' pursuit of flexible work organization and greater worker commitment to quality and efficiency should be seen as parallel developments that reinforced each other and began to converge in the wake of the Codetermination Act of 1976.

Legislative Processes and Outcomes

In anticipation of the LO congress, a Social Democratic parliamentary motion submitted in January 1971 called for a commission of inquiry to review the legal framework of industrial relations and propose legislation that would strengthen the influence of employees and unions. The upshot of this motion was the appointment of the Labor Law Commission (Arbetsrättskommittén, or ARK), which included representatives of the four major parties as well as SAF, LO, and TCO.

Eager to achieve something tangible, LO and TCO singled out board representation as a reform that could be introduced while awaiting the result of ARK's deliberations (see Hadenius 1983:94–105; Simonson 1988, chap. 4). Whereas LO had previously demanded that the unions be allowed to appoint one-third of the directors in all corporations with more than fifty employees, the bill the government introduced in fall 1972 (government bill 116, 1972) provided for two board members in corporations with more than one hundred employees during a trial period of three years. Enacted in spring 1976, while the Social Democrats still held government power, the legislation making board representation permanent extended its scope by requiring all corporations with more than twenty-five employees to comply and also stipulated that the unions were entitled to participate in the managing committee (*arbetsutskott*) of boards of directors (government bill 169, 1975–76). Yet the bill completely ignored LO's and TCO's suggestion that union-appointed members be able to veto board decisions if they had not been given adequate opportunity to consider the issues at hand. Whereas the Communists alone voted against the initial legislation on board representation, the Center party and the Conservatives objected to the new provisions of the 1976 legislation, which passed thanks to the support of the Liberals.

By the time the Labor Law Commission (ARK) began its delibera-

2. In the 1970s, teamwork experiments were promoted by the SAF Technical Department through a program known as "New Factories"; see Augurén and Edgren (1979).

tions in 1973, the employers recognized that they would not be able to resist legislative reform of industrial relations. Seeking to influence the way codetermination would be organized, from the very beginning the employer representatives on ARK conceded the principle of managerial prerogatives. LO and TCO became increasingly ambitious in the course of ARK's deliberations, however, and the representatives of the Center party and the Liberals became more sympathetic to their position. Initially the bourgeois parties, the employer representatives, and the chairman (a former LO vice president) formed a moderate majority, favoring consensual solutions, while the representatives of SAP, LO, and TCO formed a minority. When the Center party and the Liberals began to vote with the unions, the government prevailed on the two Social Democrats on the commission to vote for the recommendations of the "bourgeois" majority so as to finish the commission's work quickly.

Thus it happened that the majority recommendations of ARK's report (SOU 1975), submitted in December 1974, were formally supported by the Social Democrats, the Conservatives, and the employer representatives. The LO and TCO representatives jointly signed a lengthy dissent, and the representatives of the Center party and the Liberals also dissented from the majority view. The minister of labor said publicly that he considered the LO-TCO dissent to be the true majority view of the commission and that it would provide the basis for the government's legislative proposals. But in fact the bill Parliament enacted in spring 1976 (government bill 105, 1975–76) rejected some of the more radical proposals advanced by LO and TCO, constituting a compromise between their views and those of the elusive ARK majority.[3]

All the members of ARK concurred that codetermination legislation should be enabling; that it was to be a legal framework complemented by a negotiated agreement (or agreements) on codetermination procedures. The ARK majority proposed to abolish paragraph 32 of the SAF statutes by stipulating in law that if the unions so demanded, collective agreements had to include procedural arrangements for "employee influence in matters pertaining to the management and allocation of work" (SOU 1975:39). To enforce this stipulation, it proposed that unions should retain the right to engage in industrial conflict (strikes, overtime bans, etc.) over such matters even after they had signed a collective bargaining agreement. Although the LO and TCO

3. In its official commentary on the ARK report, SAF actually objected to some of the recommendations of the majority that included its representatives. My account of the preparation of the Codetermination Act draws primarily on Hadenius (1983:106–64), Broström (1982, chaps. 4–5), Schiller (1988, chap. 8), and Simonson (1988, chap. 5).

representatives endorsed this approach to enforcement, they objected to confining codetermination rights to work-related issues, arguing that employees should in principle have the right to participate in *all* matters of interest to them. On this score the government bill adopted the LO-TCO position.

The ARK majority proposed further that employers should, even in the absence of procedural codetermination agreements, be required to initiate negotiations with local unions before any major decision affecting working conditions or terms of employment. This stipulation did not require employers to reach an agreement with the unions, however; should the negotiations fail, the management would be free to decide the matter unilaterally. In their dissent, LO and TCO insisted that the "primary duty of negotiation" should apply to decisions pertaining to individual employees as well as the work force as a whole and that, if the local parties failed to agree, negotiations between national unions and their employer counterparts should be required if the unions so demanded. The LO-TCO dissent suggested that the unions be given veto power in certain matters, though they did not specify precisely which matters, and in their official commentaries (*remissvar*) on the ARK report LO and TCO proposed that the law give local unions decision-making rights ("self-determination") concerning occupational health and employee training.

The government bill endorsed the unions' view of the "primary duty of negotiation" but rejected their demands for veto power and self-determination rights.[4] To justify its rejection of these demands, the government invoked the principle, previously endorsed by LO and TCO, that legislation should establish a framework for negotiated codetermination arrangements instead of regulating industrial relations in detail.

Whose interpretation should prevail in contractual disputes also divided the Labor Law Commission. The majority proposed modifying established procedures by stipulating that the employer's interpretation would take priority for only ten days; if the employer failed to submit the dispute to the Labor Court within this period, priority of interpretation would pass (indefinitely) to the union side. In their dissent, LO and TCO argued that the union interpretation should take priority from the beginning. Again, the government agreed with LO and TCO but restricted the scope of this reform to codetermination issues: the employers retained priority of interpretation concerning wages and benefits.

4. In the interest of accuracy, note that the Codetermination Act provided for a restricted union veto of the use of subcontracted labor (as distinct from subcontracting for parts).

Finally, the Codetermination Act went further than the ARK majority with respect to the unions' right to information about corporate affairs, much as LO and TCO had demanded. The Codetermination Act clearly satisfied most of LO's and TCO's demands, yet the legislation did not challenge management's right to determine corporate policy unilaterally if it so wished. Again, the act established a duty to negotiate, but *not* a duty to reach agreement. (Moreover, it included no provisions about bargaining in "good faith"). As Anders Broström (1982) notes, the ARK report and government's legislative proposal tried to fudge the problem of how the codetermination rights of wage earners affected the rights of owners as enshrined in corporate law. Since labor's codetermination offensive did not translate into any changes in corporate law, codetermination rights were necessarily subordinated to ownership rights.

Related to this fundamental limitation, the rights of employees as established by the Codetermination Act pertained only to decisions of their immediate employer. The act ignored the fact that many corporations were subsidiaries of other corporations. Indeed, the 1970s marked the beginning of a major reorganization of the corporate sector as many large corporations have reconstituted themselves as groups (or combines) of many separate legal entities. The Codetermination Act may well have contributed to this development. In any case, the act was premised on a corporate structure that has become increasingly obsolete (Broström 1982:39–41; Dahlström 1989).

Collective Bargaining and Legislation in the Aftermath of Labor's Offensive

Again, the Codetermination Act was conceived as an enabling law, to be complemented by negotiated procedural arrangements. To ensure that SAF would bargain fairly, the government immediately appointed a new Labor Law Commission (*Nya arbetsrättskommitén*, NARK) to follow up the implementation of the act and to consider whether further legislation, possibly including revisions of corporate law, would be necessary. The bourgeois victory in the election of September 1976 altered the political context of codetermination bargaining, however. Though the Center party and the Liberals remained committed to codetermination, they now had to govern with the Moderates. The threat of legislation to enforce employer compliance with the spirit of the Codetermination Act waned at the same time as the onset of the economic crisis weakened the bargaining position of the unions (Simonson 1988:155–57).

In December 1976 SAF, LO, and PTK (the bargaining cartel of private sector white-collar unions) issued a joint statement affirming their intention to negotiate a peak-level codetermination agreement, but it quickly became apparent that they could hardly agree on anything else. Although public sector agreements were struck in 1978 (central government) and 1980 (local governments), several rounds of private sector negotiations failed, and it was not until 1982 that LO, PTK, and SAF finally signed an agreement on codetermination procedures, the so-called Development Agreement (Utvecklingsavtalet or UVA).[5]

As Bernt Schiller (1988, chap. 12) argues, the Development Agreement might be seen as a synthesis of the unions' quest to establish codetermination rights at the national level with the employers' quest to engage employees and unions in a joint effort to improve corporate performance at the local level. In emphasizing the common interests of employees and employers, the rhetoric of the agreement was reminiscent of the Works Council Agreement of 1966. Rather than treating codetermination as an end in itself, the Development Agreement treated it as a means of improving efficiency, profitability, and competitiveness.

Though the unions had sought a comprehensive codetermination pact, the Development Agreement was restricted to three areas: work organization, technical development, and the corporation's financial and economic situation. Whereas the agreement affirmed employees' right to participate in the development of new work practices and technical innovation, its economic provisions were couched in terms of access to information and the expertise needed to make sense of corporate accounts. Among other things, the agreement entitled local unions to engage outside consultants to examine corporate accounts, on certain conditions.

The agreement did not make provision for codetermination bargaining over personnel policy and training, nor did it give the unions any form of veto power or self-determination rights. These omissions were closely related, for it was in the area of personnel policy that LO and PTK had sought to go beyond the right to negotiate in previous bargaining rounds. For instance, they had demanded that local unions be entitled to determine who would participate in courses offered by corporations and to approve the curricula of such courses.[6] In connection with the signing of the Development Agreement, LO and PTK declared they would seek a second agreement that would specify pro-

5. SAF-LO-PTK (1982). Simonson (1988:157–87) provides a detailed account of the negotiations leading to the Development Agreement.
6. The public sector agreements on codetermination procedures signed in 1978 and 1980 did accommodate such demands; see Edlund and Nyström (1988:52–55).

cedures for the codetermination of personnel policy, but no such settlement materialized in the 1980s.

The Development Agreement also fell short of the unions' expectations in that it did not prescribe specific codetermination procedures. Conforming to SAF's view that each corporation must be allowed to develop procedures suited to its particular circumstances, the agreement simply presented a menu of possible forms of codetermination: formalized negotiations as prescribed by the Codetermination Act, direct union participation in management decision making, bipartite collaborative organs such as works councils, and union participation in development projects.

For all these shortcomings (from the unions' point of view), the Development Agreement did clearly take the Codetermination Act as its point of departure. In previous bargaining rounds, SAF had proposed to vest negotiated codetermination rights in "employee representatives" (*kontaktombud*) directly elected at the shop level and had insisted on codetermination procedures that would have preempted some of the provisions of the Codetermination Act. By contrast, the Development Agreement stipulated that employees were to be represented through their unions in all matters covered by the agreement and that the employee rights prescribed by the Codetermination Act would apply fully in these matters. If corporations developed codetermination procedures based on works councils or direct union participation in corporate decision making, the unions would retain the right to revert to formal negotiations and to strike during them. And though the agreement stipulated that codetermination should occur primarily at the level of the individual corporation, it stated that the "primary duty of negotiation" also applied to the decisions of top management in corporate groups.

In signing the Development Agreement, LO abandoned its challenge to managerial authority. It may have done so to achieve some influence over ongoing corporate efforts to reorganize industrial work. According to Simonson (1988:178–79), firms began to negotiate local codetermination agreements with their unions as the centralized negotiations dragged on, and this put pressure on LO to settle with SAF.

The New Labor Law Commission submitted its final report (SOU 1982d) in December 1982, shortly after the Social Democrats returned to power. The commission argued that further legislation should not be contemplated for the time being. Rather, the system of codetermination that had been agreed on by LO, PTK, and SAF should be allowed to develop. The new government took this recommendation to heart. Indeed, in the 1980s the Social Democrats undertook only two legislative initiatives bearing on codetermination: first, the renewal funds of

1984, and second, the revision of the law governing union representation on corporate boards of directors enacted in 1987. Providing for three union-appointed board members in corporations with more than one thousand employees, the latter measure was neither controversial nor significant, but the renewal funds deserve our attention.

Formally an extension of the existing system of investment funds, the 1984 legislation (government bill 86, 1984–85) required corporations with adjusted profits over 500,000 SEK in 1985 to deposit 10 percent of these profits in an interest-free account at the Central Bank.[7] Over a five-year period (1986–91), these funds would be available for financing employee training and R&D projects on condition that union locals approved these projects. Any funds that remained at the end of this period would revert to the corporation and become subject to regular profits taxation.

The basic idea behind this scheme was conceived by Leif Blomberg, president of the Metalworkers Union. The government agreed to introduce legislation along the lines Blomberg proposed during the wage bargaining round of 1984. As with the 1983 wage-earner funds legislation, the government sought to promote wage restraint by absorbing corporate liquidity and giving the unions influence over the use of corporate profits (Elvander 1988:162–63, 282–83; Feldt 1991:175–78). In contrast to wage-earner funds, however, the RF scheme avoided the issue of ownership.

Whereas the system of investment funds had until recently been restricted to investment in fixed capital, the system of renewal funds was designed to promote "immaterial" investment in R&D and human capital. (The funds could also be used for buildings and equipment related to such purposes, however.) Most important, the construction of renewal funds differed from that of investment funds in two respects: first, corporations were *required* to set them up; and second, the unions were given a veto over their use.[8] The 1984 legislation went beyond the Codetermination Act by affirming the principle that management and unions should share decision-making authority equally, and it also remedied the Development Agreement's omission of codetermination procedures pertaining to personnel training.

Despite subsequent union demands that corporations be required to set aside profits in renewal funds each year, the government did not follow up the 1984 legislation, and so the funds came to be based exclusively on profits set aside in 1985. All together, 5.2 billion SEK was set

7. See also *Affärsvärlden*, May 7, 1986; Meidner (1987); and Eriksson, Nilsson, and Ohlsson (1991).

8. In both respects, the renewal funds were modeled on the extraordinary work environment funds (*arbetsmiljöfonder*) enacted in 1974, also to encourage wage restraint.

aside, of which 4.2 billion SEK had been used up by the end of 1989. During the initial three years, the use of renewal funds was evenly divided between training and R&D: roughly 2 billion SEK went to each. The limited significance of renewal funds emerges clearly when we consider that the total cost of employee training by Swedish business has been estimated at 18–25 billion SEK per year and that total R&D expenditures of corporations with renewal funds were 15 billion SEK in 1986 (Eriksson, Nilsson, and Ohlsson 1991, chap. 12). Nonetheless, the RF scheme provides an interesting alternative to investment funds as well as wage-earner funds, and I shall return to its implementation after my analysis of the practice of codetermination at Volvo.

THE PRACTICE OF CODETERMINATION AT VOLVO

Again, I propose to explore the practice of codetermination at the firm level by looking at the case of Volvo. I first provide an overall picture of codetermination arrangements at Volvo and give some indication of the limited extent of union influence over strategic corporate decisions at the group level. Second, I address the role of local unions in the development of new forms of work organization, specifically the redesign of final assembly work at Volvo.

Institutional Arrangements

Volvo and its unions signed their own Development Agreement in spring 1983 (Volvo 1983). For the most part this agreement simply reproduced the provisions of the SAF-LO-PTK pact of 1982, adding commentary on their application to Volvo. Volvo management and unions characterize the Development Agreement(s) as a codification of existing practices rather than a new departure. Arguably, the whole point of the central Development Agreement of 1982 was to bring codetermination practices in other firms, especially smaller firms, up to Volvo's level. The same might be said of the 1972 legislation providing for union representation on corporate boards of directors, for Volvo decided in 1971 to allow its unions to appoint two board members (Stråth 1988:93).

At the national level, the approach to codetermination that LO and TCO adopted in the 1970s focused on formal bargaining between unions and management. Recognizing that it had to accommodate the thrust of labor's demands—to allow local unions a greater say in corporate decision making—SAF argued that codetermination should instead occur through bipartite bodies, providing for more informal, consensus-oriented interactions between unions and management. The private employers wanted codetermination to develop as an extension of the existing system of works councils. The Development Agreement of 1982 left this debate over the organization of codetermination unsettled, and so did the Volvo version of it. Yet there can be little doubt that in practice the employers' approach to codetermination has prevailed at Volvo.[9]

Bipartite collaborative bodies exist at three levels: the group level, the company level (the level of subsidiary corporations), and the plant level. Meeting four times a year, the Group Council (*koncernnämnden*) dates back to 1971. Its executive committee (*arbetsutskott*) meets more frequently, and it is in this committee that formal codetermination negotiations take place if they become necessary. The Group Council and its executive committee deliberate on the appointment of the group's executive officers, the acquisition or sale of subsidiaries, and large investment projects that concern the group as a whole.

When Volvo's divisions and other subsidiaries became separate corporate entities in the early 1980s, each instituted its own bipartite council, modeled on the Group Council. At the plant level, finally, there exists a Plant Council (known as Arbetsutskottet), that typically meets every other week. Since the early 1980s, large plants have instituted "collaboration and codetermination groups" within each of their departments as well as bipartite committees to deal with specific plantwide issues (safety, personnel development, new technology, etc.). Whereas the structure of union participation at the group and company levels entirely predates the Development Agreements of 1982–83, the structure of union participation at the plant level has undergone significant changes since the early 1980s. In essence, the locus of information and consultation has shifted from the Plant Council to smaller bipartite bodies, with a more specific mandate and without bargaining authority. At the same time, codetermination has come to involve many more people, on the management side as well as the union side (Hellberg 1988:113–14).

Alongside these arrangements for regular union participation in corporate decision making, the Volvo unions have taken part in various development projects since the mid-1970s, most notably the planning of new plants. I shall return to the significance of this type of "project participation" in the next section.

9. The following description of formal codetermination arrangements draws primarily on Hellberg (1988). Formalized negotiations have been a more prominent feature of codetermination in the public sector: see Melin's (1988) case study of the Postal Service and Edlund and Hellberg's (1988) summation of the differences between Volvo and the Postal Service.

At Volvo, codetermination has rarely involved formal negotiations, and the unions have never tried to use their right to strike to pressure management in such negotiations. In a handful of cases the unions have demanded that codetermination bargaining be elevated to the industry level—that it take the form of negotiation between the Metalworkers Union and the Engineering Employers' Association. In each of these cases, however, industry-level negotiations led nowhere, and in the end Volvo management decided the matter unilaterally.

The secretive nature of top-level corporate decision making makes it difficult to assess the influence the unions wield at the group and company levels, but most observers seem to agree that they have had very little, if any, influence at these levels.[10] In the words of Edmund Dahlström (1989:82), "Union representatives at Volvo have had difficulty getting into the settings in which strategic decisions are made. It is not until top management informs the company's boards of directors and bipartite bodies that union representatives are allowed to influence more overarching corporate issues." To cite only a couple of examples, the unions were not informed of management's negotiations with the Norwegian government in 1978 until they were nearly completed (trading Volvo shares for oil concessions; the deal was subsequently defeated by shareholders). In 1985 Volvo publicly announced a major corporate deal (with Fermenta, a pharmaceuticals corporation) before any consultations with the unions (Hellberg 1988:108). Most important perhaps, the multinationalization of Volvo's operations since the early 1970s has in no sense been a subject of codetermination bargaining.

The Redesign of Assembly Work

Since the early 1970s, Volvo has been developing new working practices, departing from traditional ("Fordist") principles of assembly-line production.[11] We can distinguish three stages in the workplace reform movement at Volvo. The famous Kalmar assembly plant, which came on line in 1974, represents the first stage. The design of the Kalmar plant was far less innovative than Volvo management and outside observers made it out to be at the time. Kalmar and other Volvo plants experimented with stationary "dock assembly" on a small scale in the mid-1970s, but these experiments were abandoned as the world eco-

10. See Alarik (1979) and Levinson (1979) on union participation at the group level in the 1970s. It is itself significant that no one has pursued this line of research: more recent research on codetermination at Volvo has almost exclusively focused on work organization and new technology.

11. Berggren (1990) provides a comprehensive and detailed account of this development. In English, see Berggren (1989), Auer and Riegler (1990), and Pontusson (1992).

nomic crisis hit Volvo. More generally, management retreated from reformist ambitions articulated earlier and tightened its control over the work process at Kalmar in the second half of the 1970s.

Three new plants that began operations in 1980–81 represent the second stage of workplace reform. In addition to a new body plant (known by the acronym TAÖ), Volvo constructed a small assembly facility (TUN) at its main plant complex at Torslanda in connection with the launch of its new model (the 700 series) in 1980. Also, Volvo opened a new assembly plant for heavy trucks at Tuve in 1981. These three plants were conceived to operate on teamwork principles that went beyond the Kalmar model by providing work teams with more collective responsibilities and decision-making autonomy.

The new assembly plant at Uddevalla, starting production in 1988, goes further beyond the Kalmar model by linking the new conception of teamwork to dock assembly. At Uddevalla, teams of eight to ten workers are supposed to build an entire car. The third stage of workplace reform also involves modernizing the main final assembly plant at Torslanda (TC), which until recently operated on completely conventional lines. It remains to be seen how far the TC modernization will go in the direction of the Uddevalla model. Nonetheless, the workplace reforms at Volvo to date can be viewed as a cumulative process of innovation, with a path that is quite distinctive from a comparative perspective (Streeck 1987; Pontusson 1992). Volvo's approach to the redesign of assembly work might well be characterized as a "worker-friendly" alternative to Japanization. At least this is how union officials at Volvo conceive it.

Volvo's approach involves job enlargement (each worker performs more assembly operations) as well as job rotation. Whereas the average job cycle at traditional car assembly lines is about two minutes, job cycles at Volvo's Kalmar plant range between twenty and twenty-five minutes, and job cycles at the Uddevalla plant might be as long as four hours. What is most distinctive about Volvo's approach, however, is its pursuit of job enrichment within the framework of (relatively) autonomous work teams and the elimination of machine pacing. In the 1980s Volvo has extended the range of tasks assigned to work teams to include administrative chores previously carried out by foremen, routine machine maintenance, and "housekeeping" in the team area. Certain tasks, such as machine maintenance, require special qualifications, but the official goal is that all team members be able to perform all team tasks. Training programs are provided to workers who wish to gain the necessary qualifications.

Whereas the work teams at Kalmar originally had no shared tasks to perform or any decision-making authority, the new team concept of the 1980s requires work teams to allocate their collective responsibilities among their members (within the constraints of qualification requirements set by management). The teams are also responsible for scheduling vacation time and other personal leaves, and they participate in hiring and training new workers. Each team has an *ombud* who organizes team meetings, handles administrative matters, and represents the team to management, and this position can rotate among team members. At least formally, Volvo's approach to teamwork stands in marked contrast to the Japanese approach, in which teams are organized around foremen appointed by management.

As noted above, the Uddevalla plant essentially combines the conception of teamwork introduced in the early 1980s with the idea of dock assembly. Without abandoning machine pacing, previous workplace reforms at Volvo used buffers to introduce an element of self-pacing.

The ideas behind the Kalmar plant were almost completely a product of management thinking. In no way did the unions help decide on plant design and technology. They were consulted about work environment and organization, but even here their role seems to have been limited and essentially passive. This reflected the attitudes of the unions as well as management. At the time the Kalmar plant was designed, the Metalworkers Union and its Torslanda local had yet to think seriously about work organization and job redesign. Organized labor focused on institutional arrangements for codetermination at the firm level, and the unions feared that teamwork and other innovations associated with Kalmar were intended as an alternative to codetermination (Ellegård 1986:21–22).

Local union officials were more important in the planning of the TUN, TAÖ, and Tuve plants, which came on line in 1980–81. They were not brought in until rather late in the game, however. At Volvo, the conception and construction of new plants typically involves three stages. First, a "red book" sets out the objectives and parameters of the project. Its approval by the board of directors leads to the appointment of a team that will draft a "blue book," providing basic specifications for the plant to be built, including the type of technology to be used, and cost estimates. A project group is then appointed to plan in detail and to supervise actual construction. The red book for each of the plants inaugurated in 1980–81 had already been approved before consultations with the unions began, and prior management decisions constrained the scope of these consultations. Once the unions were brought in, they were represented on the project group as well as its various subcommittees. Specific decisions by the project group were also subject to formal codetermination negotiations.

In accordance with the Volvo Development Agreement of 1983, the

unions were involved in planning the Uddevalla plant from the time
the board of directors commissioned a red book.[12] The steering committee (*styrningsgrupp*) established at this time to supervise the planning
and development of the Uddevalla plant included two presidents of
Volvo locals of the Metalworkers Union as well as representatives of
white-collar unions. In addition, three Torslanda officials of the Metalworkers Union worked full time on the Uddevalla project for nearly
three years (1985–87), deliberating with the main working party (*pro-
jektledningsgruppen*) and its subgroups. Formal codetermination negotiations were avoided in this case; according to union officials, consensual
decision making by the working party and steering group made such
bargaining superfluous.

The working party's initial proposals were inspired by the Kalmar
model. To begin with, the union officials included in the working party
did not object, but discussions among union officials, including the research department of the Metalworkers Union, subsequently led to a
series of demands that ran counter to the working party's proposals. At
this juncture Volvo's top management prevailed on the steering committee to pursue alternative schemes, and academic consultants and industrial engineers committed to more far-reaching industrial innovation were given the opportunity to develop their ideas.

In the first instance, the process whereby Volvo developed its distinctive approach to job redesign was clearly driven by management
choices rather than union demands. It was not until the 1980s that the
unions became fully part of the process and articulated a coherent conception of what kind of workplace reforms they wanted.[13] There can be
no doubt, however, that the Volvo unions did indeed come to play an
active and important role in the process of innovation in the 1980s and
that the rights provided by the Codetermination Act of 1976 and the
Development Agreement of 1982 allowed them to do so. The unions
were never able to impose their solutions on management, but they
were able to influence management preferences and, in the case of
Uddevalla, to tip the balance in favor of innovators within management. Simply put, the Uddevalla plant would have been quite different
had the unions not been involved in its development.

The circumscribed character of the unions' influence through codetermination arrangements must again be emphasized. When Volvo de-

12. Ellegård (1989) describes the role of the Metalworkers Union in the Uddevalla
project; see also Ellegård, Engström, and Nilsson (1991). In addition, my treatment of
this project and of earlier experiences of union participation in the planning of new
factories draws on interviews with Ingemar Göransson of the Metalworkers research department and local union officials at Torslanda (May 1988).
13. This conception emerges most clearly in Svenska Metallindustriarbetarförbundet
(1987, 1989). See also LO (1991) and Mahon (1991).

cided to build the Uddevalla plant, the alternative was to expand capacity at its plant in Ghent, Belgium, which remains a very conventional assembly yet has achieved excellent productivity in recent years. The expansion of the Ghent plant remains a viable option for Volvo, and this obviously puts pressure on the union organizations at Uddevalla to help plant management deliver the kind of performance the group management expects.

RENEWAL FUNDS IN OPERATION

Keeping in mind their limited size, how were the renewal funds of 1985 actually used? To what extent did the funds strengthen the position of unions in codetermination bargaining? In what follows, I summarize the findings of a research project carried out by the Swedish Center for Working Life (Eriksson, Nilsson, and Ohlsson 1991; see also Ohlsson 1991).

In the bill that proposed creating renewal funds, the government stated that the funds were meant to "encourage [corporate] measures that would not otherwise be undertaken" (government bill 86, 1984–85, p. 16). Noting that "women frequently hold jobs that may be eliminated through the introduction of new technology," the government also affirmed that corporations should give special consideration to the training needs of employees lacking in educational background and skills (p. 15). The bill did not propose any legal requirements in these respects, however, nor did it stipulate how renewal funds were allocated between training and R&D. So long as expenditures were for either training or R&D and the unions agreed, corporations were free to use the funds as they saw fit.

While the government avoided political interference with corporate decision making, the 1984 legislation itself affected the interfirm allocation of renewal funds in ways that were not entirely consistent with the idea that they should especially serve the training needs of disadvantaged employees. Although corporations with adjusted profits of less than 500,000 SEK in 1985 were let off the hook, the size of renewal funds would depend on corporate profitability. As a result of these provisions, renewal funds, just like investment funds before them, came to be concentrated in large, successful manufacturing corporations—corporations that were already distinguished by high levels of spending on employee training and R&D. Within manufacturing, renewal funds ranged between 1,000 SEK per employee in the textile industry and 4,000 SEK per employee in the chemical and engineering industries at the end of 1985 (Eriksson, Nilsson, and Ohlson 1991, chap. 10). This result, apparently perverse from the point of view of manpower policy, must be related to the incomes policy origins of the RF scheme; in a sense, its immediate and overriding purpose was to reward the Metalworkers for wage restraint.

It is by no means clear that the RF scheme did in fact increase corporate investment in employee training or R&D. In the survey carried out by Eriksson, Nilsson, and Ohlsson (1991, chap. 12), 57 percent of corporations with renewal funds denied that they had devoted more resources to training, and 80 percent denied that they had devoted more to R&D as a result of the funds' existence. More significant perhaps, Eriksson, Nilsson, and Ohlsson found no correlation between increased training efforts (measured by the number of employees involved) and the size of renewal funds in 1986–87. The discrepancy in R&D intensity between corporations with and without renewal funds increased in 1986–87, but this trend predates 1985.

Turning to the intrafirm allocation of renewal funds, table 11 shows management and union assessments of their relative influence over the use of the funds. Since the unions typically consider management dominant in most matters of corporate policy, the fact that more than 50 percent of LO locals considered their influence to have been at least equal to that of management is surely significant. Yet Eriksson, Nilsson, and Ohlsson's survey shows that the unions, and the LO unions in particular, were consistently less satisfied with the allocation of renewal funds than was management.

The use of renewal funds involved three allocation decisions on which the preferences of management and unions tend to diverge. First, management and unions had to agree on the allocation of funds between employee training and R&D, and we would expect the unions to prefer a greater emphasis on training than would management. Indeed, the original proposal of the Metalworkers Union was that the funds should be exclusively devoted to training, and after the legislation extended their purposes to include R&D, the Metalworkers insisted that at least half should be devoted to training. The second issue concerns the kind of training to be financed by renewal funds. In principle we would expect the unions to push for general education or training, strengthening the marketplace power of wage earners (as sellers of labor power), whereas management would prefer to develop skills pertaining to its immediate needs (plant- or firm-specific skills). This divergence of interests was expressed most clearly in the LO unions' demand that renewal funds be used for basic education in Swedish, English, and mathematics.

Finally, and closely related to the second point, the use of renewal funds involved the allocation of training resources among groups of

Table 11. Union and management perceptions of the relative influence of unions and management over the use of renewal funds

Perception	LO unions	TCO unions	Management
Management influence greater than union influence	36%	36%	25%
Union influence greater than management influence	11	6	5
Management and union influence roughly equal	46	43	66
Unable to say	7	15	4

Source: Eriksson, Nilsson, and Ohlsson (1991, chap. 17, p. 6).

employees. At least at the national level, the LO unions adopted an explicitly redistributive approach: the funds should primarily benefit blue-collar workers, and among blue-collar workers, priority should be given to the needs of the least educated. Being primarily concerned with training as a means of improving efficiency, management was presumably less preoccupied with such considerations.

How, then, were these conflicts of interest settled? The actual allocation of renewal funds might be summarized as follows. From an aggregate point of view, just about half of the renewal funds that were used up in the first three years (1986–89) were devoted to training, the other half being spent on R&D; but within industry, training accounted for only 38 percent of total expenditures financed by renewal funds. As for the kinds of training financed by the funds, only 24 percent of corporations with renewal funds used any for basic education in Swedish, English, and mathematics, and only 4 percent devoted more than half of RF-financed training expenditures to this purpose. By comparison, in 39 percent of corporations more than half of the RF-financed training expenditures were for vocational training; 24 percent devoted more than half to "education" about the corporation itself, and 17 percent spent more than half on basic computer training (Eriksson, Nilsson, and Ohlsson 1991, chap. 14). The results of Eriksson, Nilsson, and Ohlsson's corporate survey also suggest that upper-level white-collar employees and immigrants received a smaller share of RF-financed training than their share of regular training, but that all other categories of employees received roughly the same share of training as they normally would have received (chap. 13).

Significantly, very large corporations (with more than five hundred employees) consistently diverged from this general pattern. Relative to the average response, these corporations claimed to have devoted a larger share of their renewal funds to employee training, to basic education, and to disadvantaged groups of employees. Management in these corporations also thought unions had greater influence over the use of renewal funds. The responses of industrial corporations similarly diverged from those of service corporations. The unions in large corporations appear to have been more able to take advantage of the renewal funds scheme because codetermination procedures were more thoroughly institutionalized, and these unions had more resources for developing alternative proposals on the use of renewal funds. The contrast between industry and services may also reflect the dominance of LO unions within the industrial sector, with their distinctive preference for redistributing training opportunities.[14]

To sum up, the RF scheme did indeed create opportunities for labor to influence corporate decision making, but the extent and significance of this experiment were limited on two counts. The funds created in 1985 were quite small in relation to total corporate expenditures on training and R&D, and union locals in smaller corporations were often unable to take advantage of the opportunities offered. The government could have provided for a more sustained learning experience for local unions by requiring corporations to periodically refurbish their renewal funds. It could also have strengthened the unions' bargaining position by specifying the purposes of renewal funds more precisely.

CONCLUSIONS

The experience of codetermination at Volvo illustrates two basic points that appear to hold true for large manufacturing corporations in general. The first point has to do with the kinds of decisions unions have been able to influence through codetermination. To repeat, the Volvo unions have come to wield fairly significant influence over corporate decisions pertaining to plant design, work organization, and personnel policy, but they have thus far had little if any influence over strategic investment decisions at the group level. Volvo's international engagements have never been a subject of codetermination bargaining.

14. The 1984 legislation stipulated that using renewal funds required the approval of the local union representing the majority of employees in a corporation. On the whole, the LO and TCO unions appear to have adopted a common position in bargaining with management over the use of renewal funds, but the compromises involved in their collaboration were presumably affected by the majority principle. It is also noteworthy that the 1984 legislation enabled corporate groups to transfer renewal funds from one subsidiary to another. According to Eriksson, Nilsson, and Ohlsson (1991), such transfers were common practice and tended to equalize RF resources across corporations with different rates of profit.

The second point is that union influence at the plant level has been predicated on a convergence of interests between labor and management (Stråth 1988). Again, Volvo management began to experiment with new forms of work organization on its own initiative in the early 1970s, and the unions were only gradually brought in. Management's pursuit of innovation was in the first instance driven by market pressures rather than union demands; that is, pressures to improve quality and flexibility, on the one hand, and to reduce labor turnover and absenteeism, on the other. While management came to view union collaboration as needed to achieve these goals, the unions became increasingly concerned with "work humanization" as an end in itself and also grew more sensitive to more flexible organization of production as a way to secure Volvo's competitiveness. As labor's legislative offensive of 1972–76 broadened the scope of collective bargaining and strengthened the position of local unions, new economic circumstances thus created a material basis for labor-management collaboration at the plant level.[15]

From this perspective, the practice of codetermination in the 1980s might be compared with that of industrial policy in the 1970s. Industrial policy, as noted in the previous chapter, also involved a convergence of interest between labor and certain segments of business. In both cases labor's reformist ambitions were implemented through and thwarted or deflected by the politics of class compromise. Whereas the practice of industrial policy was supported by an alliance between labor and business in declining sectors of industry, however, the practice of codetermination is above all supported by an alliance between labor and business in competitive sectors. For this reason, it is likely to prove more durable.

Why has codetermination been confined, in practice, to plant-level issues? The obvious answer is that business has not wanted to bargain with unions about overarching strategic decisions and that it has been under no legal compulsion to do so. The limits of codetermination may also reflect the unions' lack of the information and expertise needed to influence higher-level decisions, as well as their limited capacity to mobilize their members concerning such decisions. It is primarily at the plant level that the unions have the organizational resources to exercise the codetermination rights established by law (Stephens and Stephens 1982). In support of this line of reasoning, unions and management alike consider union influence over the use of renewal funds to have been much greater in the area of employee training than in research and development (Eriksson, Nilsson, and Ohlsson 1991).

15. Elsewhere I have emphasized the importance of high rates of labor turnover as a reason behind Volvo's approach to the redesign of assembly work (Pontusson 1992). Turnover is a problem not only for management, but also for local union organizations.

As we have seen, the codetermination legislation enacted in 1972–76 fell short of LO's and TCO's demands on several counts. Most notably, it did not give the unions veto power or self-determination rights. The renewal funds legislation of 1984 did give the unions veto power, but again, this scheme was an extraordinary measure of very limited scope. Since the Social Democratic governments of the 1980s did not undertake any further measures to beef up the codetermination rights of labor, it is hardly surprising that labor's influence over corporate decisions remains limited.

For whatever reasons, the SAP leadership was clearly more concerned about avoiding a confrontation with business over codetermination reform than the LO leadership was in 1972–76 (Åmark 1988:75). But LO did not begin to articulate demands for veto power and self-determination rights until very late in the legislative process, and it couched these demands as exceptions to the rule that management would retain final decision-making authority. Even in its most radical incarnation, LO itself did not demand across-the-board parity between employees and management/shareowners. Instead, LO looked to collective shareownership as the way to provide for union influence over corporate investment decisions of a strategic, overarching character.

CHAPTER SEVEN

Collective Shareownership

Elaborated by a committee chaired by Rudolf Meidner, the proposal for collective profit sharing endorsed by the LO congress of 1976 was the culmination of labor's reform offensive. Had the Meidner Plan been implemented, a gradual yet inexorable transfer of ownership from private individuals and institutions to collective "wage-earner funds" (*löntagarfonder*) would have ensued. According to Meidner (1975: 79), it would have taken thirty-five years for wage-earner funds to acquire 49 percent of the shares in a corporation operating at an average profit of 10 percent. (The higher the rate of profit, the more rapid the transfer of ownership.)

The Meidner committee conceived collective profit sharing as a means to facilitate the implementation of solidaristic wage policy, but the labor movement also looked to wage-earner funds as institutional mechanism for controlling capital. The promise of wage-earner funds was that they would link industrial policy and codetermination and would strengthen labor's bargaining position at the level of the state as well as the firm.

The Meidner committee derived its mandate from the LO congress of 1971, which decided to investigate various schemes for profit sharing and collective capital formation. The 1971 congress also decided that LO should petition the government to let the AP funds buy corporate shares. In 1973 this action ushered in a separate pension fund, the Fourth AP Fund, to invest a portion of ATP savings in the stock market.

From the beginning the SAP leaders were wary of the challenge to private ownership that the Meidner Plan entailed, and the wariness increased as the issue became a source of intense political controversy in the late 1970s and early 1980s. Opponents of the funds clearly won the struggle for public opinion. When the Social Democrats returned to power in 1982, they introduced a very limited wage-earner funds reform, with little resemblance to the original Meidner Plan. In an effort to reassure the business community and depoliticize the matter, the government took as a model the Fourth AP Fund, by now widely accepted as an integral part of the mixed economy. Indeed, the 1983 legislation might be said to have created five smaller Fourth AP Funds.

Having prevailed in the 1985 election and apparently put the issue of wage-earner funds behind them, in 1988 the Social Democrats established a Fifth AP Fund, organized exactly like the Fourth. All together, then, there now exist seven collective shareholding funds. At the end of 1990 the combined assets of these funds corresponded to 7 percent of the total value of all corporate shares listed on the stock exchange and 9 percent of the total assets of the AP funds (Ministry of Finance 1991:72).

The first part of this chapter focuses on legislative outcomes and situates the existing legal-institutional framework of collective shareholding funds in the context of the origins of and motives behind labor's pursuit of collective shareownership, successive proposals by the labor movement, and the political struggles these proposals gave rise to. What did labor hope to accomplish by introducing collective shareownership? How and why does the legal-institutional framework diverge from labor's initial proposals?

The second part focuses on institutional practices: How have collective shareholding funds behaved as institutional investors? And how have they behaved as owners of corporations? Since the wage-earner funds have operated for only six years, this analysis draws extensively on the experience of the Fourth AP Fund. (The Fifth AP Fund did not begin to operate until fall 1989 and will be ignored.) As we shall see, the experience to date falls far short of the ambitions articulated by the labor movement in the 1970s. The funds' activities have been institutionally separated from codetermination bargaining as well as industrial policy-making, and the funds are simply too small to have any significant effect on corporate decisions.

THE POLITICS OF COLLECTIVE SHAREOWNERSHIP

The story behind the 1983 wage-earner funds legislation will be presented more or less chronologically. I first describe the origins of LO's new concern with collective capital formation, then set out the legal-institutional framework of the Fourth AP Fund as established in 1973 and subsequently revised. Thereafter I turn to the Meidner Plan, subsequent wage-earner funds proposals, and the 1983 legislation. Finally, I briefly mention more recent Social Democratic initiatives bearing on these funds and the issue of collective shareownership.

The Origins of Labor's Offensive

The idea of wage-earner funds must first be situated within the logic of the Rehn-Meidner model. We saw in chapter 3 that the Rehn-Meidner model prescribed that the profits of inefficient firms or sectors be squeezed through central agreements that provided above-average wage increases for low-wage workers. The expansion of more efficient firms or sectors, benefiting from the restraint exercised by high-wage workers, would offset the employment losses caused by this profits squeeze. The crux of this strategy was to get high-wage workers and their employers to go along with solidaristic central agreements. As Martin (1979, 1984, 1985) argues, maintaining coordinated wage bargaining required that LO allow a certain amount of wage drift, but too much would defeat the whole point of solidaristic wage policy. Insofar as LO compensated low-wage workers for wage drift in the subsequent round of central bargaining, solidaristic wage bargaining might raise the average wage and squeeze corporate profits in general.

In their early writings, Rehn and Meidner assumed that a sufficiently restrictive fiscal policy would curtail wage drift by limiting the ability of the most profitable employers to bid up the price of labor. Of course this policy orientation might also generalize the profits squeeze implied by solidaristic wage policy, putting downward pressure on the overall level of industrial investment. But such effects could be at least partly offset by the pro-investment bias of corporate tax policy. Also, public sector savings might be lent to the corporate sector at low interest rates. Again, the decision to use the ATP system as a mechanism of collective savings conformed to this logic.

The report the research department presented to the LO congress of 1961 tentatively advanced the idea that excess profits generated by solidaristic wage policy should be set aside in "sectoral rationalization funds" jointly administered by unions, employers, and representatives of the public. Such funds would encourage wage restraint and could also promote the restructuring of capital (LO 1963:156–62). In its report to the 1966 congress, the LO research department reiterated the idea of sector funds, but it again did so in a most tentative manner and made no policy recommendations on this score (LO 1967:220–21). Neither in 1961 nor in 1966 did the idea become a subject of discussion at the congress itself (Åsard 1978, chap. 3).

By contrast, profit sharing and collective capital formation were discussed at length and with considerable urgency at the LO congress of 1971. Numerous motions from union locals raised the problem of excess profits and recalled the sector funds as a potential remedy. Other motions argued the case for collective capital formation to extend democratic control of investment and give wage earners more influence in industrial restructuring. No fewer than ten motions addressed the legal-institutional framework of the AP funds, arguing that the funds should be allowed to buy corporate shares and thereby assume a more active and influential role (LO 1973:10–13; see also Simonson 1988: 140–41).

Why, then, did profit sharing and collective capital formation emerge, quite suddenly, as a central concern of the union movement in the early 1970s? It was not until the second half of the 1960s that LO began to implement solidaristic wage policy in a consistent and effective manner. Also, the inherent problem of reconciling the interests of high-wage and low-wage LO members was exacerbated by the growing wage militancy of white-collar unions and the uneven development of corporate profits beginning in the late 1960s. What had previously been an intellectual problem, preoccupying the LO research department, now assumed immediate relevance for the unions, brought home most forcefully by the wildcat strikes of 1969–70, which were in part a reaction to the implementation of solidaristic wage policy by high-paid workers (cf. chap. 6).

The debate at the LO congress of 1971 was also informed by the Long-Term Economic Survey of 1970 (SOU 1970), which argued that the decline of industrial investment in the later 1960s contained a secular as well as a cyclical component, and pointed out that the self-financing capacity of industry had declined. LO explicitly invoked the survey when it subsequently petitioned the government to lift the restrictions on investment by the AP funds. Allowing the AP funds to purchase corporate shares would improve the solidity of corporations without redistributing income from workers to private owners, LO argued. It would also extend societal influence over the pattern of investment. LO's 1971 petition (reprinted in SOU 1972:19–24) affirmed that technological and economic development "necessitates a higher degree of planning and coordination within industry" and that "the union movement aspires to real influence not only over the volume of investment, but also over how, when, and where investments are made."

The Fourth AP Fund

The government responded to LO's petition regarding equity investment by the AP funds by instructing the capital market commission appointed in 1968 (Kapitalmarknadsutredningen; KMU) to consider the matter. In a special report (SOU 1972), KMU recommended that investing ATP savings in equity assets be tried, but it emphasized its risky character and proposed a series of restrictions to preserve the soundness of the ATP system as an insurance scheme. Proposing that a separate pension fund be established to invest ATP savings in the stock market, the KMU report insisted that its investment decisions should be independent of public policy considerations and that the fund should not assume an active ownership role.

The government bill that created the Fourth AP Fund (bill 97, 1973) was a compromise between LO's initial petition and KMU's report (LO 1973:16–24). The government adopted KMU's proposal of a separate fund for this purpose as well as its suggestion that the new fund initially be alloted 500 million SEK, less than 1 percent of the total assets of the AP funds at the end of 1972. But the government rejected KMU's recommendation for a ceiling on individual ownership engagements by the Fourth AP Fund. Although the government bill stipulated that the Fourth AP Fund could not purchase shares in banks and insurance companies, it did not preclude the purchase of shares in investment companies as KMU had recommended. And though it failed to provide the "clear wage-earner majority" that LO had demanded, the bill also modified KMU's recommendations on the composition of the board of directors of the Fourth AP Fund, strengthening trade-union representation.

Organized business opposed the Fourth AP Fund as a threat to market allocation of capital and the autonomy of corporate management and held that the proposed reform would simply divert public savings from the bond market to the stock market, pushing share prices up rather than increasing the supply of risk capital. While the Liberals and the Conservatives essentially reproduced these objections in the parliamentary debate, the Center party sought to project itself as a "third force" by advocating that the voting rights gained through ownership engagements by the Fourth AP Fund be exercised by the employees of the firm in question. Once the government bill had been passed, the Liberals also embraced this proposal, which challenged LO's idea of the Fourth AP Fund as an instrument of industrial policy in the name of industrial democracy (Nordfors and Herrström 1976).

After the 1973 election, which ended in a perfect tie between the two parliamentary blocs, the Social Democrats made several concessions to the Center party and the Liberals to avoid further confrontation over the constitution of the Fourth AP Fund. Most notably, the government supported a motion that let the Fourth AP Fund delegate up to 60 percent of its shareholder votes to local union representatives.

Submitted in 1978, KMU's final report (SOU 1978a) presented no evidence to support the fears voiced by opponents of the Fourth AP Fund. The only legal-institutional change KMU recommended was that the fund should, as a matter of principle, be subject to the same restriction on individual ownership as were insurance companies, but it proposed raising this restriction from 5 percent to 10 percent of shareholder votes. In an omnibus bill on capital-market arrangements (government bill 165, 1978–79), the government adopted KMU's 10 percent recommendation for the Fourth AP Fund but left the restriction on insurance companies at 5 percent. The bourgeois parties thus retreated somewhat from the principle that the same rules should apply to both. The 1979 legislation also affirmed the principle that the Fourth AP Fund shared fiduciary responsibility for the ATP system by stipulating that 80 percent of its annual earnings (now tax exempt) be used for pension payments.

The 1979 legislation marked the end of the bourgeois parties' opposition to the Fourth AP Fund. Having previously cut back each of the fund's requests for new capital allotments, in 1981 they approved an unprecedented allotment of 600 million SEK. KMU's final report seems to have legitimated the Fourth AP Fund in their eyes, and the legal-institutional changes introduced in 1979 presumably further reassured them. The bourgeois parties' ability to appoint their own representatives to the fund's board of directors may also have been significant, giving them a better sense of how the Fourth AP Fund actually operated.

The Meidner Plan

The report Meidner and his collaborators submitted to the LO congress of 1976 (LO 1976) proposed, in essence, that ownership of a share of corporate profits be transferred from private shareholders to wage earners as a collective group. By law, corporations above a certain size would be required to issue new shares corresponding to some portion of their annual profits to a central fund representing all wage earners. The Meidner committee suggested fifty or one hundred employees as the threshold for obligatory participation in the system and proposed that the portion of annual profits to be issued in new stocks be set at 20 percent. The share of the equity capital of a corporation that wage earners would acquire each year would be determined by the relationship between 20 percent of the corporation's profits and its net value (in real terms). Consequently the transfer of ownership would be more rapid the higher the rate of profit.

The Meidner committee proposed that the capital the wage-earner

collective acquired remain part of the working capital of the corporation that generated it. Only in exceptional circumstances would wage-
earner shares be traded. The central fund to which shares would be
issued would simply allocate the dividends these shares yielded. Voting
rights and other ownership prerogatives would be exercised exclusively
by local unions until wage-earner shares represented 20 percent of a
corporation's equity capital. Above that threshold, ownership would be
vested in sectorally based fund boards appointed mainly by the national
unions but including representatives of other societal interests.

The Meidner committee rejected the idea of individual ownership
claims and also the idea that the dividends yielded by collectively
owned shares should be distributed to individual wage earners. A portion of the dividends would have to be set aside to purchase newly
issued shares, so that new share issues would not reduce the wage earners' stake in a given firm. The rest of the dividends should finance
adult education, wage-earner consultants, and various other programs
to help wage earners, and union activists in particular, take advantage
of the new labor laws and exercise their ownership role. The gradual
transfer of ownership would thus be accompanied by new competence
within the ranks of the union movement.

The Meidner committee identified three basic goals this scheme was
designed to achieve. First, the proposed system would bolster the
unions' solidaristic wage policy by neutralizing "excess profits." Second,
it would counteract the concentration of wealth and reconcile the need
to improve the financial solidity of industry with labor's redistributive
ambitions. Finally, the scheme would complement the industrial democracy reforms of the early 1970s by giving organized labor direct
influence over corporate decision making (LO 1976:15–19).

As Meidner himself pointed out (Meidner 1975:112–13), the proposed scheme would not enhance labor's influence over the interfirm
allocation of investment capital, for the capital to be owned by the
wage-earner collective would remain as working capital in the firms
that had generated it. Yet the buildup of wage-earner funds would
make it possible to democratize corporate investment decisions of strategic significance for society at large. As conceived by the Meidner
committee, this represented a "new level of wage-earner influence" between overall planning (the primary concern of labor's industrial policy
offensive) and concrete workplace conditions (the primary concern of
the labor laws promulgated in the early 1970s). In particular, the committee emphasized that wage-earner funds might help prevent multinational firms from moving employment and R&D abroad (LO 1976:68–
76, 87–88).

The Meidner committee clearly did not see "wage-earner influence" simply in terms of employees' ability to sway management decisions directly affecting them. Corporations with significant wage-earner ownership could be expected to be "more sensitive to the demands of industrial policy," it argued, and collaboration with "societal organs of industrial policy" would be one of the wage-earner funds' overarching tasks: "One can imagine the increased effectiveness that even today's industrial policy [as distinct from a future, more ambitious industrial policy?] would have if its intentions were actually followed up on the boards of directors of individual firms" (LO 1976:107). These formulations suggest that the Meidner Plan was informed by a sense of the inadequacy of the institutional reforms associated with labor's industrial policy offensive. At the same time, it rested on the premise that corporate profitability should determine the allocation of capital among firms and sectors.

Subsequent Wage-Earner Fund Proposals

The LO leaders apparently decided to recommend endorsing the Meidner Plan to the LO congress of 1976 without consulting the SAP leaders. Whereas the bourgeois parties attacked the Meidner Plan on ideological grounds, the Social Democrats sought to sidestep the issue of wage-earner funds in the election campaign that began shortly after the LO congress. The official SAP line was that no legislative action could be undertaken until a public commission appointed in 1975 had investigated the matter. It soon became apparent, however, that Olof Palme and other prominent figures in the SAP had serious reservations about the Meidner Plan.[1]

After the 1976 election, LO and SAP appointed a joint working group to resolve their differences and come up with a new proposal for wage-earner funds, and this group submitted a report to the SAP congress of 1978 (LO-SAP 1978). Although the congress committed the party to the idea of wage-earner funds, it raised a number of objections to the scheme proposed by the LO-SAP group, and the Social Democrats contested the 1979 elections without a firm position on what the proposed wage-earner funds should look like. In a second report, the LO-SAP group presented yet another proposal (LO-SAP 1981) whose principles were endorsed by the SAP and LO congresses of 1981.[2]

---

1. This emerges most clearly in the recently published memoirs of Kjell-Olof Feldt (1991).

2. Useful discussions of successive wage-earner fund proposals, and the debate surrounding them, include Åsard (1978, 1985), Meidner (1981), Himmelstrand et al. (1981), Albrecht and Deutsch (1983), Martin (1984), Heclo and Madsen (1986, chap. 6), Swenson (1989, chap. 5), and Olsen (1990).

Though they retained elements of the original Meidner Plan, the 1978 and 1981 proposals retreated from its more radical ambitions. These changes manifested the distinctive concerns of the SAP leaders, but they were also a response to critics outside the labor movement and a joint LO-SAP effort to set the stage for a broad-based compromise on wage-earner funds.

To begin with, the 1978 and 1981 proposals shifted the argument for wage-earner funds from redistributing wealth and power to increasing the rate of investment. Whereas from the very beginning the SAP leaders were interested in wage-earner funds primarily for wage restraint, the investment slump in the late 1970s convinced LO that to restore economic growth a portion of national income would have to be shifted from labor to capital. The problem of raising the level of savings and investment without redistributing income from wage earners to capitalists was exacerbated by the rapid decline of the ATP system as a mechanism of collective savings after 1974.

To promote savings and make the link to wage restraint more direct, the 1978 and 1981 proposals both stipulated that wage-earner funds should partly be built up through a special payroll tax. At the same time, they scaled down collective profit sharing substantially. The 1978 proposal restricted obligatory profit sharing to firms with more than five hundred employees, and the 1981 proposal reduced the program further by restricting it to "excess profits"—profits above a certain (variable) level to be determined by the government.

The 1978 proposal comprised two separate fund schemes. Based on collective profit sharing, wage-earner funds would be built up through the obligatory issue of new shares. The payroll tax introduced by the 1978 proposal would provide the basis for a second set of funds, "development funds," which would acquire corporate stocks through market transactions. The 1981 proposal restored a unitary structure by replacing obligatory share issues with a tax on excess profits. Like the payroll tax, the revenues generated by this form of collective profit sharing would be transferred to twenty-four regional wage-earner funds (one in each county), and these funds would in turn invest the money by purchasing corporate shares. Ownership would thus be collectivized entirely through market transactions.

While reaffirming the Meidner committee's rejection of individual ownership claims, the 1981 proposal sought to give individual wage earners a stake in the proposed reform by linking wage-earner funds to the ATP system. The tax revenues that would build up wage-earner funds would now be channeled via the ATP system, and the funds would be required to plow some of their earnings back into it. Shoring up the fiscal solvency of the ATP system thus became another justification for introducing wage-earner funds. The other side of this innovation was that dividends would no longer be used to promote union activities and codetermination at the firm level. In contrast to the 1978 proposal as well as the original Meidner Plan, the 1981 proposal made no mention of using dividends this way.

By substituting share purchases for obligatory share issues, the 1978 and 1981 proposals made wage-earner funds conform to the market economy. Yet this change enhanced the potential for investment steering by making it possible to move capital between firms or sectors. The so-called development funds proposed in 1979 were explicitly part of an offensive industrial policy. These funds were to promote investment, technical development, and the establishment of new firms in close coordination with government bodies and to play "an important role" within "the active sectoral planning on behalf of society required to overcome sectoral problems" (LO-SAP 1978:52–54). Wage-earner funds were thus presented as part of the Social Democratic alternative to the industrial policy measures undertaken by the bourgeois parties in 1976–78.

The connection between the labor movement's pursuit of wage-earner funds and the experience of industrial policy emerges most clearly in the report on industrial policy submitted to the 1981 LO congress (LO 1981). This report treated the introduction of wage-earner funds as a precondition for an offensive industrial policy based on direct negotiations between the state, organized labor, and big corporations in the advanced sectors of the economy. While the ownership influence of wage-earner funds was supposed to make these corporations more willing to collaborate with the government, the report suggested that managing the funds would provide the unions with the information and technical-administrative competence needed to participate in industrial policy negotiations.

By contrast, the joint LO-SAP wage-earner funds proposal of 1981 did not discuss problems of industrial policy. It reaffirmed the ambition to extend "wage-earner influence" but apparently conceived it entirely in terms of influence within the firm. Whereas the 1978 proposal spoke of the need to provide risk capital for specific corporations or investment projects, the 1981 proposal cited the need to improve the solidity of export-oriented corporations in general (LO-SAP 1981:31–32, 64–68).

The industrial policy report to the 1981 LO congress and the joint LO-SAP proposal of 1981 support two different interpretations of labor's pursuit of wage-earner funds. On the one hand, wage-earner funds can be seen as an institutional reform designed to enhance the labor movement's ability to restructure capital selectively. On the other hand, they can be seen as an effort to escape protectionist pressures and other problems associated with selective industrial policies through a "social contract" that would restore market incentives for private business to increase domestic investment and employment. From the latter perspective, wage-earner funds are designed primarily to encourage wage restraint by neutralizing its regressive distributive effects.

These two conceptions can be identified with different currents within the labor movement, but they also reflect a basic ambivalence pervading the outlook of the labor movement as a whole. The wage-earner funds legislation of 1983 resolved this ambivalence in favor of the market-oriented, distributive approach, yet it represented a further retreat in the scale of the reform.

The Wage-Earner Funds Reform of 1983

The initial response of organized business to the Meidner Plan was guarded. Although critical of the Meidner committee's proposals, business leaders expressed an interest in employee shareholding and advertised their willingness to discuss the forms it might take. It was not until 1978–79 that organized business turned against the whole idea of funds and seriously began to mobilize public opinion against them. As table 12 shows, the media campaign against wage-earner funds was very successful. Clearly, the Social Democrats won the 1982 election despite rather than because of the issue of wage-earner funds.[3]

The shift of public opinion against wage-earner funds was especially pronounced in the white-collar unions. Having initially adopted a positive view of the idea of collective profit sharing, the TCO leadership

Table 12. Voters' views of wage-earner funds, 1976–82

	For	Against	Undecided
All voters			
1976	33%	43%	24%
1979	32	45	23
1982	22	61	17
SAP voters			
1976	55	18	27
1979	58	15	27
1982	43	29	28

Source: Holmberg (1984:170, 186).

3. See Gilljam (1988) for a detailed analysis of public opinion about wage-earner funds.

was forced to retreat to neutrality by 1979–80. This in turn under-mined Social Democratic efforts to strike a deal with the Liberals or the Center party. In marked contrast to the traditional pattern of public commissions of inquiry, the commission to investigate wage-earner funds thus completely failed to obtain a consensus (see Åsard 1985). The commission's final report, submitted in 1981 (SOU 1981b), consis-ted of background information and analysis and did not include any discussion of principles, let alone any legislative recommendations.

The change of government in 1982 did not resolve the political deadlock over wage-earner funds. Shunning another public commis-sion of inquiry representing a broad range of interests, the new gov-ernment instructed three committees of experts to develop legislative proposals dealing with specific aspects of wage-earner funds. When these committees had completed their work in August 1983, the gov-ernment invited twenty-five organizations to individual consultations. This initiative plainly failed: every single business organization declined the government's invitation, the bourgeois parties announced before-hand that they were not prepared to negotiate over wage-earner funds, and the TCO leaders showed up only to inform the government that they would neither support nor oppose any forthcoming reform. Un-der pressure from LO, the government nonetheless submitted a bill (government bill 50, 1983–84), which Parliament passed in December 1983.

It should come as no surprise that the 1983 legislation was much less ambitious than any of the wage-earner funds proposals previously ad-vanced by the labor movement. To reassure the business community and remove the issue of wage-earner funds from electoral politics, the government relied on the Fourth AP Fund as a model for wage-earner funds (Ministry of Finance 1983).

Like the wage-earner funds proposal adopted by the LO and SAP congresses of 1981, the 1983 legislation provided for the buildup of wage-earner funds through a payroll tax and a tax on excess profits, linking the funds directly to the ATP system. The payroll tax was set at 0.2 percent (compared with 1 percent in the 1981 proposal) and the profits tax at 20 percent of inflation-adjusted profits above 500,000 SEK (1 million SEK as of 1986) or 6 percent of a firm's total payroll, whichever would be higher. Each fund would get one-fifth of the an-nual revenue generated in this fashion, but no more than an inflation-adjusted amount, set at 400 million SEK for 1984. (Any revenue above the total capital allotment to the five wage-earner funds was to be ab-sorbed by the ATP system.) Most important, the 1983 legislation re-stricted the buildup of wage-earner funds to seven years (1984–90).

Although the five wage-earner funds created in 1983 were constituted regionally, the government bill emphasized they should not assume any responsibility for regional employment. To prevent the funds from subsidizing, the 1983 legislation stipulated that each must pay back 3 percent of the current value of the money it has received from the ATP system. If a fund fails to realize a real rate of return of 3 percent, its assets will shrink. The 1983 legislation also stipulated that individual ownership engagements by any one wage-earner fund must not exceed 8 percent of shareholder votes in corporations listed on the stock exchange, and that the funds should delegate 50 percent of their votes to local unions if the latter so requested.

As part of the 1983 legislation, the government dropped the provision that the Fourth AP Fund should pay 80 percent of its annual earnings into the ATP system and instead subjected the fund to the same real rate of return requirement as the wage-earner funds (3 percent). The legislation preserved the 10 percent limit on the Fourth AP Fund's ownership engagements that the bourgeois parties had imposed in 1979, but it exempted ownership in unlisted corporations from this limit (an exemption that also applies to the wage-earner funds).

At the time, LO argued that the 1983 legislation was an interim measure. At the end of the seven years during which the wage-earner funds were to be built up, the experience of the funds would be assessed and the infusion of new capital considered. The minister of finance (Kjell-Olof Feldt) and the prime minister (Olof Palme), however, both stated explicitly in the parliamentary debate that they considered the 1983 reform a one-shot deal.

Toward a Further Extension of Collective Shareownership?

The economic recovery of the 1980s, as we saw in chapter 4, did not resolve the problems LO sought to address by introducing wage-earner funds. While high corporate profits fueled wage drift, the multinationalization of Swedish business accelerated during the 1980s. For the labor movement, these developments underscored the limits of the wage-earner funds legislation of 1983. Rather than pushing for the continued buildup of wage-earner funds, however, LO now began to advocate legislation that would let the original AP funds acquire corporate shares. Apparently LO thought that collective shareownership might thus be extended without reviving the wage-earner funds debate.

As expressed in a report presented in 1988 (LO 1988), LO's case for reform of the AP funds avoided the issue of control over capital (see also LO 1991). Instead, LO couched this new initiative in terms of the need to increase the revenues of the ATP system and make the financial system more efficient. Adjusting itself to the prevailing ideological climate, LO argued that the restrictions on investment of ATP savings were inconsistent with the government's policy of deregulating capital markets. If banks and insurance companies were to be allowed a broader range of investment opportunities, why shouldn't this principle also apply to the AP funds? Noting that the existing rules prevented the AP funds from realizing a return commensurate with that of private insurance companies, LO argued further that allowing the funds to purchase corporate shares would improve the solvency of the ATP system and make it possible to keep the rate of ATP contributions down (LO 1988:56–57).

The programmatic report endorsed by the 1989 congress of the Metalworkers Union (Svenska Metallindustriarbetarförbundet 1989) echoed these themes but also argued the case for reform of the legal-institutional framework of the AP funds in terms of the multinationalization of Swedish business. Anticipating a further rapprochement with the European Community, this report argued in effect that governments could no longer control the movement of private capital across national borders. Allowing the AP funds and other forms of "national capital" to supply Swedish industry with risk capital would counteract the consequences of this development (see also LO 1991).

In response to LO's demands, the government introduced legislation in 1988 (government bill 167, 1987–88) that created a Fifth AP Fund with the same organizational structure and subject to the same rules as the Fourth AP Fund. In so doing it invoked KMU's final report, which had argued that the Fourth AP Fund had reached an optimal size relative to the stock market and that any further investment of ATP savings in the stock market should be channeled through a new fund (SOU 1978a:486–87; see also Ministry of Finance 1988). To maintain the same overall (50 percent) ceiling on collective shareholding funds' ownership of individual corporations, the 1988 legislation lowered the limits on ownership engagements by wage-earner funds from 8 percent to 6 percent of shareholder votes. Nonetheless, organized business and the bourgeois parties opposed the Fifth AP Fund as yet another encroachment on the principles of private ownership and free enterprise and as a betrayal of the government's promise that the wage-earner funds reform of 1983 was a one-shot deal (see, e.g., Widén 1990).

In March 1991 the government suddenly presented a proposal for a comprehensive reorganization of the AP funds (Ministry of Finance 1991), to be sent out for official commentaries before a legislative bill is drafted. Under this proposal, the original three AP funds, the Fourth and Fifth AP Funds, and the five wage-earner funds of 1983 would be reorganized into five entirely separate pension funds of equal size (and with equal responsibility for meeting ATP payments). The new funds would be required to hold 40 percent of their assets in bonds but would be free to invest the remaining 60 percent as they saw fit—for example, in real estate or corporate shares. Since the total assets of the existing funds were 430 billion SEK at the end of 1990, this would mean they could invest some 260 billion SEK outside the bond market—equal to 47 percent of the current value of the stock market! The proposal stated that the new funds should not seek an active ownership role; rather, their efforts should be "oriented toward efficient portfolio management [*effektiv kapitalförvaltning*] to a greater extent than is the case today."

For all the government's assurances that the proposed scheme was meant solely to promote more efficient market allocation of capital and to increase the return on ATP savings, its proposal had radical implications for the structure of ownership, and it is hardly surprising that organized business and the bourgeois have denounced it. Why, then, did the Social Democrats apparently cave in to LO pressure and introduce a reform proposal that was bound to precipitate a new debate about collective ownership?

The proposal to reorganize the AP funds must be situated in the context of the collapse of public support for the Social Democrats in 1989–90.[4] The polls showed that it was primarily traditional Social Democratic voters, and LO members in particular, who abandoned the Social Democrats, and that they did so in reaction against the tax reform of 1989 and subsequent austerity measures implemented through agreements with one or several of the bourgeois parties. The party leaders seem to have figured that a polarizing debate over collective shareownership would bring back some of these deserters and that such a debate would be preferable to abandoning the tax reform or reorienting macroeconomic policy.

The proposal to reorganize the AP funds might thus be seen as a somewhat desperate election ploy. Though the Social Democrats did indeed recover a great deal of popular support in the 1991 election campaign, their share of the vote fell below 40 percent for the first time since 1928 (and by quite a margin, as their share was only 37.6 percent). Not surprisingly, the policy declaration of the new coalition government reaffirmed the bourgeois parties' commitment to dismantling the wage-earner funds of 1983 by distributing their shares to the citizenry.

---

4. As late as fall 1990, the Ministry of Finance presented a proposal for new rules for the AP funds that did not involve shareownership (Ministry of Finance 1990).

The significance of the Social Democrats' 1991 proposal to reorganize the AP funds extends beyond short-term electoral considerations, however. As widely noted at the time, the proposal spoke quite explicitly to the potential problem that EC membership poses to Swedish capitalists' ability to maintain control over their corporations. Traditionally, Swedish capitalists have enjoyed legal protection against foreign takeovers and maintained control over their corporations by issuing new shares ("B shares") with less voting power than their own shares ("A shares"). EC membership makes such restrictions doubtful, and ownership engagements by the AP funds could be seen by at least some capitalists as a way to counter the threat of hostile takeovers by foreign interests.[5] From this perspective, the Social Democrats were angling for a new compromise with business.

COLLECTIVE SHAREHOLDING FUNDS IN OPERATION

As the new government intends to dismantle the wage-earner funds, this is a good time to take stock of the experience of such funds. How have collective shareholding funds behaved as institutional investors? And how have they behaved as (part) owners of corporations? Since 1980, the Fourth AP Fund has bought shares not only in corporations that are listed on the stock exchange, but also in unlisted corporations. The wage-earner funds have also invested outside the stock exchange. Though unlisted assets account for only a small share of their assets, this is an important aspect of the funds' investment activity, which must be considered separately. I will first make some preliminary remarks about the size, performance, and organization of collective shareholding funds. Subsequent sections deal with their role as portfolio investors, their role as owners of listed corporations, and their engagements in unlisted corporations.[6]

5. See Sven-Ivan Sundkvist, "Staten bättre än uppstickarna," *Dagen Nyheter*, February 10, 1991.
6. Again, the following analysis ignores the fifth AP Fund, which began to operate in 1989. The analysis of the Fourth AP Fund covers 1974–89, and the analysis of the wage-earner funds covers 1984–89. (Annual reports for 1990 have yet to appear.) For reasons of space, I shall ignore differences among the five wage-earner funds, and for simplicity I shall refer to the wage-earner funds by number. All but one fund have adopted names that reflect their regional affiliation. From one to five, their names are Sydfonden, Fond Väst, Trefond Invest, Mellansvenska Löntagarfonden, and Nordfonden. In addition to the published sources cited below, my analysis draws on interviews with Lennart Dahlström, executive director of the Fourth AP Fund from 1974 to 1979 (June 1, 1983); Sten Wikander, executive manager of the Fourth AP Fund from 1979 to 1988 (May 10, 1983); Lars Ljung, LO representative on the board of the Fourth AP Fund from 1974 to 1982 (May 4, 1983); Kurt Lanneberg, TCO representative on the board of the Fourth AP

Size and Performance

From 1974 through 1988, any new transfer of capital from the ATP savings system to the Fourth AP Fund had to be approved by Parliament. As of 1989, the Fourth AP Fund and the newly created Fifth AP Fund are each entitled to dispose of 1 percent of the assets of the original three AP funds. For 1989 this amounted to an upper ceiling of 3,291 million SEK for each fund. By the end of the year the accumulated transfer of ATP savings to the Fourth AP Fund equaled 3,000 million SEK. The Fifth AP Fund requisitioned 500 million SEK during 1989, its first year of operation.

The 1983 legislation provided each wage-earner fund with an annual inflation-adjusted capital allotment of 400 million SEK. The Fourth Wage-Earner Fund requisitioned only part of its allotment in 1987–89 (saving the rest for future use), but the other four funds have requisitioned their entire allotments each year. All together, the five wage-earner funds had received 13,032 million SEK out of an accumulated allotment of 14,290 million SEK at the end of 1989.

Thanks to an unprecedented stock market boom, the Fourth AP Fund and each of the wage-earner funds realized a real rate of return far above 3 percent in the 1980s. In 1989 prices, the Fourth AP Fund received 5,835 million SEK from the ATP system from 1974 through 1989. At the end of 1989, it held securities with a market value of 22,310 million SEK and liquid assets worth 1,346 million SEK. The real value of the fund's assets thus quadrupled in fifteen years. The Fourth AP Fund also contributed 1,253 million SEK (in 1989 prices) to ATP payments during this period. The corresponding figures for the five wage-earner funds (again treated jointly) are as follows: in 1989 prices, the funds received 15,234 million SEK from the ATP system from 1984 through 1989. At the end of 1989 they held securities with a market value of 22,683 million SEK and an additional 932 million SEK in liquid assets. At the same time, the funds contributed 1,234 million SEK (1989 prices) to ATP payments during their first five years in operation.

Despite a major setback in 1984 and the worldwide crash of October 1987, the index of shares listed on the stock exchange increased from

Fund since 1974 (May 31, 1984); Dan Anderson, LO representative on the board of the Fourth AP Fund since 1982 (April 26, 1990); and Lennart Låftman, executive director of the Fourth Wage-Earner Fund (April 25, 1990). Sten Wikander also provided extensive written comments on an earlier version of my analysis of the Fourth AP Fund. Unless otherwise noted, all quantitative data come from the following sources: AP Fund 4 (1974–89), Wage-Earner Funds 1–5 (1984–89), and RRV (1988, 1989).

120 at the end of 1979 to an all-time peak of 1,689 in August 1989 (AP Fund 4 1979, 1989). Having underperformed the market in the 1970s, the Fourth AP Fund outperformed it for most of the 1980s. The wage-earner funds' performance varied markedly, but altogether they underperformed the market slightly in the second half of the 1980s. Had their portfolios performed exactly like the stock exchange index, their assets would have been worth 3 percent more than they in fact were at the end of 1989.

For our present purposes, of course, it is the relative size of collective shareholding funds that matters most. Again, the combined assets of the Fourth AP Fund, the Fifth AP Fund, and the five wage-earner funds corresponded to about 7 percent of the total value of all corporate shares listed on the stock exchange at the end of 1990 (6.4 percent at the end of 1989). The Fourth AP Fund accounted for roughly half of this figure. In the early 1980s the Fourth AP Fund became the second largest owner of listed shares—the largest being Skandia, a private insurance company—but by the end of 1989 it had fallen to seventh place (Sundkvist 1990).

Board Representation and Decision Making

Nothing ever came of LO's original notion that the Fourth AP Fund should be part of the institutional framework of industrial policy. Investment decisions by the Fourth AP Fund have never been a subject of consultation, let alone bargaining, between the fund and the Ministry of Industry (or any other ministry). The fund's managing directors have avoided such consultation, and neither Social Democratic nor bourgeois governments have made any effort to integrate the fund's investment activities into the industrial policy-making process.

The structure of interest representation on the board of the Fourth AP Fund (and the Fifth AP Fund as well) is tripartite. Today the board has fourteen members. Five board members represent organized labor, three of them nominated by LO and two by TCO. Three board members represent private business, nominated by SAF, the Federation of Industry, and a small-business association. Two board members represent cooperative business, and two others represent municipal governments. Finally, the government appoints the chairperson and deputy chairperson without soliciting nominations.

Compared with the boards of the original AP funds, the deliberations of the board of the Fourth AP Fund have been lively. Different views have been counterposed, and when efforts to reach consensus have failed, the majority view has prevailed. However, such conflicts have been narrow in focus and have occurred within the framework of a broad consensus on the overall orientation of the fund's investment policy as well as its role as owner. What distinguishes the Fourth AP Fund from the original AP funds is not the lack of consensus or collaboration among different interests, but rather that the fund has had more meaningful choices to make.

The legislation that established the Fourth AP Fund was accompanied by an amendment of the Company Statute allowing firms to bypass the provision that new shares first had to be offered to existing owners. Volvo immediately took advantage of this amendment by offering the Fourth AP Fund new shares for 108 million SEK, a deal that accounted for more' than half of the fund's total investment in its first year, but no firms have subsequently exercised the option to issue new shares directly to the Fourth AP Fund. While the fund has typically subscribed to new share issues that it is entitled to buy in its capacity as an existing owner, it has had to rely on the secondary market for new ownership engagements.

Transactions in the secondary market require quick decisions, which are made by the managing director based on an ongoing staff effort to identify firms whose stocks the fund might want to buy. Typically the board of directors, which meets five times a year, discusses the overall orientation of investment policy and makes general decisions (e.g., to alter the portfolio's sectoral composition), but it approves individual investment decisions only ex post. When individual transactions exceed a certain sum of money or might be construed as controversial, the managing director consults the board's executive committee (Wikander 1988:95).

The wage-earner funds bill of 1983 did not dwell on board representation. In practice, the provision that a majority of board members should be "wage-earner representatives" has meant that the unions got to nominate five members of each board (LO three and TCO two). Whereas the union representatives on the board of the Fourth AP Fund include the presidents of LO and TCO, those on the boards of the wage-earner funds tend to be local union officials.

The other members of the wage-earner fund boards are not directly nominated by any organization. Thus far, private business has boycotted participation on such boards (LO 1987:17). In 1988 twelve out of forty-five board members were corporate executives, but they were drawn entirely from state-owned and cooperative firms. In addition to twenty-five union officials and twelve corporate executives, the boards include an assortment of politicians and civil servants. Generally speaking, the boards of the wage-earner funds appear to have been more active in fund management than the board of the Fourth AP Fund. In at least one case, all investment decisions must be approved in advance by the board's executive committee.

The Funds as Portfolio Investors

The legislation that set up the Fourth AP Fund prohibited the fund from acquiring shares in banks and insurance companies but otherwise left it free to decide what shares to acquire, stating simply that the basic purpose of the reform was "to provide business with more equity capital for the benefit of industrial expansion and increased employment" (government bill 97, 1973, p. 65). Similarly, the new legislation adopted in 1983 affirmed that investments by the wage-earner funds as well as the Fourth AP Fund should "aim to improve the supply of risk capital for the benefit of Swedish production and employment," adding that their capital should be invested to satisfy three requirements: good return on investment, long-term orientation, and diversification of risks (law 1092, 1983, par. 34). Although the law specified the return-on-investment requirement, it left the other two requirements unspecified. The wage-earner funds were from the beginning allowed to acquire bank and insurance shares, and this restriction on the Fourth AP Fund was subsequently lifted.

The Fourth AP Fund never formally adopted an investment policy, but its managing directors and board members consistently articulate four general policy principles the fund has adhered to. First, the fund has always conceived of itself as a portfolio investor: it seeks to invest in a fairly large number of firms and avoids direct involvement in their day-to-day management. Second, the bulk of the fund's investments should be based on long-term commitments rather than on speculative considerations. Third, its portfolio should emphasize manufacturing firms, especially those that are export oriented and employ many people. Within these bounds, finally, individual investment decisions should aim for maximum return on investment.

Four out of five wage-earner funds adopted, and sometimes amended, explicit statements on investment policy in the second half of the 1980s (see Wage-Earner Funds 1–5, 1984–89). Concerning the portfolio of listed firms, however, the policy statements say very little, and what they do say does not add much to the general and rather vague provisions of the law. Although the rhetoric of the wage-earner funds frequently echoes the policy principles of the Fourth AP Fund, their actual investments differ from those of the Fourth AP Fund in three respects: their portfolios are more diversified; they have traded more actively; and their sectoral profile is less distinctive.

Portfolio concentration. At the end of 1978, the Fourth AP Fund held shares in thirty-one corporations listed on the stock exchange. Unlisted corporations were added to the portfolio in the 1980s. By the end of 1983 the portfolio included fifty-seven corporations (eleven unlisted), and by the end of 1989, this figure had risen to seventy-nine (twenty-six unlisted). On the average, the portfolios of the wage-earner funds included sixty-two corporations (eleven unlisted) at the end of 1989.

Measured in terms of the relative importance of the five or ten largest holdings, the concentration of the Fourth AP Fund's portfolio declined markedly from 1973 to 1983 but has subsequently remained stable. At the end of 1989, the five largest holdings accounted for 40 percent and the ten largest for 61 percent of portfolio worth. In a recurrent formulation, the fund's annual reports refer to the ten to fifteen largest holdings as "strategic" in the sense that "their evolution is decisive for the evolution of the portfolio as a whole," but they insist the fund "does not have any holdings that are strategic in the sense that they are intended to secure control of business or that they constitute part of a permanent ownership constellation" (AP Fund 4 1985:9). The latter part of this formulation is meant to distinguish the Fourth AP Fund from investment companies.

On average, the five largest holdings of the four major investment companies accounted for 50 percent of their share portfolios in 1983, compared with 41 percent for the Fourth AP Fund. The corresponding figure for the four largest insurance companies was 37 percent (Hedlund et al. 1985:90–91, 101). In this particular respect, then, the Fourth AP Fund might be said to occupy a middle ground between investment and insurance companies.

Whereas the portfolio of the First Wage-Earner Fund is more concentrated than that of the Fourth AP Fund, those of the other four funds are significantly less concentrated. On average, the five largest holdings accounted for 31 percent of the wage-earner funds' portfolios at the end of 1989. This discrepancy is all the more remarkable because the wage-earner funds are so small compared with the Fourth AP Fund.[7]

The lower ceiling imposed on individual ownership engagements by the wage-earner funds (6 percent as of 1988) does not seem to explain this discrepancy. At the end of 1989, the voting rights of the First Wage-Earner Fund, the one with the most concentrated portfolio, exceeded 3 percent in only two listed corporations. The more concentrated character of the Fourth AP Fund's portfolio may reflect a

7. In 1978 the five largest holdings accounted for 47 percent of the Fourth AP Fund's portfolio, which may constitute a more appropriate benchmark for comparison with today's wage-earner funds.

greater willingness to take risks. But this argument must be qualified by noting that the Fourth AP Fund has concentrated its assets in large, well-established corporations with a strong long-term performance. Over the ten years from 1974 to 1983, only seventeen firms figured among the ten largest ownership engagements by the Fourth AP Fund, and only thirteen firms did so for more than one year. Eleven of these thirteen firms rank among Sweden's fifteen largest multinational corporations, measured by employment abroad (see SOU 1983:183–84). The "risk" the Fourth AP Fund has taken by concentrating its portfolio in blue-chip shares is not that it might suffer dramatic losses, but rather that other shares might perform better.

Portfolio turnover. The Fourth AP Fund sold very few shares in the 1970s. Under Sten Wikander, the executive director appointed in 1979, the fund began not only to disengage from certain firms, but also to engage in various short-term transactions. In a sense the Fourth AP Fund became more of a "market player" in the 1980s. The extent of this reorientation should not be exaggerated, however. Although the turnover in the Fourth AP Fund's portfolio increased markedly in the 1980s, its share of total turnover in the stock market did not increase, and compared with the average stock market investor, the Fourth AP Fund remains distinguished by its limited short-term transactions.

The same cannot be said for the wage-earner funds. In 1987–89 the average annual portfolio turnover for the wage-earners funds (30 percent) was more than twice as high as that of the Fourth AP Fund (14 percent). To some degree this discrepancy reflects differences in portfolio size as the wage-earner funds were still in a buildup phase in the late 1980s. But the average turnover rate of the wage-earner funds also exceeded that of the stock exchange as a whole (23 percent in 1987–89). Three out of five wage-earner funds still had significantly higher turnover than the stock exchange as late as 1989 (see RRV 1989:22–26).

What, apart from size, might account for the apparent "short-termism" of the wage-earner funds? The high turnover might reflect efforts to outperform the market. The funds have been preoccupied with gaining legitimacy and may have conceived of their performance relative to the stock market index as a test of their legitimacy. From this perspective two factors distinguish the Fourth AP Fund's first five years from those of the wage-earner funds. First, the political controversy surrounding the creation of the Fourth AP Fund was much less intense, and Volvo's directed share issue of 1974 immediately gave the fund a great deal of legitimacy. Second, the stock market boom of the 1980s has been accompanied by "performance consciousness" among stock market investors and the public at large. In the sluggish market conditions of the 1970s, all institutional investors had to emphasize long-term goals. The plurality of wage-earner funds may also be relevant. That government auditors and the mass media commonly evaluate the funds' performance by comparing them with each other might have accentuated their concern with short-term performance.

The sectoral composition of the portfolio. Table 13 shows the sectoral distribution of the portfolio of the Fourth AP Fund, the average portfolio of the wage-earner funds, and the index of all stocks listed on the stock exchange. The interesting question here is how the Fourth AP Fund and the wage-earner funds differ from the stock market as a whole. The distinctiveness of the Fourth AP Fund emerges clearly: whereas engineering and chemical/pharmaceutical firms are heavily overrepresented in its portfolio, banks and investment companies are heavily underrepresented. Although the law prohibited the fund from owning bank shares from 1974 through 1988, the fund itself has always adhered to the policy that it should not hold shares in "pure" investment companies (companies solely engaged in managing securities portfolios).

In the 1970s the Fourth AP Fund's commitment to export-oriented manufacturing industry manifested itself above all in the purchase of engineering shares. Giving priority to engineering shares ran directly counter to short-term profit maximization during the second half of the 1970s, when engineering shares in general, and Volvo shares in particular, did very poorly compared with other shares. Yet nobody on the board of directors seems to have questioned the policy.

Table 13. Sectoral composition of portfolios of the Fourth AP Fund and the wage-earner funds as compared with the Stock Exchange index, end of 1989

Sector	Index	Fourth AP Fund	Wage-earner funds average
Engineering	32%	42%	28%
Chemicals and pharmaceuticals	10	22	6
Forest products	7	7	12
Other manufacturing	11	12	13
Real estate and construction	13	11	14
Wholesale and retail	1	1	4
Shipping	1	0	4
Development corporations	2	2	2
Holding corporations	14	2	9
Banks	9	2	8

Source: RRV (1989, app. 5).

In addition, in 1974–77 the Fourth AP Fund acquired major holdings in two pharmaceutical firms, Astra and Pharmacia. These proved
to be extremely successful investments. As their market value increased
steadily and rapidly, the Fourth AP Fund continued to buy shares in
both firms (which together accounted for 15 percent of its portfolio at
the end of 1989). While it has made very large, long-term engagements
in engineering and pharmaceutical firms, the Fourth AP Fund has
made sure that its portfolio has included other industrial sectors in
roughly the same proportion as the stock market as a whole. In 1981
the fund decided that forestry corporations were underrepresented in
its portfolio and increased their share. Significantly, the strongest segments of the forestry industry had by this time recovered from the
slump of the late 1970s. The Fourth AP Fund has consistently avoided
investing in firms or sectors with uncertain prospects and has sought to
disengage itself before structural problems have assumed serious proportions. It has done so, it seems, to avoid losing money, but also to
avoid becoming entangled in industrial policy-making.

Although the Fourth AP Fund has invested in construction companies, it has avoided companies engaged in real estate management
and speculation. In this respect its investment orientation has also run
counter to that of the average stock market investor.

Turning now to the wage-earner funds, their portfolios conform
more closely to the stock market index with respect to each of the features that distinguish the Fourth AP Fund. According to table 13, the
only truly distinctive feature of the average portfolio of the wage-earner
funds, relative to the stock market index, is the overrepresentation of
the forestry industry (which consistently outperformed the stock market index in the mid-1980s). This average portfolio conceals important
variations among the wage-earner funds, however. Whereas the Second Wage-Earner Fund has explicitly affirmed the principle that the
fund's portfolio should broadly conform to the sectoral composition of
the stock exchange index (Wage-Earner Fund 2, 1986:3), the First and
the Fifth Funds have both sought to diverge from the sectoral composition of the index in order to "beat the index" (Wage-Earner Fund 1,
1989, and Wage-Earner Fund 5, 1986–87). That approach is in
marked contrast to the Fourth AP Fund's long-standing commitment to
the engineering industry.

The Funds as Owners

The government bill that proposed creating the Fourth AP Fund
(bill 97, 1973) noted that the fund would provide "society and wage-
earners" with a "share of the ownership influence over corporations"
(p. 64), but it did not specify how or for what purposes this influence

was to be used. Having affirmed that wage-earner funds should "not assume continuing principal responsibility for the management of any firm," the 1983 legislation went on to say that they were expected to assume "the kind of co-owner responsibility that this type of share-holder [portfolio investors] normally assumes," which meant they should, in concert with other owners, "identify the goals of the corporations and ensure that the corporations are well managed" (government bill 50, 1983–84, p. 79).

When we inquire about ownership by the Fourth AP Fund and the wage-earner funds, the first question to ask is obvious: How much of the corporations they hold shares in do the funds own? In other words, What is their potential influence as owners? Table 14 provides a rough answer, showing each fund's average share of capital and votes in the listed corporations included in its portfolio.[8]

Again, since 1979 ownership engagements by the Fourth AP Fund have been restricted to 10 percent of shareholder votes. Ownership engagements by the wage-earner funds were initially restricted to 8 percent, and this ceiling was lowered to 6 percent in 1988. In theory, collective funds could come to control as much as 50 percent of the votes in any one corporation, but in practice the wage-earner funds seem to have done the opposite of coordinating their acquisitions to maximize influence. In fact, at the end of 1989 there were only nine listed corporations in which two wage-earner funds each held more

Table 14. Fourth AP Fund's and wage-earner funds' shares of capital and votes in listed corporations, end of 1989

	Average shares		Number of firms in which votes exceeded		
Fund	Capital	Votes	4%	6%	8%
AP 4	4.9%	3.4%	21	10	3
WE 1	1.7	1.0	1	1	1
WE 2	2.8	1.6	6	2	1
WE 3	4.4	3.3	14	6	1
WE 4	1.7	1.2	4	2	0
WE 5	3.0	1.8	4	1	1

Sources: AP Fund 4 (1989); Wage-Earner Funds 1–5 (1989).
Note: The wage-earner funds' vote shares may exceed 8 percent if the engagement occurred before a firm was listed on the stock exchange.

8. The distinction between share of capital and share of votes arises because of the practice of differential voting rights. Since many "A shares" still belong to the original owners or their descendants, institutional investors typically own more capital than votes.

than 2 percent of the vote, and none in which three wage-earner funds each held more than 2 percent of the vote. The Fourth AP Fund and the five wage-earner funds together held more than 8 percent of shareholder votes in twenty-five corporations at the end of 1989. Their average share of votes in these twenty-five corporations was 11.8 percent.

Typically, effective control of a corporation requires much less than 50 percent of shareholder votes. On the average, 2 percent of shareholders and 45 percent of shareholder votes were represented at the 1976 shareholders' meetings of listed Swedish corporations (SIND 1980:44–49). Hence voting blocs in the eight-plus range, and even in the 4 to 6 percent range, could give collective funds a significant voice in corporate affairs. Yet this depends, of course, on the distribution of the remaining votes. In every one of the twenty corporations in which collective funds together held more than 8 percent of shareholder voters at the end of 1988, there existed a single private owner (or owner group) that held a larger percentage of the votes. The smallest vote differential between the funds and the largest private owner was 3.6 percentage points, but the average differential was 28.4 points.[9]

Three channels of ownership influence are available to institutional investors: voting at annual shareholder meetings; representation on the board of directors; and informal contacts between fund managers and corporate managers. Supplementary legislation introduced in 1973 allowed the Fourth AP Fund to delegate voting rights at shareholder meetings to employee representatives. The wage-earner funds legislation of 1983 required the new funds to delegate 50 percent of their voting rights if the unions requested it.

In 1989 the Fourth AP Fund delegated voting rights in sixteen out of forty-five listed corporations in its portfolio (AP Fund 4, 1988). On the average, the wage-earner funds delegated voting rights in thirty-seven of forty-three listed corporations. This marked discrepancy suggests that local unions are more likely to request delegation from wage-earner funds than from the Fourth AP Fund, since the latter has not rejected such requests. Local unions seem to perceive the wage-earner funds, but not the Fourth AP Fund, as "theirs." Meanwhile, several of the wage-earner funds have made a point of encouraging local unions to exercise their right to be represented at shareholders' meetings.

The voting blocs controlled by collective funds are typically so small that delegating half the voting rights does not give local unions much influence over management decisions. The representation of local unions at shareholder meetings provides them with greater insight into

9. The differential was less than ten percentage points in four out of twenty corporations. Based on data in Widén (1989) and Sundkvist (1989).

corporate affairs and perhaps greater legitimacy in the eyes of management (Anderson 1988; Låftman 1988). But the codetermination legislation of the 1970s already gives the unions representation on boards of directors as well as extensive information and participation rights. According to the Fourth AP Fund's executive director, the real significance of employee representation at shareholders' meetings is negligible by comparison with board representation and codetermination (Wikander 1988:109). This assessment seems equally applicable to the wage-earner funds.

During its early years, the Fourth AP Fund typically demanded the right to nominate a member of the board of directors once its share of the votes in a corporation exceeded a certain level. By 1979 the fund was thus represented on the boards of fourteen out of thirty-six corporations. Whereas the Fourth AP Fund has made no effort to increase its representation on the boards of listed corporations since 1979, the wage-earner funds are not yet large enough to justify demands for board representation except in a couple of cases.

That the Fourth AP Fund has not demanded board representation since 1979 does not necessarily represent a retreat from active ownership. It may indicate a shift toward direct contact with corporate management. According to Wikander, the fund's managing director, such contacts represent a more effective and appropriate way to exercise influence. By law, anybody who sits on a firm's board of directors is responsible to its shareholders as a collective, and virtually everything discussed at board meetings is strictly confidential. The Fourth AP Fund cannot give directives to "its" board representatives, and they cannot provide the fund with inside information. Also, board representation restricts the fund's ability to disengage itself from a corporation (Wikander 1988:100).

The Fourth AP Fund has had neither the administrative capacity nor the political will to involve itself in ordinary management questions. As indicated above, it has sought to avoid or disengage from sectors and firms with major structural problems. But the large size of the fund's ownership engagements restricts how far it can opt for "exit" rather than "voice" when corporations experience difficulties. Beyond a certain size, even a portfolio investor aiming solely to maximize returns may be forced to assume an active ownership role. According to Wikander (1988:97), the Fourth AP Fund belongs to a group of institutional investors that is characterized by a relatively strong inclination toward "exit," but it is more inclined toward "voice" than most of the institutions in this group.[10]

In view of their closer links to local unions, we would expect wage-

10. To go beyond these generalities we would have to consider ownership influence in specific cases. Apart from space limitations, corporate secrecy makes such an exercise difficult, and the cases we know about (see Wikander 1988) are all extraordinary.

earner funds to be more constrained in taking the exit option, and at least two of the wage-earner funds have expressed a desire for a more active ownership role than the Fourth AP Fund.

The Funds as Promoters of Industrial Innovation

Although the legislation that created the Fourth AP Fund did not formally rule out investments in unlisted corporations, the government made it quite clear that it expected the fund to acquire publicly traded shares. To invest outside the stock exchange involved too much risk taking and required competence and administrative resources the fund could not, and should not, develop. At the initiative of the new managing director, the board of directors of the Fourth AP Fund decided in 1979 that the fund would begin, tentatively and in a limited way, to invest in unlisted corporations—in the first instance, innovative and expanding corporations that could be introduced on the stock exchange within five to ten years.

The capital needs of rapidly expanding corporations that have started out on a small scale are typically very great relative to their own equity capital. The 10 percent ceiling on individual ownership engagements imposed by the bourgeois parties in 1979 forced the Fourth AP Fund to invest in unlisted corporations by buying shares with lower voting rights and by assuming convertible promissory notes. In connection with the wage-earner funds legislation of 1983, the board of the Fourth AP Fund petitioned the government to exempt unlisted corporations from the 10 percent ceiling, stressing that the fund could not acquire shares in unlisted corporations unless the principal owner(s) agreed to sell. On these grounds the 1983 legislation exempted unlisted corporations from the ceiling on individual ownership engagements applied to the wage-earner funds as well as to the Fourth AP Fund.

The Fourth AP Fund acquired stakes in fifty unlisted corporations from 1980 through 1989 and held stakes in twenty-six such corporations at the end of 1989. As table 15 shows, the wage-earner funds have to varying degrees followed the Fourth AP Fund's lead in this respect.[11] As a percentage of the funds' total assets, investment outside the stock exchange remains peripheral, but its significance should be assessed relative to the total supply of external risk capital to unlisted corporations. Venture-capital corporations and new share issues on the over-the-counter market each raised roughly 1.5 billion SEK in new capital

11. The Fourth AP Fund's supply of risk capital to unlisted corporations has taken two basic forms: first, the fund has purchased shares in a number of unlisted corporations, and second, it has helped establish several venture-capital corporations or bought newly issued shares in such corporations (themselves unlisted). The wage-earner funds' involvement with unlisted corporations has exclusively taken the form of direct investment.

Table 15. Fourth AP Fund's and wage-earner funds' unlisted assets,
end of 1989

Fund	Number of firms	Purchase price or estimated value (million SEK)	Unlisted assets as percent of total
AP 4	26	627	2.8
WE 1	11	48	1.5
WE 2	12	159	3.2
WE 3	6	67	1.4
WE 4	17	184	5.2
WE 5	8	82	1.6

Sources: AP Fund 4 (1989); Wage-Earner Funds 1–5 (1989).

from 1981 to 1986, and the Fourth AP Fund held unlisted assets with a purchase price of 341 million SEK at the end of 1986 (AP Fund 4 1989). Although it is extremely difficult to estimate the size of the un-organized capital market, it seems clear that the share of this market held by the Fourth AP Fund and the wage-earner funds is significantly larger than their share of assets listed on the stock exchange. As table 16 shows, collective shareholding funds hold, on average, much higher shares of both the capital and the shareholder votes in unlisted than in listed corporations.

The Fourth AP Fund's decision to invest in unlisted corporations was taken independently of the government, but it was shaped by the public debate about industrial policy, which increasingly came to emphasize the role of small and medium-sized business in the 1980s. At least two of the wage-earner funds, the Second and the Fourth, have consciously approached investment in unlisted corporations as a matter of industrial policy, broadly conceived. The Second Wage-Earner Fund has done so from a distinctly regional point of view: its statement on investment policy explicitly affirms that it is primarily interested in investing in unlisted corporations within four western counties, and it specifies further that such corporations should be engaged in manufacturing or in services directly linked to manufacturing (Wage-Earner Fund 2 1987). In practice, three out of five wage-earner funds have almost entirely concentrated their investments outside the stock exchange to corporations from their own region (see RRV 1988, app. 2).

At the same time, the Fourth AP Fund clearly looks at investments in unlisted corporations as an opportunity to make money. According to Wikander (1988), the fund enjoys comparative advantages in this segment of the capital market by virtue of its public character. First, an investment by the Fourth AP Fund represents a means for expansive firms in need of new capital to remain independent. Second, the fund

Table 16. Fourth AP Fund's and wage-earner funds' shares
of capital and votes in unlisted corporations, end of 1989

Fund	Average shares		Number of firms in which votes exceeded		
	Capital	Votes	15%	25%	40%
AP 4	22.0%	23.7%	15	11	3
WE 1	20.5	18.2	8	2	1
WE 2	19.9	17.2	5	3	1
WE 3	28.5	21.0	4	2	1
WE 4	NA[a]	NA	NA	NA	NA
WE 5	18.0	15.2	3	1	0

Sources: AP Fund 4 (1989); Wage-Earner Funds 1–5 (1989).
[a]NA = not available

is willing to forgo immediate dividends, and third, it takes a long-term
view of its engagements. In principle these advantages apply to the
wage-earner funds as well, but there are at least a few cases in which
private entrepreneurs have shunned the wage-earner funds because of
the political controversy surrounding their creation.

Investment in unlisted corporations does not necessarily equal investment in small, innovative firms. In 1987 the Fourth AP Fund was one
of six institutional investors that bought shares offered by the state-
owned Swedish Steel Corporation (Svenskt Stål AB; SSAB). Also, it is
noteworthy that three wage-earner funds (the second, fourth, and
fifth) each acquired an 8.33 percent stake in UV Shipping when this
state-owned corporation was wholly privatized and set up for a stock
market flotation in 1988. This appears to be the only instance in which
wage-earner funds have coordinated their acquisitions. If privatization
of state enterprise is considered a form of industrial policy, the Fourth
AP Fund and the wage-earner funds became, for the first time, direct
participants in implementing industrial policy in 1987–88.

While it exempted unlisted corporations from the ceiling of individual ownership engagements, the 1983 legislation also stated that collective shareholding funds should not assume "entrepreneurial responsibility" (*företagaransvar*) for these corporations. Whereas the Fourth AP
Fund has taken this to mean that its ownership engagements must not
exceed 50 percent shareholder votes, three out of five wage-earner
funds operate with a self-imposed limit of 25 percent.

When the Fourth AP Fund assumes a stake in an unlisted corporation, it invariably demands representation on the board of directors.
All but one of the wage-earner funds (the third) appear to have followed this practice. According to Wikander (1988:106), board representation not only is necessary to keep the Fourth AP Fund abreast of

the corporation, it also represents a kind of service that attracts unlisted corporations to the Fourth AP Fund.

It is noteworthy that the Fourth AP Fund delegated shareholder rights to employee representatives in only one out of the twenty-seven unlisted corporations in which it held voting rights in 1988. This is all the more remarkable since the fund's share of the votes exceeded 20 percent in eighteen corporations, providing a significant potential for union influence in corporate affairs. Although it is tempting to conclude that the Fourth AP Fund's success as a co-owner of unlisted corporations has been predicated on an implicit understanding that the fund will not serve as a channel of union influence, there are two immediate reasons why delegating voting rights in unlisted corporations is so rare. First, local unions tend to be poorly organized in these cases. Second, the unions have little incentive to attend shareholder meetings, because the presence of a single, very dominant owner means that such meetings are brief and entirely formal affairs where no real decisions are made.

CONCLUSIONS

What are we to make of the experience of collective shareholding funds described above? The proponents of wage-earner funds commonly invoke the funds' performance to vindicate their position. Clearly, the funds have not subsidized inefficient production, as their opponents suggested they would. In the words of LO economist Dan Anderson (1988:24), "The wage-earner funds have already been a success because they have shown that collective capital can work just as well as other capital owners" (see also LO 87). But how do collective shareholding funds measure up against the ambitions of the labor movement in the 1970s? As we have seen, creating the Fourth AP Fund was part of labor's industrial policy offensive, and the fund was meant as an instrument of industrial policy. Wage-earner funds were also supposed to give employees some influence over corporate decision making.

The industrial policy report to the LO congress of 1981 summarized the experience of the Fourth AP Fund by saying that "the fund has provided a certain influence for the employee representatives [to which shareholder votes have been delegated] but none of significance for industrial policy" (LO 1981:196). Although this formulation seems to exaggerate the importance of delegating voting rights, we can make a more positive assessment of the fund's contribution to industrial policy. As we have seen, the Fourth AP Fund can be said to have "steered" the allocation of capital to manufacturing industry, particularly export-oriented engineering and pharmaceutical firms. More recently it has been rather important in providing external risk capital to smaller firms that do not have access to the stock exchange. Although the wage-earner funds' investment in listed firms has conformed more closely to prevailing market forces, they too have sought to promote small and innovative business, typically on a regional basis.

These "industrial policy functions" have not been part of any broader effort to plan the process of industrial restructuring, however. Except for recent privatizing measures, the Fourth AP Fund and the wage-earner funds have never participated directly in formulating or implementing government policy. They have acted autonomously from the government and have consistently sought to avoid firms or sectors with major structural problems. Moreover, the investment steering implied by the fund's emphasis on export-oriented manufacturing has not involved any systematic attempt to influence corporate investment decisions. The industrial policy functions of collective shareholding funds have been very general, not serving the distinctive interests of labor in any direct sense. LO's hope that such funds might counteract Swedish multinationals moving production abroad has never been realized.

It seems fair to conclude that delegating shareholder votes is of minor significance compared with the codetermination laws introduced in the 1970s. Investment strategy and working conditions seldom come up at shareholder meetings, and collective shareholding funds do not represent a large enough voting bloc to influence such issues through them. (To reiterate, the funds have *not* coordinated their investments to gain greater ownership influence.) The activities of collective equity capital funds have been institutionally separated from codetermination bargaining as well as industrial policy-making.

The Fourth AP Fund is distinguished from private insurance companies in that its ownership engagements tend to be larger, both in absolute terms and as a share of the corporation's equity capital, and more long-term. Its portfolio is also more concentrated. In each of these respects, the Fourth AP Fund is more akin to private investment companies; but in marked contrast to investment companies, it does not seek to be an active owner. The wage-earner funds occupy a different position relative to private insurance and investment companies. Considered as portfolio investors, they resemble insurance companies more than the Fourth AP Fund does, but at least a couple of the wage-earner funds seem to want to be more active owners than the Fourth AP Fund or private insurance companies.

Why have the labor movement's ambitions not been realized? We can identify four limits on the funds as instruments of industrial policy or industrial democracy. First, the funds' potential significance is limited by their size. Second, certain limits derive from their institutional-legal framework. The most important formal restriction of this sort is the ceiling on individual ownership. The tripartite structure of interest representation on the board of the Fourth AP Fund has also hampered labor's ambitions. But the importance of these formal arrangements should not be exaggerated. Had they so wished, the funds could easily have achieved significant ownership stakes in particular corporations despite the ceiling on ownership.

A third set of limits has to do with the power structure of capital markets. The power of private capitalists in the stock market perhaps represents a far greater obstacle to public investment steering than does the representation of organized business on the board of the Fourth AP Fund. Needless to say, large private owners and corporate managers would seek to keep out collective shareholding capital funds if they perceived them as a threat, presumably by competitive bidding for the shares of smaller shareholders. It would be very expensive, if not impossible, for the funds to undertake ownership in the face of hostile owners and management. This logic is particularly pertinent to unlisted corporations.

Finally, the limits of collective equity capital funds might be attributed to the labor movement's failure to pursue an alternative conception of what the funds should be doing, partly because of limited administrative resources and technical expertise, but more broadly because it lacks any other model of economic development that might guide their investments.

The limited size of collective shareholding funds, and the legal restrictions on their investments, must thus be viewed as a product of politics—in particular, the struggles surrounding wage-earner funds. The obvious questions arise: Why did the politics of wage-earner funds turn out this way? Why did the labor movement lose the struggle for public opinion? There are many possible answers. First, one might explain the outcome of the wage-earner funds debate in terms of bourgeois control of the mass media or the hegemony of capitalist values beneath the Social Democratic veneer of Swedish political culture. Second, one might argue that the Social Democratic leaders never wanted wage-earner funds and that lack of LO-SAP coordination let the mobilization against them succeed. Third, one might argue that the LO leaders failed to recognize the political nature of the issue and did not begin to mobilize popular support for their position until it was too late. Fourth, one might argue that wage-earner funds were not in the interest of wage-earners, at least not in any direct or immediate sense.

This list of arguments could be extended, but we have no way of determining the relative importance of the various factors identified here or their relation to each other. How can we gain analytical leverage on the outcome of the wage-earner funds debate? We can make at least some progress by contrasting the political failure of labor's wage-earner funds initiative to the success of its codetermination offensive in the 1970s. I explore this contrast in the next chapter.

CHAPTER EIGHT

The Limits of Social Democracy

My introductory discussion raised two basic questions: Why did the Swedish labor movement begin to challenge private control of investment? And why did the challenge fail? I shall not rehearse my explanation of labor's radicalization. Rather, I concentrate here on the results of labor's reform offensive and the reasons things turned out as they did. Clearly our three cases of reformism differ in outcomes as well as processes; that is, they vary in what the labor movement achieved as well as the mechanisms by which its ambitions were curtailed. I aim for an explanation of the limits of Social Democratic reform that is parsimonious yet flexible enough to take these variations into account, and I begin by further specifying my assessment of labor's reform offensive.

OUTCOMES

The labor movement saw its industrial policy in 1968–73 as an extension of the principles of active labor market policy. Selective state intervention in industrial restructuring did indeed increase significantly in the 1970s, but the orientation of industrial policy and the pattern of policy-making diverged markedly from the model of labor market policy, and hence from labor's expectations. On the one hand, the orientation of industrial policy was from the very beginning "defensive" in the twofold sense that it focused on the problems of declining industrial sectors and that it consisted primarily of ad hoc reactive measures. On the other hand, the industrial policy-making came to depend on direct negotiations between state officials and corporations, and organized labor never gained the prominent place it had assumed in the arena of labor market policy.

The aim of labor's codetermination offensive was to give unions a significant voice in all corporate decisions affecting the work force. The Codetermination Act required management to negotiate with the unions but left it free to act unilaterally if such negotiations failed and if the private employers refused to make further concessions in subsequent bargaining. In practice, the system of codetermination has given local unions in at least some corporations fairly significant influence over decisions pertaining to plant design, work organization, and personnel policy. But it has given them little if any influence over overarching strategic decisions (notably decisions about foreign investment). Also, union influence at the plant level has been predicated on a convergence of interests between labor and management.

As conceived by Meidner, wage-earner funds provided for a gradual extension of workers' influence over corporate decision making through ownership-based representation at shareholder meetings and on boards of directors. While conceding a slower pace of ownership collectivization, proponents of wage-earner funds within LO subsequently proposed that the funds should also be instruments of a union-orchestrated industrial policy, an ambition already articulated for the Fourth AP Fund. To date, however, collective shareholding funds rarely have enough shareholder votes to influence significantly corporate investment decisions. As for their importance to industrial policy, we can readily make the following observations: the funds have never been part of the government's industrial policy apparatus; they have not coordinated their investment strategies; and none of the wage-earner funds have expressed their overall investment strategy in terms of industrial policy.

In each case, labor movement initiatives led to new institutions or new institutional practices, but the results fell short of the labor movement's hopes. The gap between expectations and outcomes is most striking for wage-earner funds. Though the codetermination legislation of 1972–76 did not go as far as the unions wanted, it did broadly conform to their demands, and it did represent a dramatic change in the legal-institutional framework of industrial relations. Even in terms of "final outcomes"—that is, actual institutional practices as distinct from legislative provisions—labor's pursuit of codetermination rights must be considered more successful than its pursuit of ownership-based influence.

The changes associated with industrial policy in the 1970s were more far-reaching than those associated with codetermination in the 1980s, but the practice of codetermination has conformed more closely to the purposes its proponents had in mind than did the practice of industrial policy. Furthermore, codetermination has proved more enduring. On these grounds, industrial policy might be characterized as an intermediary case—less of a failure than wage-earner funds, but more of a failure than codetermination.

Thus summarized, my analysis compares the results of labor's reform offensive with the goals the labor movement articulated in 1968–76. The conclusion is that the reform offensive largely failed. This conclusion seems even more warranted if we consider the combined effects of the three reform initiatives I have so far treated separately. Arguably, the key to any major advance toward union influence over allocative investment decisions hinges on the meshing of codetermination on the shop floor and the firm level with influence "from above." The proponents of wage-earner funds within LO treated the funds not only as a complement to codetermination, but also as a means of bringing about closer cooperation with the state and enhancing unions' part in industrial policy-making. In a sense, wage-earner funds were conceived as a bridge between codetermination and industrial policy, but in practice, they came to be divorced from codetermination bargaining as well as industrial policy-making.

There is, however, a serious problem with relying on labor's stated goals as the yardstick for assessing the reform offensive. Radical ambitions may lead us to "devalue" achievements that are, by some objective criterion, considerable—using labor's own goals as the standard may create a bias in favor of moderate reformism. That the gap between expectations and outcomes was much greater for wage-earner funds than for codetermination does not necessarily mean that the wage-earner funds legislation of 1983 had less significance for the balance of power between labor and business than the Codetermination Act of 1976. By the same token, it is conceivable that a comparative perspective would yield a different assessment of labor's reform attempts. Even though the Swedish labor movement failed to realize its most radical ambitions, did it perhaps achieve a great deal more than labor movements in other countries? The problem becomes especially acute if leaders of the labor movement deliberately overstated their goals to mobilize rank-and-file support (or public opinion) for reform. Perhaps the leadership never realistically expected more than it got?

We can only speculate about the "real" goals and expectations of the proponents of reform. It seems more useful to correct for the bias of using labor's stated goals as a standard by applying a comparative perspective. Industrial policy and codetermination lend themselves readily to cross-national comparisons. A systematic analysis lies beyond this book, but let me briefly make some comparative points.

The orientation of Swedish industrial policy in the 1970s was more defensive than that of larger West European countries in that declining sectors absorbed a larger share of state aid to industry. Although it is more difficult to generalize about whether other states have pursued more coherent, forward-looking industrial policies, this certainly appears to have been the case in France and Japan (Zysman 1983) and possibly in West Germany as well (Katzenstein 1988). On the other hand, organized labor has been almost completely excluded from industrial policy-making in France and Japan (Pempel and Tsunekawa 1979; Pontusson 1991). In terms of labor's ability to influence policy outcomes, it would be more appropriate to compare the Swedish experience with that of other small "corporatist" countries. Peter Katzenstein's (1985) analysis provides no indication that the Swedish labor movement has been especially successful in this regard.

As for codetermination, the West German experience is the most obvious comparative reference point. We have seen that the approach to codetermination LO and TCO adopted in the early 1970s was intended to avoid the threat posed by "dual representation" along the German model and that the Codetermination Act conformed to this approach. The legal framework of Swedish codetermination is more favorable to the unions than the German counterpart, but does this really matter? Whereas German unions have been able to dominate the system of works council representation (Streeck 1984; Thelen 1992), Swedish corporations have largely practiced codetermination through bipartite consultations rather than formalized negotiations. On the other hand, Lowell Turner's (1991) study suggests that German auto manufacturers have not gone as far as Volvo in their pursuit of job enlargement, job enrichment, and teamwork autonomy.

Collective shareholding funds constitute a unique experiment, with no obvious parallels in other advanced capitalist countries. That such funds have been created in Sweden and not elsewhere is itself testimony to the strength of the Swedish labor movement. The significance of this achievement might be assessed by comparing the behavior of collective shareholding funds with that of private institutional investors. (In contrasting the experience of industrial policy to that of labor market policy, I have already engaged in another "intranational" comparison.) To reiterate, the Fourth AP Fund has behaved more like a private investment company than like an insurance company if we consider it as a portfolio investor. Its investment strategy differs from that of the average insurance company in that manufacturing industry is over-represented in its portfolio, its ownership engagements are more long term, and its portfolio is more concentrated. Considered as an owner, however, the Fourth AP Fund has assumed the passive posture characteristic of insurance companies. Whereas several of the wage-earner funds have expressed an ambition to be more active as owners, their ability to do so is limited, and the investment strategies of the wage-earner funds have been more akin to the market-driven strategies of the insurance companies.

In sum, I believe that the systematic application of a comparative perspective would not significantly alter my overall assessment of labor's offensive or of the successes and failures of its three components. I do not deny that the experience of Social Democratic rule has profoundly affected the workings of Swedish capitalism; my point is that the distinctive features of Swedish capitalism are not a product of purposive union influence or democratic control over allocative investment decisions. To explain them, we should look to more traditional elements of Social Democratic reformism—wage solidarity, active labor market policy, and the welfare state.

As stated above, my assessment of labor's reform offensive focuses on how much institutional reforms increased union influence over investment decisions. To round out this discussion, let me make a few remarks about the broader political consequences of institutional reforms. The crucial issue from a democratic socialist perspective is not the immediate results of a given reform, but what possibilities it opens up for further reforms by altering the terms of public debate or encouraging popular mobilization. What John Stephens (1979) refers to as the "mobilizing effects" of reforms may operate independently of their immediate results.

Selective state intervention did indeed open up a new arena of political contest in the 1970s, but the way the issues of industrial policy came to be framed did not elicit class-based mobilization of wage earners. Instead, it elicited their community-based mobilization in defense of jobs, frequently involving an implicit alliance with the managers and owners of firms in competitive troubles. Such mobilization weakened the cohesion of the labor movement, and it was partly for this reason, along with budgetary considerations, that the Social Democrats abandoned selective industrial policy in the 1980s.

The wage-earner funds legislation of 1983 was clearly designed to depoliticize collective shareownership. This effort was not entirely successful, for the bourgeois parties have continued their campaign against wage-earner funds; yet the actual investment practices of collective shareholding funds have not been the subject of much public debate. Participation on fund boards may have given some union officials a better understanding of the stock market and the world of corporate affairs. But one would be hard put to argue that the experience of collective shareholding funds has in any meaningful sense broadened the perspective of rank-and-file activists, let alone wage earners in general.

Labor's codetermination offensive was more successful than its other reform initiatives not only in yielding influence over corporate decision making, but also in contributing to a cumulative reform process. Clearly, codetermination practices have involved union activists far more than either of the other reform initiatives, and there is at least some evidence that they have enhanced wage earners' expectations. In a series of employee surveys in the early 1980s, Volvo found that job satisfaction in its new factories was not significantly greater than in its Torslanda plant. Why didn't better working conditions yield greater satisfaction? Further surveys showed that workers' expectations were significantly higher in the new factories (Berggren 1990). In this sense the experience of codetermination has perhaps prepared the ground for further reform initiatives. At the same time, however, codetermination, along with new management practices, may have confined workers' demands to the firm level and thereby contributed to the spread of "firm-level corporatism" (Brulin 1989).

EXPLANATIONS

Why did the labor movement fail to realize its reform ambitions? We can distill four arguments from my analysis:

1. The reform offensive failed legislatively because business mobilized against it.
2. The reform offensive failed legislatively because the SAP leaders and the government did not share labor's ambitions.
3. The reform offensive failed because the systemic power of capital thwarted the effects of the legislation that labor achieved.
4. The reform offensive failed because labor lacked an alternative industrial strategy and hence failed to take advantage of the opportunities created by the new legislation.

As figure 8 (which repeats fig. 1) illustrates, these arguments are distinguished on two dimensions. The first pertains to the point in the reform process where outcomes diverged from labor's goals. Simply put, did labor's offensive fail because labor failed to secure the legislation it wanted, or did it fail because of something that happened after the legislative phase? The second dimension pertains to the mechanisms that account for why outcomes diverged from labor's goals. Did the offensive fail because of the resistance of business (business-cen-

	Capital	Labor
Legislation	Political mobilization	Party-union divisions
Implementation	Exit options	Lack of altern- ative model

Figure 8. Explanations of the limits of reformism.

tered explanations) or because the labor movement was divided, lacked a coherent strategy, or made tactical errors (labor-centered explanations)?

Now, there is empirical evidence to support each of the arguments above. Moreover, any one of them might plausibly be construed as a sufficient explanation of why labor's reform offensive failed. What then are we to do? Should we simply conclude that our outcomes are "overdetermined"? Alternatively, we might weigh the explanatory factors that these arguments stress and explore the relations among them. Can we characterize one factor (or some factors) as "primary" in that its (their) operation is a necessary and sufficient condition for other factors to come into play?

As we have seen, the relative importance of the politics of legislation and the politics of implementation varies across our three cases. In the case of collective shareownership, reform clearly failed in the legislative or, more accurately, the "prelegislative" phase. Given the provisions of the 1983 legislation, it is not surprising that wage-earner funds have not significantly enhanced union influence over investment allocation. The gap between labor's original goals and the 1983 legislation is much greater than the gap between the 1983 legislation and the actual practices of wage-earner funds. For codetermination, by contrast, the gap between goals and outcomes emerges primarily in the course of implementing new legislation (in the "postlegislative" phase of the reform process). Again, industrial policy represents an intermediary case.

In other words, the politics of legislation deserves analytical primacy in the case of collective shareownership, and the politics of implementation deserves it in the case of codetermination. It follows that if we want to explain the limits of labor's reform offensive as a whole, we must attend more or less equally to the politics of legislation and the politics of implementation.

In my view, the importance of business resistance relative to labor politics, and the relation between the factors that fall in these two categories, is a more significant question than the relation between legislation and implementation. Though business-centered and labor-centered arguments are by no means mutually exclusive, their political implications differ: whereas business-centered arguments suggest that any reformist challenge to private control of investment is bound to fail, labor-centered arguments suggest that reforms of this kind might have been significantly more successful if labor acted differently.

How tight are the constraints that the power of business imposes on labor reformism in advanced capitalist societies? To answer this question with confidence, we need at least one case of a strong, unified labor movement pursuing a coherent strategy to introduce collective ownership or otherwise democratize investment decisions. From this point of view, the Swedish case is far from ideal. The preferences and strategies of the Social Democratic party and the LO unions have tended to diverge on each set of reform initiatives treated here, and the proponents of institutionalized union participation in investment decisions have largely failed to articulate a coherent conception of the purposes that union representatives should pursue. Unfortunately, I can think of no other national labor movement that fulfills the requirements of the ideal case.

At least in the politics of legislation, business- and labor-centered factors co-vary across our three cases of reformism. Relatively speaking, business mobilization and labor-movement divisions were weak in the case of codetermination and strong in the case of wage-earner funds; and both might be characterized as "moderate" in the case of industrial policy. We cannot weigh the relative importance of these factors here by playing them off against each other, but this may be a generic analytical problem, for the persistence of covariation suggests a causal relation between them.

In what follows, I put forth two tentative arguments for the analytical primacy of capital-centered explanations of the limits of reformism: that business mobilization is a plausible explanation of labor-movement divisions; and that the systemic power of capital is a plausible explanation for labor's lack of an alternative industrial strategy. Both these causal links are, I believe, far more likely than their opposites: it is far less reasonable to invoke labor-movement divisions to explain business mobilization or to invoke labor's lack of an alternative industrial strategy to explain the systemic power of capital.

The Politics of Legislation

To explore the politics of legislation further, let us try to unravel the contrast between the politics of codetermination reform (initiated by

LO in 1971) and the politics of wage-earner funds (initiated by LO in 1976). The contrast between these experiences might be summarized as follows:

1. Organized business opted for an accommodationist response to labor's codetermination offensive and never sought to mobilize public opinion or the bourgeois parties against codetermination. By contrast, business mobilized early and heavily against wage-earner funds.

2. The politics of codetermination generated a "united wage-earner front," since LO and TCO agreed on virtually all substantive questions and closely coordinated their activities. By contrast, the Meidner Plan was strictly an LO initiative. Though TCO had previously expressed sympathy for the idea of collective profit sharing, it ended up assuming a neutral position in the wage-earner funds debate.

3. Though it resisted some of the unions' more radical proposals, the Social Democratic party and government basically supported the codetermination offensive. By contrast, wage-earner funds were a source of major disagreements between SAP and LO.

4. Whereas the Liberals and the Center party also supported the push for codetermination, these parties joined with the Moderates in a "united bourgeois front" against wage-earner funds.

Taken together, these four considerations provide a fairly exhaustive explanation of why LO got the kind of legislation it wanted for codetermination but not for wage-earner funds. Again, can we generate a more parsimonious explanation by establishing a "hierarchy of causes"? It is common to invoke TCO's position to explain the Liberals' and the Center party's support for the Codetermination Act. (Recall that the Parliament that enacted this legislation was perfectly divided between the socialist and bourgeois blocs.) The argument here also sheds a great deal of light on the positions the SAP leaders adopted in the codetermination and wage-earner funds debates. By the early 1970s, TCO's growing membership had emerged as the pivotal terrain of electoral competition between the Social Democrats and the centrist bourgeois parties. As I suggested earlier, the divisions between LO and SAP over wage-earner funds largely expressed a growing tension between the logic of (class) unionism and the logic of electoral competition. On issues that unite LO and TCO, this tension is much less pronounced (assuming these organizations do indeed represent the views of their members).

By this line of thinking, the contrast between the politics of codetermination and the politics of wage-earner funds boils down to one question: Why did TCO support codetermination but not wage-earner funds? There is no obvious answer in terms of the interests of TCO members. Quite the contrary, the contrast between TCO's positions on codetermination and on wage-earner funds seems paradoxical from this point of view, for codetermination is about the democratization of corporations, and such a reform could easily be construed as a threat to the power and prerogatives of a sizable stratum of TCO members (Fry 1986). By contrast, the collectivization of ownership should be an issue on which all wage earners would converge in opposition to the owners of capital.

One can argue that the mobilization against wage-earner funds by organized business and the bourgeois parties neutralized TCO in the debate over wage-earner funds. Although it seems hard to derive the different positions adopted by TCO from the interests of its members, there is a straightforward interest-based explanation of why business responded differently to these LO initiatives. Quite simply, the wage-earner funds posed a more direct threat to the systemic interests of business than did the proposed system of codetermination. The Code-termination Act of 1976 was premised on the employers' willingness to accommodate the unions' demands in subsequent bargaining over procedural arrangements, and it left management with the authority to act unilaterally in the absence of any collective agreement.

In unfavorable political circumstances, it made sense for organized business to avoid a major political confrontation and instead use post-legislative bargaining to define codetermination. By contrast, the Meidner Plan and subsequent wage-earner funds proposals left very little room (if any) for postlegislative bargaining. In other words, the code-termination offensive was a legislative success for the same reason that the implementation of the new legislation became a disappointment for labor.

The argument here is that the radical nature of the Meidner Plan mobilized the business community; that the campaign against wage-earner funds neutralized TCO; and that the neutralization of TCO in turn created tensions between LO and SAP. But is this argument consistent with an interest-based approach to politics? After all, it treats TCO's behavior entirely as a function of outside ideological influences. The reader may well ask, What happened to "organized class interests" (cf. chap. 2)? If this is a useful way to conceive the behavior of LO and SAF, shouldn't it also apply to TCO?

This is certainly not the place to analyze the class-structural position of TCO's members. But TCO's membership is clearly more hetero-genous than LO's (whatever conception of class we adopt), and many TCO members occupy what Erik Olin Wright (1976) calls "contradic-tory class locations." Following Wright, one might well assume that people in such locations are torn between the interests of labor and capital and that their choices are especially influenced by political and ideological factors. Thus it might be possible to develop a materialist explanation of the apparent indeterminacy of TCO politics.

It is not sufficient, however, to explain why business mobilized against wage-earner funds and to show that its mobilization neutralized TCO. What is perhaps the crucial question remains: Why did the mobilization against wage-earner funds succeed? There are at least two quite different ways to answer this question. First, one might argue that the mobilization succeeded because business was able to muster greater power resources than labor. Second, one might argue that it succeeded because the idea of wage-earner funds was fundamentally flawed from a political point of view.

According to Sven Ove Hansson (1984:156), organized business spent about as much on its advertising and media campaign against wage-earner funds in 1982 as the five parliamentary parties spent on the election campaign of the same year. Also, newspapers affiliated with the bourgeois parties account for 80 percent of total circulation. The editorial pages of these papers inveighed heavily against wage-earner funds. Finally, the campaign relied in part on the influence corporate management exercises over employees. Business organizations urged affiliated firms to explain the dangers of wage-earner funds to their employees. Although some firms shied away from this politicization of industrial relations, many did send out personal letters or otherwise communicate with their employees about wage-earner funds, frequently claiming that the funds threatened employment security.

Jörgen Hermansson and Jon Elster both suggest that the success of the mobilization should be seen as an expression of basic flaws in the labor movement's proposal to collectivize ownership. Hermansson (1988: 51) argues that the wage-earner funds initiative diverged from traditional Social Democratic reform politics by not appealing to the immediate interests of electoral constituencies of strategic importance, and that this accounts for its failure. In Hermansson's (1988:54) words, wage-earner funds were conceived "solely for the working class, industrial workers in the traditional sense." Elster (1987) makes a similar point while denying that successful reformism must appeal to immediate material interests. In his interpretation, the wage-earner funds initiative failed because it did not rest on a compelling conception of social justice. According to Elster (1987:99), it is "perverse" to "give employee voting rights only to workers in firms which for some reason happen to be chosen as investment objects for the funds" and "ridiculous" to "argue that 'the working class' as a whole would have control over the firms through trade union representatives in the funds," since "real power would be vested in the trade union bureaucracy."

Hermansson and Elster alike seem to think their critiques encompass all the successive wage-earner funds proposals advanced by the labor movement. Considered as a critique of the original Meidner Plan, are their arguments accurate? And most important for our purposes, do they provide a plausible explanation for its demise? To begin with, it is true that the Meidner Plan did not appeal directly to the immediate material interests of wage earners, let alone the interests of electoral constituencies of strategic importance. But this also seems to hold for the codetermination reforms LO proposed in the early 1970s, which nonetheless received strong support from white-collar as well as blue-collar employees. Support for structural reforms like these clearly must rest on different premises than support for redistributive reforms, but we ought not to preclude the possibility that wage earners can recognize and act on long-term collective interests.

As for Elster's contention that "real power would be vested in the trade union bureaucracy," this is certainly how the critics protrayed the Meidner Plan, but the plan actually provided that local unions would wield all shareholder voting rights until wage-earner funds came to control 20 percent of the voting rights in any one corporation. Again, the experience of codetermination provides an instructive counterpoint. LO's and TCO's successful approach to codetermination emphasized that employee interests would be represented by unions. Elster's argument fails to explain how "employee representatives" suddenly came to be perceived as "union bureaucrats."

Under the Meidner Plan, the voting rights that accrued to wage-earner funds would be exercised by white-collar as well as blue-collar unions. It is simply not true that the plan would have empowered only industrial workers. Also, there was nothing arbitrary about the investment of wage-earner funds under the Meidner Plan: the rate of profitability was to determine where collective capital would be formed.

Based on profit sharing, however, the Meidner Plan and subsequent wage-earner funds proposals did not empower public sector employees. It is on this score that Elster's argument about justice becomes relevant to the contrast between the experiences of codetermination and wage-earner funds, for labor's codetermination offensive catered to the interests of all wage earners. Yet the attitudes of private and public sector employees toward wage-earner funds hardly diverged at all in the election surveys of 1982 and 1985 (Gilljam 1988:180), and the opposition to wage-earner funds within TCO came primarily from SIF (the Association of Industrial Employees). Public sector employees and unions may have tended to be indifferent to wage-earner funds, affecting the terms of public debate more generally.

The arguments advanced by Hermansson and Elster fail to explain why a third of all voters supported the idea of wage-earner funds in

1976 and 1979 and why it was not until the early 1980s that public support plummeted (see table 12 above). The mobilization against wage-earner funds provides the most plausible explanation of why popular support decreased in the early 1970s. Significantly, popular support dropped at the same time as the SAP leaders sought to impose the traditional mold of Social Democratic reform politics on the wage-earner funds issue (Feldt 1991).

I do not deny that the Meidner Plan had flaws. But any proposal that entails such a far-reaching collectivization of ownership is bound to precipitate a major countermobilization by private business. LO did not recognize this point until it was too late. Instead of launching the struggle for public opinion, LO in effect looked to elite-level bargaining among parties and interest groups to achieve its objectives. Apparently it figured it would be able to get the support of TCO and thereby put pressure on SAP and the centrist bourgeois parties. In other words, LO failed to recognize that collectivizing ownership required a political strategy different from the one it had used to achieve codetermination legislation.

Also, LO never clearly articulated, in the public debate, how wage-earner funds would behave differently from private investors or owners. By relying on market forces to allocate capital, the Meidner Plan sought to sidestep this problem. Such a posture became untenable, however, as the opponents argued forcefully that collective share-ownership would inevitably lead to less efficient use of society's resources. In sum, the proponents of wage-earner funds made strategic errors, and divisions between LO and SAP weakened their position, but these labor-centered variables must be seen in the context of business resistance to labor's reformist ambitions.

The Politics of Implementation

The case for focusing on the politics of legislation is very persuasive when we consider the potential mechanisms of investment control the labor movement introduced in the postwar period. My analysis of the operation of the original AP funds demonstrates that these funds have not served to steer the allocation of capital within the corporate sector, but it adds little if anything to explain why. To a very large extent, the operation of the original AP funds has been determined by the legal-institutional framework adopted in 1959. The legislative measures produced by labor's reform offensive of 1968–76 also entailed important limits on union influence over the allocation of investment, but it is less credible to claim that legislative provisions adequately explain institutional practices in the case of industrial policy, codetermination, or even collective shareholding funds. We must also ask, why did labor fail to realize the potential influence provided by the new institutional arrangements?

Again, we can answer either in terms of the power of business or in terms of labor politics. Business assumes a different guise in this context, however. The argument about the power of business in the realm of legislative politics focused on the ability of business to influence public opinions and the positions adopted by political parties. As we turn to implementation, and to policy-making within institutions with a particular mandate, business appears as an economic actor. As such, it enjoys "systemic power" embedded in the institutional substructure of the economy. In contrast to the political power of business, deploying systemic power does not (at least not necessarily) require collective action.

Perhaps the simplest way to think about the systemic power of business is in terms of "exit options." Consider codetermination bargaining. Even if the law prescribed that management must reach an agreement with the unions, capital would still retain the option to exit. If codetermination yielded a bargain that was unfavorable to capital—or was perceived as such by management or owners—management would very likely decide to locate new investment in plants with more pliable unions, perhaps abroad. Alternatively, capitalists would divest themselves of their holdings in the firm in question. To be sure, individual workers may also have exit options, but this presupposes favorable macroeconomic conditions and may involve considerable costs. And from the point of view of the union organization in a particular plant or firm, there is no exit option. In formulating their demands and deciding what compromises to accept, unions clearly take into account the constraints implied by the alternative investment opportunities of capitalists.

Collective shareownership brings out the reverse side of the exit option: what we might term capital's "control of entry." As I argued above, management or existing owners may deny collective funds access to corporate shares or push prices so high that acquiring these shares would undermine the funds' ability to meet their rate-of-return requirements. Of course, such action would entail costs for management/owners, but if the firm is a successful one and collective funds pose a genuine threat to the prevailing management strategy, they should be willing to bear such costs.

Although struggles surrounding hostile takeovers (in Sweden and elsewhere) demonstrate that this is not just fanciful speculation, there is no obvious instance in which management/owners of corporations listed on the stock exchange have acted to keep collective funds out or to limit their ownership. But there are at least a few instances where owners of unlisted corporations have avoided issuing new shares to wage-earner funds. In any case, the absence of any major cases of this sort may mean that the funds have behaved according to the logic of the stock market. Certainly the funds have been very keen to demonstrate their willingness to cooperate with existing management and owners.

The experience of industrial policy illustrates both the exit options of business and its control of entry. On the one hand, state subsidies, and direct infusion of capital via state enterprise, became necessary in the 1970s to counteract private disinvestment in declining sectors and the regions they dominated. On the other hand, selective state intervention in industrial restructuring has depended on the active cooperation of corporate management and other business actors (creditors and owners). The cooperation of organized labor is less vital to the successful implementation of industrial policy, and this seems to account for organized labor's marginal role in industrial policy-making. Again, the logic of industrial policy differs from the logic of labor-market policy in this respect.

The experience of industrial policy also brings out another aspect of the systemic power of business—its control of information about corporations and sectoral market conditions. Government officials and union representatives involved in industrial policy-making have depended heavily on information furnished by firms requesting state aid. For the most part, corporate management has defined the problems to be addressed by public policy. This consideration also applies to the experience of collective shareownership and codetermination. At the plant level, unions have independent access to information on the issues at stake in codetermination bargaining, but at higher levels of corporate decision making management clearly continues to enjoy a decisive advantage in this respect, despite the provisions of the Codetermination Act and the Development Agreement.

Still, the question remains, Couldn't the labor movement have acted more decisively to take advantage of the potential of new institutional arrangements to serve as mechanisms of wage-earner influence over investment decisions? Couldn't it have devoted more resources to developing the administrative competence or technical expertise required to influence industrial policy-making and to shape the actions of institutions such as the Investment Bank, the Fourth AP Fund, and the wage-earner funds? The absence of union efforts to achieve coordination among these institutions or to prescribe general guidelines for them is striking. As we have seen, LO was very active in proposing institutional reforms and mobilizing to get them passed, but once they were introduced LO seems to have backed off, assuming a rather passive role.

Labor's failure to "follow up" on institutional reforms seems closely related to its failure to develop a coherent conception of the purposes of institutionalizing union influence over the allocation of investment. Again, the labor movement never developed anything like an "alternative model of development" that could have provided criteria for allocating public or collective capital and for identifying the type of private investment that the state should promote. The failure to develop such a model might be attributed to conflicts of interest and political divisions within the labor movement as well as to its traditional ideological commitment to free trade and Keynesian economics.

Another line of argument proceeds from the observation that in the 1980s the LO unions, notably the Metalworkers Union and its Volvo local, did begin to elaborate strategy concerning the redesign of industrial work. As I indicated in chapter 7, this change might be the outcome of a learning process in that the unions developed a conception of the kind of workplace changes they wanted, and of how to achieve them, by participating in corporate development projects and in response to management initiatives. This argument might perhaps be extended to the exercise of union influence from above. A coherent and credible union strategy to steer the interfirm allocation of capital (or to influence overarching corporate investment decisions) presupposes that unions can participate—indeed, that they have been able to participate for some time—in investment decisions at various levels of the economy.

Labor's lack of an alternative industrial strategy might thus be explained in terms of the systemic power of business—labor lacks strategic capacity because business is able to exclude it. Again, I do not claim this argument is an adequate explanation of the strategic ambiguities of labor's reform offensive. But it enables us to link business and labor-centered variables on a predictable basis. It is certainly more plausible to derive the strategic weakness of labor from the systemic power of business than vice versa.

CONCLUSIONS

If business-centered variables are indeed of primary importance, then successful reform depends on the cooperation of at least some segments of business. This perspective yields a fairly parsimonious account of the variations among our three cases of reformism. The wage-earner funds initiative was the biggest failure because it most challenged the systemic interests of business yet provided no material incentives for business to cooperate with labor. Labor's industrial policy offensive succeeded in that selective state intervention in industrial restructuring did indeed emerge. This success rested on an implicit alliance between labor and declining industry. By contrast, the limited but real success of labor's codetermination offensive was based on a convergence of interests between labor and business in advanced industrial sectors. Over the long run, the economic and political costs of the alliance with declining industry were unacceptable to the labor movement, and the Social Democrats consequently abandoned selective state intervention in industrial restructuring. The alliance between labor and advanced industry has proved more durable.

The economic recovery strategy the Social Democrats adopted in the 1980s did not secure a durable pattern of growth that satisfied labor's interests in full employment, real wage growth and reskilling in a solidaristic way. The problems that provided the impetus for the reform efforts of 1968–76 remain. At least some of them—wage drift and investment abroad—have become more acute. In the late 1980s, the LO unions again began to argue for a more active industrial policy and more extensive collective shareownership.

Does my account of the limits of the earlier reform offensive mean these new initiatives are bound to fail or that reformist labor movements elsewhere cannot possibly achieve more far-reaching institutional reforms than has the Swedish labor movement? I am not convinced of that. The systemic power of business can be curtailed through legislation, and the politics of legislation contains an important element of indeterminacy. For instance, the Meidner Plan would have short-circuited the aforementioned logic of the stock market (the control of entry) by requiring corporations to issue new shares to wage-earner funds. Without altering this feature, the idea of wage-earner funds could have been made more attractive to public sector employees by giving the citizenry at large greater representation in the exercise of ownership influence (as Walter Korpi advocated in the late 1970s). Also, the proponents of wage-earner funds could (should) have recognized the importance of mobilizing public opinion at an earlier stage. In these circumstances, the outcome of the wage-earner funds debate would surely have been more favorable to labor.

Without speculating further in counterfactuals, let me briefly identify three lessons that democratic socialists might draw from the Swedish experiences described in the second half of this book. The first lesson is that any effort to introduce collective shareownership must employ some combination of popular mobilization and incentives for business to cooperate—a "hegemonic strategy."

The second lesson is that a socialist industrial policy should avoid case-by-case intervention and direct negotiations with corporate management. Business enjoys a decisive advantage over labor when industrial policy takes this form, which also encourages protectionist pressures. I do not mean that socialists should avoid selective state intervention in industrial restructuring: selectivity can take different forms. The goals of industrial policy should be based on principled considerations rather than on bargaining with business in crises. In pursuit of such goals, industrial policy should operate by shaping the overall structure of incentives rather than by direct subsidies. To illustrate further, it is one thing for collective shareholding funds to override market forces by favoring investment in certain sectors or types of business, as the Fourth AP Fund has done, and quite another for such funds to disregard market signals when choosing among corporations within priority categories. The latter form of investment steering is likely to be self-defeating in a market economy.

The final lesson is that industrial policy, and investment policy more generally, must be linked to the immediate concerns of wage earners. In the absence of influence from above, the significance of codetermination is strictly limited; but influence from above is likely to become divorced from wage-earner interests unless it addresses the issues at stake in codetermination bargaining. Linking these spheres may be the key to sustaining the momentum of labor reform. When reforms result in institutional arrangements with no direct bearing on the wage earners' immediate concerns (for instance, when collective shareholding funds are reduced to deciding whether to buy shares in Volvo or Saab) wage earners are bound to become less supportive of further efforts to democratize investment decisions.

References

Ahlén, Kristina. 1989. Swedish collective bargaining under pressure: Inter-union rivalry and incomes policies. *British Journal of Industrial Relations* 27, no. 3:330–46.

Alarik, Björn. 1979. Facklig verksamhet i komplexa organisationer: Koncernsamverkan i Svenska Volvo. Stockholm: Arbetslivscentrum.

Albrecht, Sandra, and Steven Deutsch. 1983. The challenge of economic democracy: The case of Sweden. *Economic and Industrial Democracy* 4, no. 3:287–319.

Åmark, Klas. 1988. Sammanhållning och intressepolitik: Socialdemokratin och fackföreningsrörelsen i samarbete och på skilda vägar. In *Socialdemokratins samhälle*, ed. Klas Misgeld, Karl Molin, and Klas Åmark, 57–82. Stockholm: Tidens Förlag.

AMS. 1983. Redogörelse för avsättningar till investeringsfonder, arbetsmiljöfonder, särskilda investeringsfonder och vinstfonder under åren 1974–1980 samt meddelade beslut under åren 1975–81. *Meddelanden Från Utredningsenheten*, no. 4.

Anderson, Dan. 1988. Inledning: Om löntagare, huvudmän och brukare. In *Mitt i steget: Om ägande och inflytande inför 90-talet*, ed. Dan Anderson, 7–26. Stockholm: Tidens Förlag.

AP Funds 1–3. 1960–89. *Årsredovisning*. Annual reports.

AP Funds 4. 1974–89. *Årsredovsining*. Annual reports.

Apple, Nixon, Winton Higgins, and Michael Wright. 1981. *Class mobilization and economic policy: The struggle over full employment in Britain and Sweden, 1930–1980*. Stockholm: Arbetslivscentrum Working Papers.

Åsard Erik. 1978. *LO och löntagarfondsfrågan*. Stockholm: Rabén & Sjögren.

———. 1985a. *Kampen om löntagarfonderna*. Stockholm: Norstedts.

Auer, Peter, and Claudius Riegler. 1990. *Post-Taylorism: The enterprise as a place of learning organizational change*. Stockholm: Arbetsmiljöfonden.

Augurén, Stefan, and Jan Edgren. 1979. *Annorlunda fabriker: Mot en ny produktionsteknisk teori*. Stockholm: SAF.

Axelsson, Roger, Karl-Gustaf Löfgren, and Lars-Gunnar Nilsson. 1983. *Den svenska arbetsmarknadspolitiken under 1900-talet*. Stockholm: Prisma.

Berggren Christian. 1986. *Fack, företagsledning och besluten om företagens framtid*. Lund: Arkiv.

———. 1989. "New production concepts" in final assembly: The Swedish experience. In *The transformation of work?* ed. Stephen Wood, 171–203. London: Unwin Hyman.

References

———. 1990. *Det nya bilarbetet: Konkurrensen mellan olika produktionskoncept i svensk bilindustri, 1970–1990.* Lund: Arkiv.

Bergström, Hans. 1987. *Rivstart? Från opposition till regering.* Stockholm: Tidens Förlag.

———. 1991. "Sweden's politics and party system at the crossroads." *West European Politics* 14, no. 3:8–30.

Bergström, Villy. 1969. *Den ekonomiska politiken i Sverige och dess verkningar.* Stockholm: Almqvist & Wicksell/Industriens Utredningsinstitut.

———. 1982. *Studies in Swedish post-war industrial investments.* Stockholm: Almqvist & Wicksell International.

Birgersson, Bengt Owe, et al. 1981. *Sverige efter 1900: En modern politisk historia.* 9th ed. Stockholm: BonnierFakta Bokförlag.

Block, Fred. 1977. The ruling class does not rule. *Socialist Review,* no. 33:6–28.

Boston Consulting Group. 1978. A framework for Swedish industrial policy. Published in Swedish as *En ram för svensk industripolitik.* Uddevalla, 1978.

Broström, Anders, ed. 1981. *Storkonflikten 1980.* Stockholm: Arbetslivscentrum.

———. 1982. *MBL:s gränser: Den privata äganderätten.* Stockholm: Arbetslivscentrum.

Brulin, Göran. 1989. *Från den "svenska modellen" till företagskorporatism? Facket och den nya företagsledningsstrategin.* Lund: Arkiv.

Carlsson, Bo. 1981. Sammanfattning och syntes. In *Industrin inför 80-talet,* ed. Bo Carlsson et al., 21–82. Stockholm: Industriens Utredningsinstitut.

Carlsson, Bo. et al. 1979. *Teknik och industristruktur: 70-talets ekonomiska kris i historisk belysning.* Stockholm: Industriens Utredningsinstitut.

Castles, Francis. 1978. *The Social Democratic image of society: A study of the achievements and origins of Scandinavian Social Democracy in comparative perspective.* London: Routledge & Kegan Paul.

Crouch, Colin. 1980. Varieties of trade union weakness. *West European Politics* 3, no. 1:87–106.

Dahlkvist, Mats. 1975. *Staten, socialdemokratin och socialismen.* Stockholm: Prisma.

Dahlström, Edmund. 1989. *Arbetets maktförhållanden.* Stockholm: Maktutredningen.

De Geer, Hans. 1978. *Rationaliseringsrörelsen i Sverige.* Stockholm: Studieförbundet Näringsliv och Samhälle.

Dencik, Peter, 1974. Solidarisk lönepolitik som inkomstpolitik. In *Arbete, kapital och stat,* ed. Peter Dencik and Bengt-Åke Lundvall, 191–214. Stockholm: Rabén & Sjögren.

Edgren, Gösta, Karl-Olof Faxén, and Clas-Erik Odhner. 1970. *Lönebildning och samhällsekonomi.* Stockholm: Rabén & Sjögren.

Edlund, Sten, and Inga Hellberg. 1988. Epilog. In *Konfliktbehandling på arbetsmarknaden,* ed. Sten Edlund et al., 129–39. Stockholm: Arbetslivscentrum.

Edlund, Sten, and Birgitta Nyström. 1988. *Developments in Swedish labour law.* Stockholm: Swedish Institute.

Elander, Ingemar. 1978. *Det nödvändiga och det önskvärda: En studie av socialdemokratisk ideologi och regionalpolitik, 1940–72.* Stockholm: Arkiv.

Eliasson, Gunnar. 1965. *Investment funds in operation.* Stockholm: Liber Förlag.

Eliasson, Gunnar, and Bengt-Christer Ysander. 1983. Sweden: Problems of maintaining efficiency under political pressure. In *State investment companies in Western Europe: Picking winners or backing losers?* ed. Brian Hindley, 156–91. New York: St. Martin's Press.

Ellegård, Kajsa. 1986. Utvecklingsprocessen: Ny produkt, ny fabrik, ny arbetsorganisation. Department of Human and Economic Geography, University of Gothenburg.

———. 1989. Metalls medverkan i projekteringen av Volvos Uddevallafabrik. Department of Human and Economic Geography, University of Gothenburg.

Ellegård, Kajsa, Tomas Engström, and Lennart Nilsson. 1991. *Reforming industrial work: Principles and realities in the planning of Volvo's car assembly plant in Uddevalla.* Stockholm: Arbetsmiljöfonden.

Elster, Jon. 1987. The possibility of rational politics. *Archives Europeennes de Sociologie* 28:67–103.

Elvander, Nils. 1969. *Intresseorganisationerna i dagens Sverige.* Lund: CWK Gleerup Bokförlag.

———. 1988. *Den svenska modellen.* Stockholm: Allmänna Förlaget.

———. 1991. *Arbetsmarknadsrelationer i Sverige och Storbritannien.* Stockholm: SNS Förlag.

Ericsson, Bengt. 1979. *Huggsexan: Spelet kring det dukade bordet.* Stockholm: LTs Förlag.

Eriksson, Arne, Arne Nilsson, and Bengt Ohlsson. 1991. *Förnyelsefonder: Huvudrapport.* Stockholm: Arbetslivscentrum.

Erixon, Lennart. 1982a. Tillväxt och strukturförändringar i svensk industri under 70-talet. Meddelande no. 7/82. Institute for Social Research, University of Stockholm.

———. 1982b. Why did Swedish industry perform so poorly in the crisis? *Skandinaviska-Enskilda Banken Quarterly Review*, no. 4.

———. 1984. Den svenska modellen i med- och motgång: En analys av dess innehåll, effekter och förändrade förutsättningar under perioden 1960–1984. Institute for Social Research, University of Stockholm.

———. 1985. What's wrong with the Swedish model? Meddelande no. 12/85. Institute for Social Research, University of Stockholm.

———. 1988. Structural change and economic policy in Sweden during the post-war period. Working paper, Arbetslivscentrum.

———. 1989. Den tredje vägen: Inlåsning eller förnyelse? *Ekonomisk Debatt*, no. 3: 181–95.

Esping-Andersen, Gösta. 1980. *Social class, Social Democracy, and state policy.* Copenhagen: New Social Science Monographs.

———. 1985. *Politics against markets: The Social Democratic road to power.* Princeton: Princeton University Press.

———. 1990. *The three worlds of welfare capitalism.* Princeton: Princeton University Press.

Evans, Peter, Dietrich Rueschemeyer, and Theda Skocpol, eds. 1985. *Bringing the State Back In.* Cambridge: Cambridge University Press.

Feldt, Kjell-Olof. 1958. Pensionsreformen och sparandet. In SOU 1958:4, *Promemoria med förslag om fondförvaltning m.m. i samband med utbyggd pensionering*, 63–88.

———. 1984. *Samtal med Feldt.* Inteviews by Berndt Ahlqvist and Lars Engqvist. Stockholm: Tidens Förlag.

———. 1991. *Alla dessa dagar . . . I regeringen 1982–1990.* Stockholm: Norstedts.

Fry, John. 1986. The Co-determination Act in practice: The case of the mining industry. In *Towards a democratic rationality: Making the case for Swedish labour*, ed. John Fry, 122–66. Aldershot: Gower.

Fulcher, James. 1976. Joint regulation and its decline. In *Readings in the Swedish class structure*, ed. Richard Scase, 51–97. Oxford: Pergamon Press.

Furåker, Bengt. 1979. *Stat och arbetsmarknad: Studier i svensk rörlighetspolitik.* Lund: Arkiv.

Gilljam, Mikael. 1988. *Svenska folket och löntagarfonderna: En studie i politisk åsiktsbildning.* Lund: Studentlitteratur.

REFERENCES

Golden, Miriam, and Jonas Pontusson, eds. 1992. *Bargaining for change: Union politics in Europe and North America*. Ithaca: Cornell University Press.

Gourevitch, Peter. 1986. *Politics in hard times*. Ithaca: Cornell University Press.

Gustafsson, Bo. 1973. A perennial doctrinal history: Keynes and the "Stockholm school." *Economy and History* 16:114–28.

———. 1981. *I övermorgon socialism*. Stockholm: Gidlunds.

Hadenius, Axel. 1976. *Facklig organisationsutveckling: En studie av Landsorganisationen i Sverige*. Stockholm: Rabén & Sjögren.

———. 1983. *Medbestämmandereformen*. Stockholm: Rabén & Sjögren.

Hadenius, Stig. 1985. *Swedish politics during the 20th century*. Stockholm: Swedish Institute.

Hall, Peter. 1986. *Governing the economy: The politics of state intervention in Britain and France*. New York: Oxford University Press.

Hancock, Donald. 1972. *Sweden: The politics of postindustrial change*. Hinsdale: Dryden Press.

Hansson, Sven Ove. 1984. *SAF i politiken*. Stockholm: Tidens Förlag.

Heclo, Hugh. 1974. *Modern social politics in Britain and Sweden*. New Haven: Yale University Press.

Heclo, Hugh, and Hendrik Madsen. 1986. *Policy and politics in Sweden*. Philadelphia: Temple University Press.

Hedborg, Anna, and Rudolf Meidner. 1984. *Folkhemsmodellen*. Stockholm: Rabén & Sjögren.

Hedlund, Gunnar, et al. 1985. *Institutioner som ägare*. Stockholm: Studieförbundet Näringsliv och Samhälle.

Hellberg, Inga. 1988. Exemplet Volvo. In *Konfliktbehandling på arbetsmarknaden*, ed. Sten Edlund et al., 94–128. Stockholm: Arbetslivscentrum.

Henning, Roger. 1974. *Staten som företagare: En studie av Statsföretag AB:s mål, organisation och effektivitet*. Stockholm: Rabén & Sjögren.

———. 1977. *Företagen i politiken: Om selektiv politik och industrins kontakter med staten*. Stockholm: Studieförbundet Näringsliv och Samhälle.

———. 1980a. *Partierna och Stålverk 80: En studie av industripolitiskt beslutsfattande*. Stockholm: Liber Förlag.

———. 1980b. Politikernas informationsunderlag. In *Att utveckla en långsiktig industripolitik: Några specialstudier*, ed. Ministry of Industry, 80–113. DsI 1980.

———. 1984. Industrial policy or employment policy? In *Unemployment: Policy responses of Western democracies*, ed. J. Richardsson and R. Henning. Beverly Hills, Calif.: Sage.

Hermansson, C. H. 1981. *Kapitalister II: Storfinans*. Stockholm: Arbetarkultur.

Hermansson, Jörgen. 1988. Steget som kom bort: Om politisk framgång och misslyckande. In *Mitt i steget: Om ägande och inflytande inför 90-talet*, ed. Dan Andersson, 46–63. Stockholm: Tidens Förlag.

Hibbs, Douglas. 1990. *Wage compression under solidarity bargaining in Sweden*. Stockholm: Trade Union Institute for Economic Research.

Higgins, Winton. 1980. Class mobilization and socialism in Sweden: Lessons from afar. In *Work and inequality*, ed. G. Dow and P. Borehan, 153–54. South Melbourne: Macmillan.

———. 1983. Den svåra vägen tillbaka till en reformistisk marxism. *Häften för kritiska studier* 16, no. 4:41–52.

———. 1985. Political unionism and the corporatist thesis. *Economic and Industrial Democracy* 6, no. 3:349–81.

———. 1988. Swedish Social Democracy and the new Democratic socialism. In *Democ-*

racy, state and justice, ed. Diane Sainsbury, 69–90. Stockholm: Almqvist & Wicksell International.

Higgins, Winton, and Nixon Apple. 1983. How limited is reformism? *Theory and Society* 12, no. 5:603–30.

Himmelstrand, Ulf, et al. 1981. *Beyond welfare capitalism: Issues, actors and forces in societal change.* London: Heinemann.

Hodgson, Geoff. 1982. On the political economy of socialist transition. *New Left Review*, no. 133:52–66.

Holmberg, Sören. 1984. *Väljare i förändring.* Stockholm: Liber Förlag.

Israel, Joachim. 1978. Swedish socialism and big business. *Acta Sociologica* 21, no. 3:341–53.

IVI. 1984. *Economic growth in a Nordic perspective.* Stockholm: Industriens Utredningsinstitut.

Jacobsson, Bengt. 1989. *Konsten att reagera: Intressen, institutioner och näringspolitik.* Stockholm: Carlssons.

Johansson, Anders. 1989. *Tillväxt och klassamarbete: En studie av den svenska modellens uppkomst.* Stockholm: Tidens Förlag.

Johansson, Mats, and Per-Olov Johansson. 1983. Investeringsfonderna 1938–83: En översikt. Gävle: Statens råd för byggforskning.

Jones, G. H. 1976. *Planning and productivity.* London: Croom Helm.

Katzenstein, Peter. 1978. Conclusion: Domestic structures and strategies of foreign economic policy. In *Between power and plenty*, ed. Peter Katzenstein, 295–336. Madison: University of Wisconsin Press.

———. 1985. *Small states in world markets: Industrial policy in Europe.* Ithaca: Cornell University Press.

———. 1988. *Policy and politics in West Germany.* Philadelphia: Temple University Press.

King, Desmond, and Mark Wickham-Jones. 1990. Social Democracy and rational workers. *British Journal of Political Science* 20:387–413.

Kjellberg, Anders. 1981. Från industriell demokrati till medbestämmande: Fackliga utvecklingslinjer, 1917–1980. *Arkiv för Studier i Arbetarrörelsens Historia*, nos. 21/22:53–82.

———. 1983. *Facklig organisering i tolv lander.* Lund: Arkiv Förlag.

Korpi, Walter. 1978. *The working class in welfare capitalism: Work, unions and politics in Sweden.* London: Routledge & Kegan Paul.

———. 1980. Industrial relations and industrial conflict: The case of Sweden. In *Labor relations in advanced industrial societies*, ed. Benjamin Martin and Everett M. Kassalow, 89–108. New York: Carnegie Endowment for International Peace.

———. 1982. The historical compromise and its dissolution. In *Sweden: Choices for economic and social policy in the 1980's*, ed. Bengt Rydén and Villy Bergström, 124–41. London: George Allen & Unwin.

———. 1983. *The democratic class struggle.* London: Routledge & Kegan Paul.

Kuuse, Jan. 1986. *Strukturomvandlingen och arbetsmarknadens organisering.* Stockholm: SAF.

Låftman, Lennart. 1988. I en fonddirektörs huvud. In *Mitt i steget: Om ägande och inflytande inför 90-talet*, 123–31. Stockholm: Tidens Förlag.

Lancaster, Kevin. 1973. The dynamic inefficiency of capitalism. *Journal of Political Economy* 81:1092–1109.

Lash, Scott. 1985. The end of neo-corporatism: The breakdown of centralised bargaining in Sweden. *British Journal of Industrial Relations* 23:215–40.

Levinson, Klas. 1979. Facklig verksamhet i komplexa organisationer: Facklig bevakning av Volvos internationella verksamhet. Working paper, Arbetslivscentrum.

REFERENCES

——. 1990. Fackliga aktörer i strategiska beslutsprocesser: Medverkan och inflytande. Stockholm: Arbetslivscentrum.
Lewin, Leif. 1967. *Planhushållningsdebatten.* Stockholm: Almqvist & Wicksell.
——. 1975. The debate on economic planning in Sweden. In *Sweden's development from poverty to affluence, 1750–1970,* ed. Steven Koblik, 282–302. Minneapolis: University of Minnesota Press.
Lindbeck, Assar. 1974. *Swedish economic policy.* Berkeley: University of California Press.
Lindblom, Charles. 1977. *Politics and markets.* New York: Basic Books.
Lipietz, Alain. 1987. *Mirages and miracles.* London: New Left Books.
LO. 1953. *Trade unions and full employment.* Report to the 1951 congress. London: George Allen & Unwin.
——. 1961. *Fackföreningsrörelsen och företagsdemokratin.* Report to the 1961 congress.
——. 1963. *Economic expansion and structural change.* Report to the 1961 congress. London: George Allen & Unwin.
——. 1967. *Trade unions and technological change.* Report to the 1966 congress. London: George Allen & Unwin.
——. 1971. *Demokrati i företagen.* Report to the 1971 congress.
——. 1973. *Fackföreningsrörelsen och AP-fonden.* Stockholm: LO.
——. 1976. *Kollektiv kapitalbildning genom löntagarfonder.* Report to the 1976 congress. Published in English as Rudolf Meidner, *Employee investment funds.* London: George Allen & Unwin, 1978.
——. 1981. *Näringspolitik för 80-talet.* Report to the 1981 congress.
——. 1987. *3 år med fonderna: En utvärdering av löntagarfonderna.*
——. 1988. *Välfärdsstaten och sparandet.*
——. 1991. *Det utvecklande arbetet.* Report to the 1991 congress.
Lönnroth, Johan. 1974. Svensk samhällsplanering: Ett försök till idéhistoria. In *Arbete, kapital och stat,* ed. Peter Dencik and Bengt-Åke Lundvall, 52–63. Stockholm: Rabén & Sjögren.
LO-SAP. 1978. *Löntagarfonder och kapitalbildning.* Stockholm: LO-SAP.
——. 1981. *Arbetarrörelsen och löntagarfonderna.* Stockholm: Tidens Förlag.
Lundgren, Nils, and Ingemar Ståhl. 1981. *Industripolitikens spelregler.* Stockholm: Industriförbundets Förlag.
Lundmark, Kjell. 1983. Welfare state and employment policy: Sweden. In *Industrial crisis: A comparative study of the state and industry,* ed: Kenneth Dyson and Stephen Wilkes, 220–44. New York: St. Martin's Press.
Mahon, Rianne. 1991. From solidaristic wages to solidaristic work: A post-Fordist historic compromise for Sweden? *Economic and Industrial Democracy* 12, no. 3: 295–325.
Marklund, Staffan. 1982. *Klass, stat, socialpolitik.* Lund: Arkiv.
Martin, Andrew. 1975a. Labor movement parties and inflation. *Polity* 7, no. 4:427–51.
——. 1975b. Is democratic control of capitalist economies possible? In *Stress and contradiction in modern capitalism,* ed. Leon Lindberg, 13–56. Lexington, Mass.: D. C. Heath.
——. 1977. Sweden: Industrial democracy and Social Democratic strategy. In *Worker self-management in industry,* ed. David Garson, 49–96. New York: Praeger.
——. 1979. The dynamics of change in a Keynesian political economy: The Swedish case and its implications. In *State and economy in contemporary capitalism,* ed. Colin Crouch, 88–121. New York: St. Martin's Press.

———. 1981. Economic stagnation and social stalemate in Sweden. In *Monetary policy, selective credit policy and industrial policy in France, Britain, West Germany and Sweden*, 136–215. Staff study prepared for the Joint Economic Committee of the U.S. Congress. Washington, D.C.: Government Printing Office.

———. 1984. Trade unions in Sweden: Strategic responses to change and crisis. In *Unions and economic crisis: Britain, West Germany and Sweden*, ed. Peter Gourevitch et al., 189–359. London: George Allen & Unwin.

———. 1985. Distributive conflict, inflation and investment: The Swedish case. In *The politics of inflation and stagnation*, ed. Leon Lindberg and Charles Maier, 403–66. Washington, D.C.: Brookings Institution.

———. 1987. Sweden: Restoring the Social Democratic distributive regime. Working paper, Center for European Studies, Harvard University.

———. 1991. Wage bargaining and Swedish politics: The political implications of the end of central negotiations. Report to the (government-appointed) commission to study power and democracy in Sweden (*Maktutredningen*).

Meidner, Rudolf. 1973. Samordning och solidarisk lönepolitik under tre decennier. In *Tvärsnitt: Sju forskningsrapporter utgivna till LO:s 75-årsjubileum 1973*, 7–71. Stockholm: Prism.

———. 1975. *Löntagarfonder*. Stockholm: Tidens Förlag.

———. 1980. Our concept of the third way. *Economic and Industrial Democracy* 1:343–70.

———. 1981. Collective asset formation through wage-earner funds. *International Labour Review* 120, no. 3:303–17.

———. 1987. Renewal funds: A Swedish innovation. *Economic and Industrial Democracy* 8:237–42.

Melin, Tore. 1988. Exemplet Posten. In *Konfliktbehandling på arbetsmarknaden*, ed. Sten Edlund et al., 67–92. Stockholm: Arbetslivscentrum.

Ministry of Finance. 1983. *Löntagarfonder i ATP-systemet*. DsFi 1983:20.

———. 1988. *En femte AP-fondsstyrelse*. Ds 1988:12.

———. 1990. *En teknisk översyn av AP-fondens placeringsregler*. Ds 1990:90.

———. 1991. *AP-fondens förvaltning: En översyn*. Ds 1991:14.

Ministry of Industry. 1978. *Sveriges Investeringsbank AB:s framtida verksamhet*. DsI 1978:4.

———. 1981. *Bankernas roll i industripolitiken*. DsI 1981:25.

———. 1982a. *Svensk industri och industripolitik*.

———. 1982b. *Organisation för industriell förnyelse*. DsI 1982:14.

———. 1982c. *Verksamheten vid vissa organ inom den industri- och regionalpolitiska organisationen*. DsI.

———. 1982d. *The net costs of government support to Swedish industry*. DsI 1982:10.

———. 1983–89. *Svensk industri och industripolitik*.

———. 1990. *Svensk industri i utveckling*. Ds 1990:16.

Mjöset, Lars, et al. 1986. *Norden dagen derpå*. Oslo: Universitetsförlaget.

Molin, Björn. 1965. *Tjänstepensionsfrågan: En studie i svensk partipolitik*. Gothenburg: Akademiförlaget.

Nordfors, Lennart, and Staffan Herrström. 1976. Den fjärde AP-fonden: Debatten och verksamheten. Department of Political Science, University of Uppsala.

Offe, Claus, and Helmut Wiesenthal. 1980. Two logics of collective action. In *Political power and social theory*, ed. Maurice Zeitlin, vol. 1, 67–115. Greensburg, Conn.: JAI Press.

Ohlsson, Bengt. 1991. *Pengar till utbildning: Sammanfattning av Förnyelsefondsprojektet*. Stockholm: Arbetslivscentrum.

Öhman, Berndt. 1973. LO och arbetsmarknadspolitiken after andra världskriget. In

REFERENCES

Tvärsnitt: Sju forskningsrapporter utgivna till LO:s 75-årsjubileum 1973, 73–150. Stockholm: Prisma.

Olsen, Gregg. 1990. On the limits of Social Democracy: The rise and fall of the Swedish wage earner funds. Ph.D. diss., University of Toronto.

Olson, Mancur. 1982. *The rise and decline of nations.* New Haven: Yale University Press.

Olsson, Jan. 1989. *Vad ska staten äga? De statliga företagen inför 90-talet.* Stockholm: Ministry of Finance. Ds 1989:23.

Örtengren, Johan. 1981. Kapitalbildning i svensk industri under efterkrigstiden. In *Industrin inför 80-talet,* ed. Bo Carlsson et al., 83–152. Stockholm: Industriens Utredningsinstitut.

Palme, Olof. 1987. *En levande vilja.* Stockholm: Tidens Förlag.

Parris, Henry, Pierre Pestieau, and Peter Saynor. 1987. *Public enterprise in Western Europe.* London: Croom Helm.

Pempel, T. J., and Keiichi Tsunakawa. 1979. Corporatism without labor? In *Trends towards corporatist intermediation,* ed. Philippe Schmitter and Gerhard Lehmbruch. Beverly Hills, Calif.: Sage.

Petersson, Olof. 1980. Staten och kapitalet: Exemplet investeringsfonderna. Unpublished paper, Department of Political Science, University of Uppsala.

Piore, Michael, and Charles Sabel. 1983. *The second industrial divide.* New York: Basic Books.

Pontusson, Jonas. 1983a. Comparative political economy of advanced capitalist states: Sweden and France. *Kapitalistate,* nos. 10–11:43–73.

———. 1983b. Socialdemokratin och den tredje vägen. *Häften för Kritiska Studier* 16, nos. 5–6:64–73.

———. 1984a. Behind and beyond Social Democracy in Sweden. *New Left Review,* no. 143:69–96.

———. 1984b. *Public pension funds and the politics of capital formation in Sweden.* Stockholm: Arbetslivscentrum.

———. 1986. Labor reformism and the politics of capital formation in Sweden. Ph.D. diss., Department of Political Science, University of California, Berkeley.

———. 1987. Radicalization and retreat in Swedish Social Democracy. *New Left Review,* no. 165:5–33.

———. 1988. *Swedish Social Democracy and British labour: Essays on the nature and conditions of Social Democratic hegemony.* Occasional Paper no. 19. Ithaca: Western Societies Program, Cornell University.

———. 1989. The triumph of pragmatism: Nationalisation and privatisation in Sweden. *West European Politics* 11, no. 4:129–40.

———. 1991. Labor, corporatism and industrial policy: The Swedish case in comparative perspective. *Comparative Politics* 23, no. 2:163–79.

———. 1992. Unions, new technology and job redesign at Volvo and British Leyland. In *Bargaining for change,* ed. Miriam Golden and Jonas Pontusson. Ithaca: Cornell University Press.

Przeworski, Adam. 1985. *Capitalism and Social Democracy.* Cambridge: Cambridge University Press.

Przeworski Adam, and John Sprague. 1986. *Paper stones: A history of electoral socialism.* Chicago: University of Chicago Press.

Rehn, Gösta. 1952. The problem of stability: An analysis and some policy proposals. In *Wages policy under full employment,* ed. Ralph Turvey, 30–54. London: William Hidge.

———. 1977. Finansministrarna, LO-ekonomerna och arbetsmarknadspolitiken. In *Ekonomisk debatt och ekonomisk politik: Nationalekonomiska föreningen 100 år,* ed. Jan Herin and Lars Werin, 210–27. Stockholm: Norstedts.

References

———. 1980. Idéutvecklingen. In *Lönepolitik och solidaritet*, 22–69. Stockholm: LO.

———. 1984. Cooperation between the government and workers' and employers' organizations on labour market policy in Sweden. Stockholm: Swedish Institute.

Rothstein, Bo. 1986. *Den socialdemokratiska staten*. Lund: Arkiv.

———. 1987. Corporatism and reformism: The Social Democratic institutionalization of class conflict. *Acta Sociologica* 30, nos. 3–4:295–311.

———. 1990a. Marxism, institutional analysis, and working class power: The Swedish case. *Politics and Society* 18, no. 3:317–45.

———. 1990b. Svenska intresseorganisationer: Från lösningar till problem. In *Svensk demokrati i förändring*, ed. Johan P. Olsen. Stockholm: Carlssons.

RRV. 1988. Fjärde fondstyrelsens och löntagarfondstyrelsernas medelsförvaltning räkenskapsåret 1988. Annual report on collective shareholding funs by the Office of Government Auditors.

———. 1989. Fjärde fondstyrelsens, femte fondstyrelsens och löntagarfondstyrelsernas medelförvaltning räkenskapsåret 1989. Annual report on collective shareholding funds by the Office of Government Auditors.

Rudberg, K., and C. Öhman. 1971. *Investment funds: The release of 1967*. Stockholm: Liber Förlag.

Rydén, Bengt. 1971. *Fusioner i svensk industri*. Stockholm: Industriens Utredningsinstitut.

SAF-LO-PTK. 1982. *Agreement on efficiency and participation*. Stockholm: SAF.

Sainsbury, Diane. 1980. *Swedish Social Democratic ideology and electoral politics, 1944–1948*. Stockholm: Almqvist & Wicksell International.

———. 1991. Swedish Social Democracy in transition. *West European Politics* 14, no. 3:31–57.

Sandkull, Bengt. 1982. *Facket i storföretagen: En forskningsöversikt om inflytandets villkor i koncerner*. Stockholm: Tidens Förlag.

SAP. 1967. *Näringspolitiken*. Stockholm: SAP.

———. 1968. *Näringspolitik*. Stockholm: SAP.

———. 1981. *Framtid för Sverige*. Stockholm: Tidens Förlag.

SAP. 1989. *90-tals programmet*. Stockholm: Tidens Förlag.

SAP-LO. 1946. *The postwar program of Swedish labour*. Stockholm: LO-SAP. (*Artetarrörelsens efterkrigsprogram*, 1944).

Scase, Richard. 1977. *Social Democracy in capitalist society: Working-class politics in Britain and Sweden*. London: Croom Helm.

SCB. Various years. *Statistisk årsbok för Sverige/Statistical Abstract of Sweden*. Issued by SCB.

Schiller, Bernt. 1973. LO, paragraf 32 och företagsdemokratin. In *Tvärgnitt: Sju forskningsrapporter utgivna till LO:s 75-årsjubileum*, 283–398. Stockholm: Prisma.

———. 1988. *Samarbete eller konflikt*. Stockholm: Arbetsmiljöfonden.

Schön, Lennart. 1982. Det förstenade kapitalet: Det svenska industrisamhällets kris i historiskt perspektiv. *Zenit* no. 77:17–26.

Shonfield, Andrew. 1965. *Modern capitalism*. London: Oxford University Press.

Simonson, Birger. 1988. *Arbetarmakt och näringspolitik: LO och inflytandefrågorna*. Stockholm: Arbetsmiljöfonden.

SIND. 1980. *Ägandet i det privata näringslivet*. Stockholm: SIND.

———. 1981. *Selektiv eknomisk politik och industrins strukturanpassning*. PM no. 22.

Sjönander, Bo Jonas. 1974. *AP-fonden och kapitalmarknaden*. Stockholm: Handelsbankens Småskriftsserie.

———. 1981. En ännu icke oskadliggjord marknad. *Skandinaviska Enskilda Bankens Kvartalsskrift*, no. 3–4:66–76.

Söderlind, Donald, and Olof Petersson. 1986. *Svensk förvaltningspolitik*. Uppsala: Diskurs.

REFERENCES

Söderpalm, Sven-Anders. 1975. The Crisis Agreement and the Social Democratic road to power. In *Sweden's development from poverty to affluence, 1750–1970*, ed. Steven Koblik, 258–78. Minneapolis: University of Minnesota Press.

——. 1976. *Direktörsklubben: Storindustrin i svensk politik under 1930- och 40-talen.* Stockholm: Rabén & Sjögren.

——. 1980. *Arbetsgivarna och Saltsjöbadspolitiken.* Stockholm: SAF.

Södersten, Bo. 1974. Bostadsförsörjning och bostadspolitik under efterkrigstiden. In *Svensk ekonomi*, 2d ed., ed. Bo Södersten, 318–51. Stockholm: Rabén & Sjögren.

Södersten, Jan. 1977. Bolagsbeskattningens verkningar. In *Beskattning av företag: Bilagor*, 107–93. SOU 1977:87.

Söderström, Hans Tson, ed. 1990. *I Samtidens bakvatten?* Konjunkturrådets rapport. Stockholm: SNS Förlag.

——. 1991. *Sverige vid vändpunkten.* Konjunkturrådets rapport. Stockholm: SNS Förlag.

SOU. 1957. *Förbättrad pensionering: Betänkande avqivet av allmänna pensionsberedningen.* SOU 1957:7.

——. 1958. *Promemoria med förslag om fondförvaltning m.m. i samband med utbyggd pensionering.* SOU 1958:4.

——. 1965. *Arbetsmarknadspolitik.* SOU 1965:9.

——. 1970. *The Swedish economy 1971–75 and the general outlook up to 1990.* SOU 1970:71.

——. 1972. *Näringslivets försörjning med riskkapital från allmänna pensionsfonden.* SOU 1972:63.

——. 1975. *Demokrati på arbetsplatsen.* SOU 1975:1.

——. 1977a. *Beskattning av företag: Slutbetänkande av företagsskatteberedningen.* SOU 1977:86.

——. 1977b. *Beskattning av företag: Bilagor.* SOU 1977:87.

——. 1978a. *Kapitalmarknaden i svensk ekonomi.* SOU 1978:11.

——. 1978b. *Statligt företagande i samhällets tjänst.* SOU 1978:78.

——. 1980. *Långtidsutredningen 1980.* SOU 1980:52.

——. 1981a. *Att avveckla en kortsiktig stödpolitik.* SOU 1981:72.

——. 1981b. *Löntagarna och kapitaltillväxten 5: Slutrapport.* SOU 1981:44.

——. 1982a. *En effektivare kreditpolitik.* SOU 1982:52.

——. 1982b. *Tillväxt eller stagnation? Avstämning av 1980 års långtidsutredning.* SOU 1982:14.

——. 1982c. *Svensk industri i utlandet: En analys av drivkrafter och effekter.* SOU 1982:27.

——. 1982d. *MBL i utveckling.* SOU 1982:60.

——. 1983. *Näringspolitiska effekter av internationella investeringar.* SOU 1983:16.

——. 1988. *Ägande och inflytande i svenskt näringsliv.* SOU 1988:38.

——. 1989. *Reformerad företagsbeskttning.* SOU 1989:34.

Steinmo, Sven. 1984. Taxation as an instrument of public policy: Sweden. Paper presented to the European Consortium on Political Research conference at Salzburg, April 13–18, 1984.

——. 1988. Social democracy vs. socialism: Goal adaptation in Social Democratic Sweden. *Politics and Society* 16, no. 4:403–46.

——. 1989. Political institutions and tax policy in the United States, Sweden, and Britain. *World Politics* 41, no. 4:500–35.

Stephens, Evelyne Huber, and John Stephens. 1982. The labor movement, political power, and workers' participation in Western Europe. *Political Power and Social Theory* 3:215–49.

References

Stephens, John. 1979. *The transition from capitalism to socialism.* London: Macmillan.
Stråth, Bo. 1988. Verkstadsklubbarna vid Volvo och Saab: Facklig politik i två företagskulturer. In *Metall 100 År: Fem uppsatser*, 83–108. Stockholm: Svenska Metallindustriarbetarförbundet.
Streeck, Wolfgang. 1984. Co-determination: The fourth decade. In *International yearbook of organizational democracy*, 2:391–422. London: John Wiley.
———. 1985. Introduction. In *Industrial relations and technological change in the British, Italian, and German automobile industries*, ed. Streeck. Berlin: Wissenschaftszentrum.
———. 1987. Industrial relations and industrial change: The restructuring of the world automobile industry. *Economic and Industrial Democracy* 8:437–62.
Sundgren, Per. 1978. Införandet av MTM-metoden i svensk verkstadsindustri. *Arkiv för Studier i Arbetarrörelsens Historia*, 3–33.
Sundkvist Sven-Ivan. 1989. *Owners and power in Sweden's listed companies, 1989.* Stockholm: Dagens Nyheter.
———. 1990. *Owners and power in Sweden's listed companies, 1990.* Stockholm: Dagen Nyheter.
Svenning, Olle. 1972. *Socialdemokratin och näringslivet.* Stockholm: Tidens Förlag.
Svenska Metallindustriarbetarförbundet. 1987. *Rewarding work.* Stockholm: Arbetsmiljöfonden.
———. 1989. *Solidarisk arbetspolitik för det goda arbetet.* Report to the 1989 congress of the Metal Workers' Union.
Swenson, Peter. 1989. *Fair shares: Unions, pay and politics in Sweden and West Germany.* Ithaca: Cornell University Press.
———. 1991. Bringing capital back in, or Social democracy reconsidered: Employer power, cross-class alliances and centralization of industrial relations in Denmark and Sweden. *World Politics* 43, no. 4:513–44.
———. 1992. Labor and the limits of the welfare state. In *Bargaining for change*, ed. Miriam Golden and Jonas Pontusson. Ithaca: Cornell University Press.
Taylor, John. 1982. The Swedish investment funds system as a stabilization policy rule. *Brookings Papers on Economic Activity*, no. 1.
TCO. 1981. *Offensiv industripolitik—ett måste för 80-talet.* Report to the TCO congress of 1982.
Thelen, Kathleen. 1992. The politics of flexibility in the German metalworking industries. In *Bargaining for change*, ed. Miriam Golden and Jonas Pontusson. Ithaca: Cornell University Press.
Therborn, Göran. 1984. Socialdemokratin träder fram. *Arkiv för Studier in Arbetarrörelsens Historia*, nos. 27–28:3–71.
Thunholm, Lars-Erik. 1981. Affärsbankerna och den industriella utvecklingen. *Skandinaviska Enskilda Bankens Kvartalsskrift*, nos. 1–2:3–11.
Tilton, Tim. 1990. *The political theory of Swedish Social Democracy: Through the welfare state to socialism.* Oxford: Clarendon Press.
Tingsten, Herbert. 1973. *The Swedish Social Democrats.* Totowa, N.J.: Bedminster Press. Originally published 1941.
Turner, Lowell. 1991. *Democracy at work: Changing world markets and the future of labor unions.* Ithaca: Cornell University Press.
Uhr, Carl. 1977. Economists and policy-making 1930–36: Sweden's experience. *History of Political Economy* 9, no. 1:89–121.
Unga, Nils. 1976. *Socialdemokratin och arbetslöshetsfrågan, 1912–34.* Lund: Arkiv Förlag.
Volvo. 1983. AB Volvo Development Agreement. Trans. Alan Neal for *Labour Line Europe*. Mimeographed.
Waara, Lennart. 1980. *Den statliga företagssektorns expansion.* Stockholm: Liber Förlag.

REFERENCES

Wadensjö, Eskil. 1979. Arbetsmarknadspolitiken: Från rörlighetsstimulans till företagsstöd. *Ekonomisk debatt* 7, no. 2:103–9.

Wage-Earner Fund 1. 1984–89. *Årsredovisning.* Annual reports.

Wage-Earner Fund 2. 1984–89. *Årsredovsining.* Annual reports.

Wage-Earner Fund 3. 1984–89. *Årsredovisning.* Annual reports.

Wage-Earner Fund 4. 1894–89. *Årsredovisning.* Annual reports.

Wage-Earner Fund 5. 1984–89. *Årsredovisning.* Annual reports.

Walters, Peter. 1983. Sweden's public sector crisis, before and after the 1982 elections. *Government and Opposition* 18, no. 1:23–39.

———. 1985. "Distributing decline": Swedish Social Democrats and the crisis of the welfare state. *Government and Opposition* 20, no. 3:356–69.

Weir, Margaret, and Theda Skocpol. 1985. State structures and the possibilities for "Keynesian" responses to the Great Depression. In *Bringing the state back in*, ed. Peter Evans, Dietrich Rueschemeyer, and Theda Skocpol, 107–68. Cambridge: Cambridge University Press.

Wickman, Krister. 1983. Räcker AP-fonderna? Mimeographed.

Wickman, Kurt. 1980. *Makro-ekonomisk planering: Orsaker och utvecklong.* Stockholm: Almqvist & Wicksell International.

Widen, Leif. 1989. *Fem år med löntagarfonder.* Stockholm: Näringlivets Ekonomifakta.

———. 1990. *Löntagarfonderna under sex år—och de nya stegen.* Stockholm: Näringslivets Ekonomifakta.

Wikander, Sten. 1988. Har fjärde ap-fonden haft någon betydelse? In *Mitt i steget: Om ägande och inflytande inför 90-talet*, ed. Dan Anderson, 93–110. Stockholm: Tidens Förlag.

Wright, Erik Olin. 1976. Class boundaries in advanced capitalist societies. *New Left Review*, no. 98:3–42.

Zysman, John. 1983. *Governments, markets and growth: Financial systems and the politics of industrial change.* Ithaca: Cornell University Press.

Index

AB Kabi, 135 (table), 136
AB Statens Skogsindustrier (ASSI), 136, 140, 147, 148, 149, 150 (table)
Agrarian party, 4,5, 51, 64, 65, 79
  in 1930s, 37, 38, 44, 45, 54, 95
  See also Bourgeois parties; Center party
Allmännapensionsfonden. *See* AP funds
Åmark, Klas, 162
AMS. *See* Labor Market Board
Anderson, Dan, 216
AP funds, 12–13, 22, 32, 57–58, 121
  decline in, 98, 112–13
  Fifth, 187, 199, 202, 203
  and intermediary credit institutions, 89–91, 133
  legal-institutional framework of, 21, 58–59, 80–84, 89, 92–94, 233
  and lending to business, 84–85, 88–92
  proposed reorganization of, 198–201
  sectoral allocation of, 58, 84–88
  See also ATP system; Fourth AP Fund
Arbetsmarknadsstyrelsen. *See* Labor Market Board
ARK. *See* Labor Law Commission
Åsbrink, Per, 81
ASEA-Atom, 136
ASSI. *See* AB Statens Skogsindustrier
Association of Industrial Employees (SIF), 231
Astra, 209
ATP system, 12–13, 71, 92–94
  and corporate efficiency, 95
  decline in savings of, 98, 112, 113, 122
  funding of, 79–80

impact on industrial finance, 103
long-term viability of, 85
multiple funds in, 81
proposed reorganization of, 198–201
and Small Business Fund, 145
and wage-earner funds, 194–95, 197
See also AP funds; Fourth AP Fund
Australia, 106

Banks, 49, 52, 86, 133, 153
  and collective shareholding funds, 190, 205
  control of corporate equity by, 88–89
  and intermediary credit institutions, 90, 92
Bargaining, 96, 110, 128, 166
  and Basic Agreement, 38–39, 161
  employers' efforts to decentralize, 118, 119
  limitations on, 161–62, 168–70
  See also Codetermination; Wage solidarity
Basic Agreement (Saltsjöbaden Agreement), 38–39, 45, 161
Blomberg, Leif, 173
Board of Technological Development (STU), 132
Board of Industry (SIND), 132
Bonds, 85–87, 88, 89, 90, 113, 200
Borrowing
  and corporate vulnerability, 103–4, 108
  decline in, 109–10, 122
Boston Consulting Group, 152

Bourgeois parties, 13–14, 22, 110
and active labor market policy, 66
and AP funds, 81, 94, 191, 199, 213
and codetermination, 166, 168
currency devaluation by, 116
deficit spending under, 105, 112
and industrial policy, 128, 130, 138–
42, 152, 153–54, 157
and investment funds, 113–14, 115
and Myrdal Commission, 50
opposition to wage-earner funds by, 4,
15, 193, 224, 229, 230
See also Agrarian party; Center party;
Moderate Unity party; People's
party
Brazil, 106
Broström, Anders, 170
Budgets
and deficit spending, 47, 48–49, 65,
105, 112
1980s balancing of, 14, 117, 143, 149
Business
and active labor market policy, 66, 67–
68
attitude toward AP funds, 81, 94, 190,
199
campaign against planning, 50, 54
collaboration with government, 48, 52–
53
division within, during 1930s, 44–45
and historical compromise, 38–40
vs. labor's interests in investment decisions, 31–32
need for cooperation by, 236, 237
and 1979 investment fund legislation,
114
opposition to collective shareholding
by, 15, 103, 190, 196, 199, 229–32
political power of, 5, 18, 54–55
position on codetermination, 228
rationalization movement within, 41
supply of ATP savings to, 84–85, 88–
92
systemic power of, 22–24, 227–28,
233–34, 235
See also Corporations; Industry

Capital
concentration of, 74
restrictions on international movement
of, 14
Capital equipment, 107, 108, 114, 115
Capital-intensive industry, 75, 107

Capital Market Commission, 81, 82n.11,
91
Capital markets
government inability to manipulate,
152–55
and limits on collective shareholder
funds, 218
Carlson, Ingvar, 150
Carlsson, Bo, 107–8
Celsius Industries, 149, 150 (table), 151
Center party, 4n.5, 77, 130–31, 138, 141
and codetermination, 26, 166, 167,
168, 170, 228
and Fourth AP Fund, 190
and wage-earner funds, 228
See also Agrarian party; Bourgeois parties
Central Bank, 70, 90, 92, 173
and AP funds, 21, 58, 87, 112–13
regulation of credit markets by, 13,
85–86, 88
Central Organization of Salaried Employees (TCO), 1–2n.1, 67, 114
and codetermination, 26, 166, 167,
168–70, 174, 185, 223, 228
and Fourth AP Fund, 203
and labor representation in industrial
policy-making, 155–56, 157
and renewal funds, 183n.14
and wage-earner funds, 28, 196–97,
204, 228–30, 232
Chemical industry, 105, 111
Codetermination, 2, 16, 161–63, 234
commission of inquiry on, 167–70
and Development Agreement, 171–72,
174–75, 179, 234
and exit option, 22–23, 233
limitations on, 183–85
origins of LO offensive for, 163–67
and renewal funds, 163, 172–74, 180–
83, 185
success of, 6, 23, 221–22, 225
in Sweden and other countries compared, 223
vs. union representation at shareholder
meetings, 212, 217
Volvo agreement on, 174–76
and wage-earner funds legislative politics compared, 26, 226–27, 228–
29, 231
and work reorganization at Volvo,
176–80, 184, 223
Codetermination Act of 1976, 16, 170–
72, 179, 221, 229, 234

Codetermination Act of 1976 (*cont.*)
  and German codetermination law compared, 223
  importance of, 162
Collective bargaining. *See* Bargaining
Collective shareholding funds, 2
  board representation and decision making in, 203–5
  legislative politics of, 226–27, 228–32, 236–37
  limitations on, 23, 217–19, 233–34
  as owners, 209–13, 217, 218
  as portfolio investors, 205–9
  as promoters of industrial innovation, 213–16
  significance of, 223–25
  size and performance of, 202–3
  See also Fourth AP Fund; Meidner Plan; Wage-earner funds
Commercial state agencies, 134. *See also* State enterprise
Commission for Postwar Economic Planning, 49–50, 51, 55, 62
Communist party, 1n.1, 51, 54, 131, 167
Company Statute, 204
Conservatives. *See* Moderate Unity party
Coordinated Industrial Policy, 129, 130
Corporations, 2, 201, 204, 211
  access to information about, 164, 170, 171, 234
  mergers of, 107, 108, 139, 145–46
  union representation on boards of directors of, 164, 167, 173
  See also Business; Industry; State enterprise; Taxation
Corporatism, 7–8, 12, 95. *See also* Codetermination; Representation
Credit, supply of, 103, 112, 118
Credit markets, 88–92
  competition in, 81–82
  deregulation of, 14, 118
  regulation of, 13, 85–86, 88
Crouch, Colin, 30
Currency
  crisis of 1947, 52
  devaluation of, 14, 53, 116, 117, 144

Dahlström, Edmund, 176
Dahlström, Lennart, 82n.11, 86, 87
Debt-equity ratios. *See* Borrowing
December Compromise (1906), 161
Deficit spending. *See* Budgets
Democratic socialism. *See* Social democracy; Social Democratic party

Democratization
  defined, 8
  labor's interests in, 29–32
  See also specific programs
Depreciation, 70, 71–72, 75
Devaluation, 14, 53, 116, 117, 144
Development Agreement, 171–72, 174–75, 179, 234
Development funds, 195
Direktörsklubben. *See* Executives' Club

EC. *See* European Community
EEC. *See* European Economic Community
EFO model, 102, 110
Eiser Corporation, 136, 139
Electoral politics, 7, 18–20, 22, 25–26
  and retreat from planning, 50–51, 54
  and socialist rise to power, 37–38
  See also specific parties
Elster, Jon, 230, 231–32
Elvander, Nils, 67
Employment, 41, 42, 59, 70
  and active labor market policy, 12, 65, 67, 68
  as a cause of labor's radicalization, 33, 98
  and defensive orientation of industrial policy, 152, 154
  and deficit spending, 47, 48–49
  and foreign investment, 110–11
  labor's interests in, 30
  in 1980s, 14, 117, 122
  and rationalization, 42, 43, 122
  and regional policy, 77, 130, 133, 141, 147, 198
  and restructuring of state enterprise, 150
  sectoral tradeoffs in, 103, 104–5
Employment Security Act of 1974, 3
Energy, 101
Engineering industry, 73–74, 105, 106, 107, 111, 153
  foreign employment in, 108
  Fourth AP Fund investment in, 208, 217
  skill levels in, 120
  and wage bargaining in 1980s, 118
Enterprise committees, 42
Esping-Andersen, Gösta, 2, 57–58, 59, 79
Eriksbergs Mekaniska Verkstad, 139
Eriksson, Arne, 181, 182
Erixon, Lennart, 101, 109, 119

Erlander, Tage, 52n.7, 65, 133
European Community (EC), 5, 109, 121, 199, 201
European Economic Community (EEC), 76
Executives' Club, 44–45, 50, 52
Exit options, 22–23, 233
Exports, 3, 106, 116. *See also* Trade

Federation of Industry, 46, 50, 52
Feldt, Kjell-Olof, 25, 116, 117, 144, 159, 160, 198
Fifth AP Fund, 187, 199, 202, 203
Fiscal corporations, 134. *See also* State enterprise
Fiscal policy, 32, 60, 61, 103, 188
Forestry, 106, 111, 122, 136, 140, 147
   collective shareholding fund investment in, 208 (table), 209
Fortia, 151
Fourth AP fund, 132, 149, 153, 186, 216–17, 221
   creation of, 189–91
   as model for wage-earner funds, 15, 187, 197
   1983 legislation regarding, 198
   as owner, 209–11, 212, 223–24
   as portfolio investor, 205–9, 223
   as promoter of industrial innovation, 213–16
   representation and decision-making in, 203–4
   size and performance of, 153, 199, 202–3
France, 14, 39, 152–53, 154, 223
Free trade, 3

GDP. *See* Gross domestic product
Geijer, Arne, 65n.4
Germany, West, 152, 164, 223
Ghent, Belgium plant (Volvo), (180)
Götaverken shipyard, 139–40
Gränges and Stora Kopparberg, 140
Great Britain, 39, 152
Great Depression, 41, 42
Gross domestic product (GDP), 2, 14
Group Council (Volvo), 175

Hadenius, Axel, 42
Hansson, Per Albin, 44, 52n.7
Hansson, Sven Ove, 230
Harpsund conferences, 52n.7
Hedborg, Anna, 160
Henning, Roger, 78, 134

Hermansson, Jorgen, 230–31, 232
Higgins, Winton, 25, 26
"Historical compromise," 4–5, 17, 37, 38–39, 45–46
Housing, 2n.2, 85, 86, 87

IF. *See* Investment funds
Imports, 3, 111, 116. *See also* Trade
Income redistribution, 2, 70, 93–94
Industrial Credit Corporation, 90–91
Industrial democracy, 42. *See also* Codetermination
Industrial Fund, 141
Industrial policy, 2, 23
   and active labor market policy compared, 13–14, 151–58, 220–21
   under bourgeois governments, 128, 138–42
   and codetermination, 221–22
   collective shareholding funds as instrument of, 25, 193, 195, 203, 214, 216–19, 221
   defensive orientation of, 127, 128, 151–55, 158–59, 220, 223
   and expansion of state enterprise, 133–38
   and institutional reforms, 131–34
   labor's role in making, 155–58
   lessons for, 237
   origins of, 128–31
   reasons for failure of, 127–28, 158–60, 224
   and restructuring and privatization of state enterprise, 142–43, 147–51, 215
   of Social Democratic party in 1980s, 142–47
   and systemic power of business, 234
Industrial Policy Council, 131, 156, 157
Industrifonden. *See* Industrial Fund
Industry
   and AP fund investment policies, 87–88
   competitive position of, 105–7, 110–11, 121–22
   distribution of borrowing by, 89–90
   investment in, 1937–82, 100 (figure)
   and sectoral tradeoffs in employment, 103, 104–5
   subsidies to, 14
   See also Business; Corporations
Inflation, 54, 59, 60, 112
   in 1980s, 117, 118, 119, 122
Infrastructure, 85

Insurance companies, 49, 52
  and AP funds compared, 13, 58, 83–
    84, 86, 89
  and collective shareholding funds, 190,
    205, 206, 217, 223
Interest rates, 86, 103, 104, 153
Interest representation. *See* Representation
Intermediary credit institutions, 89–92,
  132–33, 135, 147, 153
Investeringsbanken. *See* Investment Bank
  of Sweden
Investment
  business power over allocation of, 22–
    23, 233–34
  and electoral politics, 19–20
  and employment patterns, 103–5
  foreign, 108–9, 110–11, 120–21, 122,
    153
  in industry, 1932–82, 100 (figure)
  by Investment Bank of Sweden, 132–
    33
  labor's interests in control of, 29–32
  levels of decision-making about, 7
  1970s slump in, 99, 101
  by State Enterprise Corporation, 137
  See also AP funds; Collective sharehold-
    ing funds; Investment funds
Investment Bank of Sweden, 90, 91 (table), 132–33, 135, 147, 153
Investment companies, 190, 206, 217,
  223
Investment Council, 51
Investment funds (IF), 21, 46, 57, 69–73,
  98, 113–15
  abolition of, 15, 115
  differential effects of, 73–75
  releases as a policy tool, 12–13, 58, 59,
    75–79, 115, 130
  and renewal funds compared, 173
Investment politics, history of, 11–17
Iron, 122, 136, 137, 147

Jacobsson, Bengt, 150, 159
Japan, 106–7, 152–53, 154, 223
Joint-stock companies, 74

Kalmar plant (Volvo), 176–78
Kapitalmarknadsutredningen (KMU),
  189–91, 199
Katzenstein, Peter, 5, 223
Keynesian economic theory, 3, 40, 41, 61
KMU. *See* Kapitalmarknadsutredningen

Korpi, Walter, 10, 17–18, 20, 32, 33, 236
  on historical compromise, 4–5, 17, 37,
    39

Labor costs
  and competitiveness, 101–3
  and foreign investment, 108
  and inflation in 1980s, 118
  1970s increases in, 99–100
Labor Law Commission (ARK), 167–70
Labor Law Commission (NARK), 170,
  172
Labor Market Board (AMS), 57, 62, 132,
  138
  and authorization of investment fund
    releases, 12, 76–77, 78
  corporatist representation on, 66–68,
    96, 155, 156
Labor market policy, 77, 96, 103
  and corporatist representation on
    AMS, 66–68
  and industrial policy compared, 13–14,
    151–58, 220–21
  opposition to, 65–66
  and Rehn-Meidner model, 12, 60, 61,
    62, 64–65
Labor movement
  alliances with business, 236
  defined, 1–2n.1, 19
  divisions within, 5–6, 16–17, 25–27,
    28, 158–59, 224, 227–28
  and electoral politics, 19, 20
  and government inability to manipu-
    late capital markets, 153, 154–55
  and historical compromise, 4–5, 17,
    38–40
  industrial policy failure of, 159–60,
    221–22
  interests in democratization of invest-
    ment, 29–32
  internal unity of, 95–96
  and investment in housing and infra-
    structure, 85
  lack of influence on investment fund
    releases, 78
  and limitations on bargaining, 161–62
  mechanisms of industrial restruc-
    turing's impact on, 99
  origins of industrial policy of, 128–31
  pension reform objectives of, 93–94
  postwar strategy of, 11–12, 32–33, 47–
    50, 94–95
  and rationalization, 41–43

Labor movement (*cont.*)
  and reasons for reform offensive of
      1968–76, 17–18, 20, 32–33, 97–
      98
  reform initiatives proposed by, 1–2, 3–
      4, 13–16
  and regulation of credit markets, 88
  retreat from planning by, 51–56
  role in making active labor policy, 155
  role in setting industrial policy, 128–
      31, 155–58
  wage solidarity as ideal of, 62–63
  See also Landsorganisationen; Unions;
      and specific reforms promoted by
Lancaster, Kevin, 30
Landsorganisationen (LO), 1n.1
  and active labor market policy, 62, 65,
      66
  and aims of wage-earner funds, 222
  and Basic Agreement, 38–39, 45
  and codetermination legislation offen-
      sive, 168–70, 185, 223, 228
  and codetermination offensive, 162,
      163–67
  and December Compromise, 161
  and Development Agreement, 171–72,
      174
  and divisions within labor movement,
      16–17, 24, 25
  and energy policy, 151
  and equity investment by AP funds,
      121, 189–90, 198–99
  and implementation of reforms, 235
  and industrial policy, 61–62, 129, 155–
      56, 157
  and 1970s wage increases, 100, 102–3
  and 1979 investment fund legislation,
      114
  1981 economic program of, 116
  and pension reform of 1959, 93
  pivotal role of, 96
  and political failure of wage-earner
      funds, 160, 218, 228, 229, 230,
      232
  Postwar Program of, 47–50, 52, 53, 54
  postwar wage restraint by, 59
  and proposal for tripartite sector coun-
      cils, 51–52
  and rationalization, 42
  and renewal funds, 181–82, 183
  representation on AMS, 66
  and representation on collective share-
      holding funds, 203, 204
  and state enterprise, 135, 150

  and wage-earner funds proposals, 3–4,
      186, 188–89, 193–96
  and wage solidarity, 63–64, 68–69,
      101, 102–3, 118
  and works councils, 53, 55n.8
Layoffs. *See* Employment
Lewin, Leif, 40, 43, 47
Liberals. *See* People's party
LKAB. *See* Luossavaara-Kirunavaara
LO. *See* Landsorganisationen
Long-Term Economic Survey of 1970,
      189
Luossavaara-Kirunavaara (LKAB), 135
      (table), 136, 137, 140, 150 (table)
  restructuring of, 147, 148, 149
  strike at, 165, 166
Luxor, 140, 148

Mammoth Commission, 43–44, 55
Management
  and limitations on codetermination,
      184–85
  and ownership, 6–7
  and renewal funds, 181–82
  at Volvo, 175, 178, 179, 184
Manufacturing sector, 72, 75
Martin, Andrew, 61, 99–100, 166, 188
Meidner, Rudolf, 57, 61, 62n.3, 160, 186,
      221
  and pension reform, 93, 94
  on wage solidarity, 74
  See also Meidner Plan; Rehn-Meid-
      ner model
Meidner Plan, 4, 21, 24, 191–93, 228,
      236
  critiques of, 231–32
  and LO-SAP wage-earner fund pro-
      posals compared, 194–95
  opposition to, 15, 186–87, 196, 229
  See also Collective shareholding funds;
      Wage-earner funds
Mergers, 107, 108, 139, 145–46
Metalworkers Union, 62, 118, 120, 181
  and industrial policy, 150, 156–57
  and legal restrictions on "national capi-
      tal," 121, 199
  and work reorganization at Volvo, 178,
      179, 235
Mining, 100 (figure), 104, 106, 111, 140
Ministry of Domestic Affairs, 156n.12
Ministry of Energy and Environment,
      150
Ministry of Finance, 78

Ministry of Industry, 131–32, 150, 151, 156, 203
  under bourgeois governments, 141–42
  and research and development, 146
  and state enterprise, 134, 147, 154
Ministry of Labor, 156n.12
Moderate Unity party, 4n.5, 138, 167, 170, 190, 228. *See also* Bourgeois parties
Molin, Rune, 150–51, 157n.15
Möller, Gustav, 52n.7
Myrdal, Gunnar, 50, 52n.7
Myrdal Commission. *See* Commission for Postwar Economic Planning

NARK. *See* Labor Law Commission
Nationalization, 39, 40, 133
  under bourgeois parties, 14, 140–41
  postwar porposals for, 49, 52
  See also State Enterprise Corporation
NCB, 148, 149, 151
Nilsson, Arne, 181, 182
Norbottens Järnverk AB (NJA), 135 (table), 136, 137, 140
Norway, 102

OECD, *See* Organization for Economic Cooperation and Development
Offe, Claus, 23
Ohlsson, Bengt, 181, 182
Ohlsson, Bertil, 65n.4
Oil crisis, 101
Olsson, Jan, 150
Organization for Economic Cooperation and Development (OECD), 99, 101, 106, 117, 118
"Organized capitalism," 42

Palme, Olof, 162, 193, 198
Pension Committee of 1957, 81, 83, 92–93
Pension reform of 1959. *See* AP funds; ATP system
Pension reserve funds, 46, 71
People's party, 4n.5, 26, 166, 168, 170, 228
  and Fourth AP Fund, 190
  and industrial policy, 138
  See also Bourgeois parties
Pharmaceutical firms, 208 (table), 209, 217
Pharmacia, 209
PK Banken. *See* Postal and Credit Bank

Planning, 11, 15, 159
  and labor's postwar offensive, 47–50
  during 1930s, 43–47
  postwar retreat from, 11, 39, 50–53
  reasons for retreat from, 53–56
  Social Democratic idea of, 41–43
Plant Council (Volvo), 175
Postal and Credit Bank, 147, 148
Postwar Program (LO-SAP), 47–50, 52, 53, 54
Pripps Breweries, 137
Privatization, 148–50, 215
Procordia, 147–49, 150 (table). *See also* State Enterprise Corporation
Productivity growth, 54, 80, 101–2, 107–8, 119–21
  labor's interest in, 30
  and Rehn-Meidner model, 60, 63
Profits, 102, 103, 109, 110, 111
  in 1980s, 117, 118, 122
Profit-sharing. *See* Collective share-holding funds; Wage-earner funds
Przeworski, Adam, 10, 18–20, 28–29, 33
PTK, 171
Public sector, 110, 231–32
  cutbacks in, 116, 117, 119
  employment in, 105, 117

Rationaliseringsutredningen. *See* Rationalization Commission
Rationalization, 41–43, 45, 54, 122
  commission recommendations on, 46–47
  and productivity growth in 1960s, 107–8
Rationalization Commission, 46–47
Raw materials, 101, 102, 104, 106, 122
R&D. *See* Research and development
Real wages, 41–42, 80, 98
Reform offensive of 1968–76, 1–6, 221–22
  business-centered reasons for failure of, 22–24, 227–28
  comparative assessment of, 223–24
  implementation as locus of failure of, 21–22, 227, 232–35
  labor-centered reasons for failure of, 24–27, 28, 227–28
  legislative reasons for failure of, 21–22, 226–27, 228–32
  lessons from, 236–37
  reasons for, 29–33, 97–98
  See also specific programs

Regional policy objectives, 77, 130–31, 145
  and state enterprise, 133, 147
  and wage-earner funds, 198, 214
Rehn, Gösta, 57, 61. *See also* Rehn-Meidner model
Rehn-Meidner model, 11–12, 32–33, 57, 60–62, 63, 64–65, 93
  and ATP system, 80
  and corporate profits taxation, 72
  and industrial policy in 1980s compared, 145
  and labor's alliance with export-oriented industry, 94–96
  and wage-earner funds, 188
Renewal funds (RF), 163, 172–74, 180–83, 185
Representation, 95
  on AMS, 67
  on AP fund boards, 13, 81, 82 (table)
  on collective shareholding funds, 203–5
  on corporate boards of directors, 164, 167, 173, 215–16
  electoral parliamentary vs. corporatist, 7–8
  in intermediary credit institutions, 91
  of labor in industrial policy making, 155–58
  of unions at shareholder meetings, 211, 212, 216, 217
  See also Codetermination
Research and development (R&D), 104, 114, 146–47
  and renewal funds, 173, 174, 180, 182, 183
Retroverse loans, 82, 83 (table), 87, 89, 90, 93
RF. *See* Renewal funds
Rothstein, Bo, 29
Rydén, Bengt, 107

Saab, 31n.10
SACO-SR. *See* Swedish Confederation of Professional Associations
SAF, 50, 66, 168, 203
  and Development Agreement, 171, 172, 174
  and managerial prerogatives, 38–39, 161, 165
  and rationalization, 42, 45, 53
  wage bargaining by, 63, 64, 110, 118
  and works councils, 53, 164

Saltsjöbaden Agreement (Basic Agreement), 38–39, 45, 161
SAP. *See* Social Democratic party
SARA, 135 (table), 136
Schiller, Bernt, 18n.5, 171
SEB. *See* Skandinaviska-Enskilda Banken
Selective state intervention, 3, 127, 237
  by bourgeois governments, 141, 152
  and defensive orientation of industrial policy, 152–53
  in labor market, 60, 61, 95, 96
  labor movement retreat from, 23–24, 25, 39, 51, 128, 160, 224
  Rationalization Commission recommendations on, 47
  and regional policy objectives, 130–31
  and regulation of credit markets, 86, 88
  and Rehn-Meidner model, 12, 60, 61
  and "third way," 14
Severin, Frans, 42–43
Shareholder meetings, 211–12, 216, 217
SHB. *See* Svenska Handlesbanken
Shipbuilding, 106, 111, 136, 139–40, 146
SIF. *See* Association of Industrial Employees
Simonson, Birger, 172
SIND. *See* Board of Industry
Sjönander, Bo Jonas, 82n.11, 87
Skandinaviska-Enskilda Banken (SEB), 88
Sköld, Per Edvin, 52n.7, 65
Small Business Fund, 145
Social democracy, lessons for, 237
Social Democratic party (SAP), 17, 20, 166
  and abolition of investment funds, 15, 115
  and active labor market policy, 65
  and AP fund investments, 84, 113
  coalitional realignments of, 95
  and codetermination legislation, 167, 168, 172–73, 185
  consolidation of power of, 37–38
  and creation of Fourth AP Fund, 190
  and defensive orientation of industrial policy, 152, 153–54
  and divisions within labor movement, 6, 25–27
  electoral vulnerability of, 22
  elements of reformism of, 224
  and failure of industrial policy, 159–60
  and historical compromise, 4–5
  idea of planning of, 41–43

Social Democratic party (SAP) (*cont.*)
ideological traditions in, 2–3, 16
joint proposals with LO for wage-
earner funds, 193–96
and labor representation in industrial
policy-making, 157
longevity of government by, 1
and Meidner Plan, 186–87
and nationalization, 14, 40
1980s industrial policy orientation of,
142–47, 155
and 1983 wager-earner fund legislation, 196–97
1990 political crisis in, 118, 200
and origins of industrial policy, 128–
29, 131
and pension reform of 1959, 79, 93
and pivotal role of LO, 96
and planning during 1930s, 43–47
and political failure of wage-earner
funds, 218, 228, 229, 230, 232
Postwar Program of, 47–50, 52, 54,
55
retreat from planning by, 11, 39, 51,
54, 55
and state enterprise, 14, 133–34, 147–
51, 153–54
support for codetermination, 16, 228
and "third way," 14–16, 97, 115, 117,
122–23
and works councils, 55n.8
Socialiseringsnämnden. *See* Socialization
Commission
Socialist parties, 14, 18–20, 22, 37–38,
51, 54. *See also* Social Democratic
party
Socialization. *See* Nationalization
Socialization Commission, 40
Söderlund, Gustav, 44
Söderpalm, Sven-Anders, 44, 45, 55
Södersten, Jan, 74
Södra Skogsägarna AB, 148
SSAB. *See* Swedish Steel Corporation
State enterprise, 132, 154
expansion of, 133–38
restructuring and privatization of, 14,
142–43, 147–51, 215
State Enterprise Corporation, 132, 134,
135–38, 140, 147–48, 151. *See also*
Procordia
Statens Industriverk. *See* Board of Indus-
try
Statsföretag AB. *See* State Enterprise
Corporation

Steel industry, 106, 137, 140, 145–46,
147, 156
Steel Plant 80, 137, 145
Stephens, John, 2, 79, 93, 224
Sträng, Gunnar, 65n.4, 159
Strikes, 44, 118, 168
of 1969–70, 24, 33, 165–66, 189
Styrelsen för Teknisk Utveckling. *See*
Board for Technological Develop-
ment
Svenska Handelsbanken (SHB), 88
Sveriges Industriförbund. *See* Federation
of Industry
Swedish Confederation of Professional
Associations (SACO-SR), 2n.1, 67
Swedish Export Credit Corporation, 91
(table), 92
Swedish Steel Corporation (SSAB), 147,
148, 149, 151, 215
employment in, 150 (table)
formation of, 140, 157
Swedish Tobacco Corporation, 135 (ta-
ble), 136
Swedyard, 140, 146, 157
Swenson, Peter, 45, 63

TAÖ plant (Volvo), 177, 178
Tariffs, 109
Taxation, 99, 105, 173
and corporate advantages of IF system,
12, 70–72
1938 reform of, 46, 69–70
1989 reform of, 14–15, 115, 200
and release of investment funds, 114
structural effects of, 73–75, 95, 111
Taylor, John, 115
TCO. *See* Central Organization of
Salaried Employees
TC plant (Volvo), 177
Teamwork, 166–67, 177–78
Thatcher, Margaret, 14
"Third way," 14–15, 97, 115–17, 122–23
Thursday Club, 52
Tingsten, Herbert, 40
Torslanda Plant (Volvo), 225
Trade, 3, 111
balance of, 105–6
1970s decline in, 99, 100, 101
and recovery of 1980s, 116, 117
Trade Policy Council, 51
Training, 171, 177, 178
and renewal funds, 173, 174, 180,
181–83
TUN plant (Volvo), 177, 178

Turner, Lowell, 233
Tuve plant (Volvo), 178

Uddcomb Sweden AB, 136
Uddevalla plant (Volvo), 177, 178, 179–80
Uddevalla Shipyard, 135 (table), 136, 139, 146, 147
Unemployemtn. *See* Employment
Unemployment insurance, 26n.8
Unga, Nils, 41
Unions, 58, 195, 231, 234, 235
  and active labor market policy, 12, 60, 155, 156
  and Basic Agreement, 38–39
  and codetermination at Volvo, 16, 162, 175, 176, 178–80, 183–84
  and Development Agreement, 171–72
  growth of white-collar, 102–3
  and interests of workers, 29–30
  and limited success of codetermination, 184–85, 221, 225
  and political parties contrasted, 25–26
  and renewal funds, 173, 181–82
  representation at shareholder meetings, 211–12, 216, 217
  representation in industrial policy making, 155–57
  representation on AMS, 67
  sources of influence on investment decisions, 7–8
  wage-earner fund links to locals, 212–13
  See also Central Organization of Salaried Employees; Labor movement; Landsorganisationen; Metalworkers Union
United States, 152
UV Shipping, 148n.9

Vänsterpartiet. *See* Communist party
Volvo, 16, 31n.10, 149, 225
  codetermination agreement at, 174–76
  Fourth AP fund investment in, 204, 207, 208
  and Uddevalla Shipyard, 146, 147
  union influence over investment decisions by, 162, 183–84
  work reorganization at, 176–80, 184, 223, 235

Wage-earner funds, 2, 3–4, 23, 24, 116, 160

and divisions within labor movement, 25, 26, 229–30
impact of, 224
legislative politics of, 21–22, 218, 226–27, 228–32, 236–37
LO-SAP proposals for, 193–96
1991 proposed reorganization of, 199–200
opposition to, 15, 22, 186–87, 196–97, 229–32
as owners, 210–13
and pension funds compared, 94
as portfolio investors, 205, 206, 207–8
as promoters of industrial innovation, 213, 214, 215, 217
provisions of 1983 legislation on, 197–98
provisions of Meidner Plan, 191–92
purposes of, 33, 186, 192–93, 194–96, 221, 222
and Rehn-Meidner model, 188
and renewal funds compared, 173
representation on, 204–5
size and performance of, 202–3
success of, 216
See also Collective shareholding funds; Meidner Plan
Wage restraint, 59, 116, 118, 119, 194
  and investment control, 30
  and renewal funds, 173, 181
  See also Wage solidarity
Wages
  real, 80, 98
Wages, real, 41–42
Wage solidarity, 62–64, 68–69, 165, 188–89
  and concentration of capital, 74
  and corporate efficiency, 94–95, 96
  and foreign investment, 109
  and 1970s wage increases, 99–100, 102–3
  theory of, 11–12, 60–61
Walters, Peter, 117
Welfare reforms, 26n.8
Wickman, Krister, 82n.11, 131, 133, 159
Wiesenthal, Helmut, 23
Wigforss, Ernst, 38, 41, 43, 45–46, 52n.7, 69–70
Wikander, Sten, 207, 212, 214, 215
Women, 64, 67, 180
Work Environment Act of 1977, 3
Work reorganization, 166–67, 176–80, 184, 223, 235
Works Council Agreement of 1966, 171

Works councils, 53, 55n.8, 161, 164, 165,
223
and Development Agreement, 171, 175

Wright, Erik Olin, 229

Zysman, John, 7n.7, 152–53, 154

Cornell Studies in Political Economy

EDITED BY PETER J. KATZENSTEIN

Collapse of an Industry: Nuclear Power and the Contradictions of U.S. Policy, by John L. Campbell

Power, Purpose, and Collective Choice: Economic Strategy in Socialist States, edited by Ellen Comisso and Laura D'Andrea Tyson

The Political Economy of the New Asian Industrialism, edited by Frederic C. Deyo

Dislodging Multinationals: India's Strategy in Comparative Perspective, by Dennis J. Encarnation

Rivals beyond Trade: America versus Japan in Global Competition, by Dennis J. Encarnation

Democracy and Markets: The Politics of Mixed Economies, by John R. Freeman

The Misunderstood Miracle: Industrial Development and Political Change in Japan, by David Friedman

Patchwork Protectionism: Textile Trade Policy in the United States, Japan, and West Germany, by H. Richard Friman

Monetary Sovereignty: The Politics of Central Banking in Western Europe, by John B. Goodman

Politics in Hard Times: Comparative Responses to International Economic Crises, by Peter Gourevitch

Closing the Gold Window: Domestic Politics and the End of Bretton Woods, by Joanne Gowa

Cooperation among Nations: Europe, America, and Non-tariff Barriers to Trade, by Joseph M. Grieco

Pathways from the Periphery: The Politics of Growth in the Newly Industrializing Countries, by Stephan Haggard

The Philippine State and the Marcos Regime: The Politics of Export, by Gary Hawes

Reasons of State: Oil Politics and the Capacities of American Government, by G. John Ikenberry

The State and American Foreign Economic Policy, edited by G. John Ikenberry, David A. Lake, and Michael Mastanduno

Pipeline Politics: The Complex Political Economy of East-West Energy Trade, by Bruce W.
  Jentleson
The Politics of International Debt, edited by Miles Kahler
Corporatism and Change: Austria, Switzerland, and the Politics of Industry, by Peter J.
  Katzenstein
Industry and Politics in West Germany: Toward the Third Republic, edited by Peter J.
  Katzenstein
Small States in World Markets: Industrial Policy in Europe, by Peter J. Katzenstein
*The Sovereign Entrepreneur: Oil Policies in Advanced and Less Developed Capitalist
  Countries,* by Merrie Gilbert Klapp
International Regimes, edited by Stephen D. Krasner
*Power, Protection, and Free Trade: International Sources of U.S. Commercial Strategy,
  1887–1939,* by David A. Lake
State Capitalism: Public Enterprise in Canada, by Jeanne Kirk Laux and Maureen
  Appel Molot
France after Hegemony: International Change and Financial Reform, by Michael
  Loriaux
Opening Financial Markets: Banking Politics on the Pacific Rim, by Louis W. Pauly
The Limits of Social Democracy: Investment Politics in Sweden, by Jonas Pontusson
The Fruits of Fascism: Postwar Prosperity in Historical Perspective, by Simon Reich
*The Business of the Japanese State: Energy Markets in Comparative and Historical
  Perspective,* by Richard J. Samuels
In the Dominions of Debt: Historical Perspectives on Dependent Development, by Herman
  M. Schwartz
Europe and the New Technologies, edited by Margaret Sharp
Europe's Industries: Public and Private Strategies for Change, edited by Geoffrey
  Shepherd, François Duchêne, and Christopher Saunders
Ideas and Institutions: Developmentalism in Brazil and Argentina, by Kathryn Sikkink
Fair Shares: Unions, Pay, and Politics in Sweden and West Germany, by Peter Swenson
Union of Parts: Labor Politics in Postwar Germany, by Kathleen A. Thelen
Democracy at Work: Changing World Markets and the Future of Labor Unions, by Lowell
  Turner
*National Styles of Regulation: Environmental Policy in Great Britain and the United
  States,* by David Vogel
International Cooperation: Building Regimes for Natural Resources and the Environment,
  by Oran R. Young
*Governments, Markets, and Growth: Financial Systems and the Politics of Industrial
  Change,* by John Zysman
*American Industry in International Competition: Government Policies and Corporate
  Strategies,* edited by John Zysman and Laura Tyson

Library of Congress Cataloging-in-Publication Data

Pontusson, Jonas.
  The limits of social democracy : investment politics in Sweden /
Jonas Pontusson.
    p.   cm. — (Cornell studies in political economy)
  Based on the author's thesis (Ph.D.)—University of California.
Berkeley, 1986.
  Includes bibliographical references and index.
  ISBN 0-8014-2652-9 (alk. paper)
    1. Sweden—Economic policy.   2. Industry and state—Sweden.
  3. Labor policy—Sweden.   4. Sweden—Politics and government—1973-
    5. Socialism—Sweden.   6. Investments—Government   policy—
Sweden.
  I. Title.   II. Series.
  HC375.P67   1992
  338.9485—dc20   92-2694